FAULKNER
in the University

F A U L K N E R
in the University

Edited by Frederick L. Gwynn

and Joseph L. Blotner

with an Introduction by Douglas Day

University Press of Virginia

Charlottesville and London

Frontispiece photo by Ralph Thompson

THE UNIVERSITY PRESS OF VIRGINIA
Copyright © 1959, 1995 by the Rector and Visitors
of the University of Virginia

First Virginia paperback edition 1995

Library of Congress Cataloging-in-Publication Data
Faulkner in the university / edited by Frederick L. Gwynn and Joseph
L. Blotner : with an introduction by Douglas Day.—1st Virginia   pbk.
ed.   p.   cm.
    Includes index.
    ISBN 0–8139–1612–7 (paper)
    1. Faulkner, William, 1897–1962—Interviews. 2. Novelists.
  American—20th century—Interviews. 3. English teachers—
Virginia—Charlottesville—Interviews. 4. University of Virginia—
History—Sources.   I. Gwynn, Frederick L. (Frederick Landis),
1916–
II. Blotner, Joseph Leo, 1923–
PS3511.A86Z7832119 1995
813'.52—dc20   94–36034
                                                             CIP

Printed in the United States of America

Oleh, Chief, Grandfather

Contents

Introduction to the 1995 Edition

Faulkner in the University is a remarkable document and a deceptive one: those of us who teach and write about Faulkner absorbed the book long ago, until its contents became almost part of a scholarly collective unconscious. Without knowing we were doing so, we became so familiar with it that we scarcely needed to think about it—especially after the deluge of critical books and articles about Faulkner that was to come after this watershed collection of 1959.

Before *Faulkner in the University* there had been a number of important works dealing with Faulkner's impressive career, to be sure. We had come to acknowledge that he was one of our greats even before his Nobel Prize (awarded the same year this book was published). Few of us had escaped undergraduate school without exposure to *The Sound and the Fury* and *Absalom, Absalom!,* even if neither we nor our professors quite knew what to make of these works. And after the publication in 1946 of Malcolm Cowley's crucial *Portable Faulkner,* a large segment of the literate population was ready to acknowledge that Faulkner was up there with Hemingway and Fitzgerald.

Today, in 1994, few would raise their eyebrows if I were to assert, as I do, that there have been only two truly great novelists in North American literary history: Herman Melville and William Faulkner. If sheer volume of scholarly and critical attention were the sole criterion, Faulkner would have to be judged the winner,

ix

hands down. My computer and I made a random count the other day and discovered that almost thirteen hundred *books* have been written about Faulkner's life and works since the appearance of *Faulkner in the University*. Assessing the number of articles and essays would have been a formidable task indeed, one depressing even to contemplate. Those of us who try to keep even marginally abreast of Faulkner scholarship know that we are doomed to failure. In this life, one has time to read Faulkner or Faulkner criticism, one or the other. Most of us, I suspect, are like me—content to concentrate on the work, especially on the major phase of fiction published between *Sartoris* in 1929 and *Go Down, Moses* in 1942; and to point ourselves and our students toward eleven or twelve scholarly books and essays that seem particularly distinguished. Suffice it here to say that there are dozens of studies, textual and critical, of the individual works, and that the whole Faulkner canon has been subjected to every sort of critical scrutiny: anthropological, Marxist, feminist, new historical, formalist, psychoanalytic. Happily, Faulkner still eludes his biographers, as his works do their exegetes.

When we mention *Faulkner in the University* we do so almost in passing, as though everyone already knew it quite by heart. But this is our mistake, because this collection of interviews and observations merits close attention and periodic reexamination. We know now, after several weighty biographies and the memoirs of old friends and lovers, that Faulkner was never, as he claimed in these talks, a bootlegger or a merchant seaman, a barnstormer or a commercial airline pilot. We smile today at this rather innocent persona-building on Faulkner's part, and save our serious attention, if we are biographically or psychologically inclined, for accounts of his drinking habits, or his philandering, or his complex and even bizarre genealogy. (A recent biographer has uncovered evidence of a black branch of his family, which adds resonance to our thinking about the prominence of miscegenation in so many of his works.) Faulkner, from today's perspective, didn't really reveal much of himself in these conferences. But we still need to pay attention to what he says here about what goes on in the mind and heart of a serious writer; about what he says, again and again, is most important to him, especially about the past (especially the Southern past); and what the writer's role in his culture ought to be. We need to hear him when he says that one cannot teach writing; that all a young writer can do is read, absorb, and steal from his predecessors. Or that sensationalism is all right when it is only a means to an end and not the end itself. Or, perhaps most importantly, that a writer finally has three qualities on which he can draw: imagination, observation, and experience—and that, when he's really writing, he scarcely can distinguish among these three. And we should listen to what he says here about his own books, even if, intentionally or not, he is not always accurate about them.

Faulkner was a tricky man, not above playing, however courteously, with his audiences. Yet few writers are bold enough to be so open—or apparently open—about what they were trying to do in their books. He tells us here, for instance, that *The Sound and the Fury* has the shape it does because it represents four failed attempts to tell a single, simple story. Though he was to tell the same story again, in Nagano, Japan, scholars have convincingly argued that the novel was much more carefully and artfully constructed than his account would suggest. Nonetheless, it is interesting to speculate why Faulkner should have chosen to remember his novel as he does here. For ease of anecdote, when a true account of what must have been the real turmoil behind the creation of his masterpiece (and favorite work) might have been too distressing or protracted—or both? Perhaps.

I was a graduate student in English at the University of Virginia during the years Faulkner served as writer-in-residence, and so had ample opportunity to observe him both in and out of the classroom. Frederick Gwynn taught me American fiction and Joseph Blotner advised me in my first efforts at scholarly writing. I suspect that, with all good will, these gentlemen often used me as a kind of go-between with Faulkner in the service of their own research. If, say, they knew I had an appointment to interview him about his flying stories of World War I, they would brief me about what I might ask him, and eagerly debrief me after the interview.

I must have been rather a disappointment to them, because Faulkner never cared to discuss his work with me or any other supplicant. Our first meeting, in his tiny office on the fifth floor of Cabell Hall, initially was very frustrating. I asked my questions; Faulkner only smiled and sucked on his pipe. But when it somehow came up that I had been a fighter pilot in the Marine Corps he livened up and began asking *me* questions. Before long I was spending time in Faulkner's office, drawing fighter combat tactics on his blackboard while he watched, beaming. I do not think that this activity was particularly fascinating to Gwynn or Blotner (both of whom, incidentally, had been aviators in World War II and, as such, probably already had their own share of tall stories to tell) but it certainly was to me, and possibly to Faulkner as well.

The man had floated a rumor years before, and allowed it to stand, that he had been wounded while flying with the Lafayette Escadrille over France in the Great War. Knowing (as we all knew) that he had done no such thing, Gwynn and Blotner tried their own form of trickery to catch him out. They built a small plastic model of a Sopwith Camel and gave it to Faulkner, and Gwynn asked, "Is this the kind of plane you flew in France, Mr. Faulkner?" Faulkner studied the model for a minute or two, smiled, and said, "Yes, that's a Sopwith Camel, all right."

Several days before Faulkner came to one of our classes, Gwynn would solicit potential questions from us. If he (or Blotner) were curious to hear a given question answered by Faulkner, one would be given a little slip of paper with the question on it, so that it might be posed to Faulkner during class discussion. By vetting our questions, Gwynn and Blotner would not only further their own research but also protect Faulkner against having to answer questions he'd already been asked, at Virginia or elsewhere. Not that Faulkner particularly minded repeating himself: I came to believe, after sitting in on many of these classes, that he enjoyed the possibilities for incremental variation in his answers, responding one way today and another way next month, especially about his own work and that of other writers. (Faulkner always distinguished between "truth" and "facts"; "facts" sometimes annoyed him.)

Tricky, as I say; but I reasoned that Faulkner had to keep from boring himself over so many interviews and conferences, and so quite understandably wished to embellish here and there, to revise the "facts" now and then, just for fun. As I followed him (and Blotner and Gwynn, lugging their heavy old tape recorder after them) from class to class, I was to hear him tell one group how much he detested Jason Compson, of *The Sound and the Fury*—and to hear him tell another group, a month later, that Jason was one of his favorite characters ("Any man who hates Babe Ruth can't be all bad"). And he enjoyed toying with Gwynn and Blotner, whom he sometimes referred to privately as "Step 'n' Fetchit." Publicly, Faulkner was unfailingly courteous to everyone he met at the University, but he never pretended to take scholarly work very seriously. He would talk about flying with me, or about horses and hunting with anyone; but if forced to talk about "literature," his own or others', he would almost unfailingly hide behind a shield of irony, amiable banter, or assumed (or real) forgetfulness.

Something else his biographers often fail to notice about the man: that his frequently adopted attitudes of hauteur, archness, or "I'm-just-a-country-boy" faux-naïveté were really functions of a radical shyness, a fear of social confrontation. I shall never forget one evening when I was to introduce him to a large audience in Alderman Library, when he was to read from his work and then respond to questions. As we waited in an anteroom for our cue, I tried to make a little small talk with him, until I realized that Faulkner was unable to speak. For what seemed an eternity the tiny man stood silently beside me, trembling, a look of real agony on his face. This was the most intense stage fright I'd ever seen.

Once clasping the lectern and beginning to read, he managed to seem relaxed and happy, quite in charge of things, and sure enough of himself to pause now and then to reach into the sleeve of his carefully tailored Harris tweed jacket, pull out an enormous chartreuse silk handkerchief, and blow his nose.

I felt like cheering when he did things like this, not only because such flamboyant gestures were a splendid way for him to poke a little fun at himself and at his very respectful and sober audience, but also because I had become aware of how painful Faulkner found such public appearances, how much they cost him, and how frightened he was of almost any sort of self-revelation or intimacy. He would have *liked* to be a Sartoris, mute and insolently gallant and perhaps a little stupid; and his occasional stabs at bonhomie and dandyism were possibly manifestations of this desire. But he was probably far closer to his other favorites, V. K. Ratliff and Ike McCaslin—small, neat witnesses and testifiers in clean and faded bib overalls, men not taken too seriously by the larger and louder men around them.

There were times, however, when one had to take Faulkner seriously, and to admire his dignity and poise. On that same night in the library, sitting behind him, I watched with dread as he nodded at one of the little old ladies who invariably occupied the front-row seats at these readings, slept through them, and then raised their hands to ask amazingly gauche questions. This little old lady squinted at Faulkner maliciously and asked, "Mister Faulkner, would you allow your daughter to marry a nigra?" Faulkner drew himself up and responded with utter gravity, "Ma'am, I would hope that Mrs. Faulkner and I would have raised her sufficiently well for her to be able to make an appropriate choice." No diplomat could have said it better.

The transcribed conferences in *Faulkner in the University* show us a man apparently enjoying himself: teasing, provocative, self-deprecatory, confident, not above toying affectionately with his avid listeners. I, who often saw him sweating and shaking before and after these meetings, remember something very poignant about the whole experience. These appearances took a lot out of him, and we must appreciate the torment this very private man was putting himself through for us, out of courtesy and his own very real kind of gallantry, far superior to that displayed by the surly and silent Sartorises. A tricky man, yes; but a brave one, too.

Douglas Day

Preface to the 1959 Edition

From February to June of 1957 and 1958, William Faulkner was Writer-in-Residence at the University of Virginia under a grant from the Emily Clark Balch Fund for American Literature. As Mr. Faulkner himself expressed it, the grant furnished him with a house to live in and someone to clean it, making his association with the University not that of a professor but rather "the mutually voluntary one of a guest accepting and returning the amenities of guesthood."

During these periods—except for short trips to Greece, to Princeton, and to Mississippi—Mr. Faulkner held thirty-seven group conferences and an uncounted number of individual office meetings with students and staff of the University. He encouraged groups to ask questions about his writing and indeed about anything, which resulted in his answering publicly over two thousand queries on everything from spelling to the nature of man. Almost every word spoken in the group conferences was recorded on tape, now deposited in the Alderman Library of the University. Because a complete transcript of this 40,000-foot record would have been prohibitively long, repetitive, and occasionally misleading, we have selected what seemed to us the most typical and significant questions and answers, indicating omissions by the ellipsis.

We first arranged the material by subject-matter for the convenience of readers, but we later agreed that the order most faithful to the fact and spirit of the sessions would be that in which the questions were actually asked and answered, and that an index would have to serve to link together comments on the same works and subjects. We have reproduced what Mr. Faulkner and his questioners said as accurately as possible, although the absence of studio recording conditions, the obscuring of parts of questions and answers by laughter or run-out tape, and the presence of natural human error in speaking and hearing have made a perfect transcription impossible. (After hiring persons to transcribe and check, we did the whole job over, and must therefore be held responsible for any imperfections.) We have restricted copy-editing chiefly to punctuation that attempts both to make meaning clear and to reproduce actual pauses in speech. We have consistently omitted the "Yes sir" and "Yes ma'am" with which Mr. Faulkner usually recognized each of his questioners, and we have not attempted to render his striking regional dialect or individualized pronunciation, although it will linger long in our ears. We have of course omitted the author's preliminary readings from his works, as well as the many introductions, conclusions, and classroom rituals by teachers and officials.

Any reader familiar with Faulkner's work will find that many of his answers illuminate an understanding of particular novels and stories, while the total dialogue of course demonstrates the working of the writer's mind and the qualities of his character. On the other hand, a reader would be ill advised to treat these answers as consistently revealed truth. In Mr. Faulkner's own words, "Since his association with the University—and in fact with literature itself during this period— was not professorially appointive but instead was voluntary and invitational, the following is not the (at the moment of speaking) definite record of the ideas and opinions of a writer on life and literature, including his own work, but is rather the self-portrait of a man in motion who also happens to be a writer." No one man's view of an artist's work, least of all the writer's own, can comprehend all views. Furthermore, the writer's memory of words and purposes conceived many years ago must of simple human frailty be faulty and probably at times downright untrue, although Mr. Faulkner always made an effort to recall exactly the facts of his fiction and its design, and even took the trouble (in 1958) to re-read *Absalom, Absalom!* for this purpose. Then too, an artist who creates new life cannot always account for the process even if he wants to, and there are some secrets of creation that he is entitled to keep forever his own. Finally, any human being speaking in public finds himself unconsciously adapting his remarks to the comparative tone and intelligence of the questioners, the sequence of questions, the questions themselves and how many times he has previously been asked them, the weather, and the condition of his digestion. Mr. Faulkner's answers, in short, must be taken as a revelation of an artist's mind at a particular moment, in a particular place, operating as honestly and painstakingly as it can, to fulfill a particular purpose: "That these"—Mr. Faulkner again—"are questions answered without rehearsal or preparation, by a man old enough in the craft of the human heart to have learned that there are no definitive answers to anything, yet still young enough in spirit to believe that truth may still be found provided one seeks enough, tests and discards, and still tries again." At Mr. Faulkner's suggestion and in his phrasing, we warn the reader that any resemblance the ideas and opinions expressed here have to ideas and opinions Mr. Faulkner has held or expressed previously, and to the ideas and opinions which— since he intends to continue to live and to test and discard for some time yet—he might hold or express in the future, is purely coincidental. Having made this admonition at length, we sum it up by simply urging readers to take the writer's comments for what they are worth.

The interested reader will note that the brief Session Three is re-created from our memory after a recording failure, but he should also know that another failure accounts for the omission of what would have been Session Thirty-Six (19 May 1958, First-Year English, on *As I Lay Dying*) and that the loss of one tape has prevented a final re-check of Session Fourteen. A version of Session Fifteen was printed in *The University of Virginia Magazine* for February 1957 and Spring 1958, and the address "A Word to Virginians" appeared in the Spring 1958 issue. A version of Session Eight was printed in *College English* for October 1957. The address "A Word to Young Writers" that begins Session Twenty-Seven appears here for the first time.

For funds to make the whole project possible, we are grateful to the University of Virginia's Research Committee, Professor C. Julian Bishko, Chairman; to the administrative officers President Colgate W. Darden, Jr. and Comptroller Vincent Shea; and to the Director of the University of Virginia Press, Mr. Charles E. Moran, Jr. For advice we are grateful to Mr. Faulkner's editor and friend, the late Saxe Commins. We are of course indebted to the dozens of here nameless students, teachers, and visitors who asked the questions that drew the answers. The greatest debt—the one to be repaid only by generations of present and future readers of his work—is finally to William Faulkner, whose special role we have tried to signify in our dedication.

Frederick L. Gwynn
Joseph L. Blotner

FAULKNER
in the University

Session One

FEBRUARY 15, 1957

GRADUATE COURSE IN AMERICAN FICTION

. . . Q. Mr. Faulkner, in *The Sound and the Fury* the first three sections of that book are narrated by one of the four Compson children, and in view of the fact that Caddy figures so prominently, is there any particular reason why you didn't have a section with—giving her views or impressions of what went on?

A. That's a good question. That—the explanation of that whole book is in that. It began with the picture of the little girl's muddy drawers, climbing that tree to look in the parlor window with her brothers that didn't have the courage to climb the tree waiting to see what she saw. And I tried first to tell it with one brother, and that wasn't enough. That was Section One. I tried with another brother, and that wasn't enough. That was Section Two. I tried the third brother, because Caddy was still to me too beautiful and too moving to reduce her to telling what was going on, that it would be more passionate to see her through somebody else's eyes, I thought. And that failed and I tried myself—the fourth section—to tell what happened, and I still failed.

. . .

Q. Speaking of Caddy, is there any way of getting her back from the clutches of the Nazis, where she ends up in the Appendix?

A. I think that that would be a betrayal of Caddy, that it is best to leave here where she is. If she were resurrected there'd be something a little shabby, a little anti-climactic about it, about this. Her tragedy to me is the best I could do with it—

unless, as I said, I could start over and write the book again and that can't be.

. . .

Q. Mr. Faulkner, I am interested in the symbolism in *The Sound and the Fury,* and I wasn't able to figure exactly the significance of the shadow symbol in Quentin. It's referred to over and over again: he steps in the shadow, shadow is before him, the shadow is often after him. Well then, what is the significance of this shadow?

A. That wasn't a deliberate symbolism. I would say that that shadow that stayed on his mind so much was foreknowledge of his own death, that he was—Death is here, shall I step into it, or shall I step away from it a little longer? I won't escape it, but shall I accept it now or shall I put it off until next Friday? I think that if it had any reason that must have been it.

. . .

Q. Sir, what sort of symbol was the snake? We discussed that in both *The Bear* and in "Red Leaves."

A. Oh, the snake is the old grandfather, the old fallen angel, the unregenerate immortal. The good and shining angel ain't very interesting . . . .

Q. Sir, what book would you advise a person to read first of yours?

A. Well, that's not a fair question to ask me because I would like anyone to try the one that I love the best, which is a poor one to start on. If you are asking me to give an objective answer I would say maybe *The Unvanquished.*

Q. Why would you select that one?

A. Because it's easy to read. Compared to the others, I mean . . . .

. . .

Q. Mr. Faulkner, I'd like to ask you about Quentin and his relationship with his father. I think many readers get the impression that Quentin is the way he is to a large extent because of his father's lack of values, or the fact that he doesn't seem to pass down to his son many values that will sustain him. Do you think that Quentin winds up the way

2

he does primarily because of that, or are we meant to see, would you say, that the action that comes primarily from what he is, abetted by what he gets from his father?

A. The action as portrayed by Quentin was transmitted to him through his father. There was a basic failure before that. The grandfather had been a failed brigadier twice in the Civil War. It was the—the basic failure Quentin inherited through his father, or beyond his father. It was a—something had happened somewhere between the first Compson and Quentin. The first Compson was a bold ruthless man who came into Mississippi as a free forester to grasp where and when he could and wanted to, and established what should have been a princely line, and that princely line decayed.

Q. Sir, how do you feel about your books after they have gone to press? Do you reread them and puzzle over them . . .?

A. No, I don't because by that time I know the book was not as good as it should have been and so I'm usually busy on another one.

Q. As a general rule, you never re-read?

A. No, that's one book the writer don't have to read any more.

. . .

Q. Mr. Faulkner, you speak of writing the one great book but in your own works you keep returning to this fictitious county you've made. You don't consider that a pageant, the whole work, from the Indians through the early settlers—?

A. No, it was not my intention to write a pageant of a county, I simply was using the quickest tool to hand. I was using what I knew best, which was the locale where I was born and had lived most of my life. That was just like the carpenter building the fence—he uses the nearest hammer. Only I didn't realize myself that I was creating a pageantry of a particular part of the earth. That just simplified things to me.

. . .

Q. In *The Bear*, Mr. Faulkner, many readers come across Part Four and find it written in quite a different style than the other parts and the conclusion—well, it gets far ahead in years beyond Part Five. Was there any conscious plan in that?

A. Only this: *The Bear* was a part of a novel. That novel was—happened to be composed of more or less complete stories, but it was held together by one family, the Negro and the white phase of the same family, same people. *The Bear* was just a part of that—of a novel.

Q. *Go Down, Moses?*

A. Yes.

Q. So that it was all right for Ike to think ahead . . . to his thirty-fifth year.

A. Yes, that's right, because the rest of the book was a part of his past too. To have taken that story out to print it alone I have always removed that part, which I have done.

Q. Yes, some of the textbooks do that.

A. As a short story, a long short story, it has no part in it, but to me *The Bear* is part of the novel, just as a chapter in the novel.

. . .

Q. In what period of development did you write that book of poems, *A Green Bough?*

A. That was written at the time when you write poetry, which is seventeen, eighteen, nineteen—when you write poetry just for the pleasure of writing poetry and you don't think of printing it until later. It may be—I've often thought that I wrote the novels because I found I couldn't write the poetry, that maybe I wanted to be a poet, maybe I think of myself as a poet, and I failed at that, I couldn't write poetry, so I did the next best thing.

Q. Mr. Faulkner, in your speech at Stockholm you expressed great faith in mankind . . . not only to endure but prevail . . . . Do you think that's the impression the average reader would get after reading *The Sound and the Fury?*

A. I can't answer that because I don't know what the average reader gets from reading the book. I agree that what I tried to say I failed to say, and I never have had time to read reviews so I don't know what impression people might get from the book. But in my opinion, yes, that is what I was talking about in all the books, and I failed to say it. I agree

4

with you, I did fail. But that was what I was trying to say—
that man will prevail, will endure because he is capable of
compassion and honor and pride and endurance.

. . .

Q. Sir, Hawthorne seemed to have found trouble in creating
good characters, whereas his more or less bad characters stand
out as works of art. Do you think that is a problem with all
writers, that it's harder to create a good character than an
evil one?

A. It's possible that that's inherent in human nature, not
so much in the character of writers but in human nature itself,
that it's easier to conceive of evil than of good or to make—
that evil is easier to make believable, credible, than good.

Q. Mr. Faulkner, when you say man has prevailed do you
mean individual man has prevailed or group man?

A. Man as a part of life.

Q. In Quentin, for instance, [he] seemed to have the cards
stacked against him . . . it seems to be inherently impossible,
and I wondered . . . .

A. True, and his mother wasn't much good and he had an
idiot brother, and yet in that whole family there was Dilsey
that held the whole thing together and would continue to hold
the whole thing together for no reward, that the will of man
to prevail will even take the nether channel of the black man,
black race, before it will relinquish, succumb, be defeated.

. . .

Q. Well, sir, you seem to have us believe in . . . the ultimate
goodness of man, that he will come through in spite of all.
How do you explain the sum of mass brutality, the things
we practice on each other, the horrible things that take place
in our life, including the lines of religion and our politics?

A. I didn't say in the ultimate goodness of man, I said only
that man will prevail and will—and in order to prevail he has
got to . . . [try to be good]. As to whether he will stay on the
earth long enough to attain ultimate goodness, nobody knows.
But he does improve, since the only alternative to progress is
death. And we can see the little children don't have to work, a
merchant can't sell you poisoned food. They are minor im-

provements but they are improvements. Nobody is hanged for stealing bread any more. People are not put in jail for debt. It's some improvement—it's not a great deal, I grant you, as matched against atomic bombs and things like that. But it's some improvement. Man is improved.

Q. You don't feel that mass manipulation by a fanatic along ideological and political lines will negate all this?

A. No, I don't. That to me is part of the ferment of man's immortality—that these people, the nuts, are necessary too.

Q. Do you think that man will prevail against destroying himself . . . ?

A. I think he will prevail against his own self-destruction, yes.

Q. What about the forces of nature . . . ?

A. Well, unless the earth gets sick and tired of him like an old dog and just scratches him off like the old dog does fleas.

Q. Mr. Faulkner, what do you think is man's most important tool—the mind or the heart . . . ?

A. I don't have much confidence in the mind. I think that here is where the shoe fits, that the mind lets you down sooner or later, but this doesn't.

Q. Mr. Faulkner, I've been very much interested in what it seems to me you did—maybe you didn't—in *The Sound and the Fury*, in the character of Caddy. To me she is a very sympathetic character, perhaps the most sympathetic white woman in the book, and yet we get pictures of her only through someone else's comments and most of these comments are quite [?] and wouldn't lead you to admire her on the surface, and yet I do. Did you mean for us to have this feeling for Caddy, and if so, how did you go about reducing her to the negative picture we get of her?

A. To me she was the beautiful one, she was my heart's darling. That's what I wrote the book about and I used the tools which seemed to me the proper tools to try to tell, try to draw the picture of Caddy.

6

Q. Mr. Faulkner, we've got a poker player over here, Mr. Jordan, who's holding back on a question I'm dying to hear the answer to.

A. Let's have it.

Q. Well, I was wondering in the short story "Was" why Mr. Hubert does not call Uncle Bud. It seems to me that must be the point of the story, and yet no one could understand why he did not call him.

A. I'll have to look at that page again. I don't remember exactly—

Q. He looks up and sees that Tomey's Turl is dealing the cards.

A. Oh, Tomey's Turl wants to be free, and so Tomey's Turl has dealt the right card to the right one, and Mr. Hubert knows that. As soon as he sees that Tomey's Turl was the one that dealt the cards, he knows that he's beat.

Q. But Tomey's Turl stood to win either way, didn't he? . . .

A. No, he was—I don't remember the story too well, but I don't think so. That Tomey's Turl had a stake in that game, too. As I remember it, Hubert Beauchamp would have taken his brother—no, what are the names? I can't even remember the names.

Q. Buck and Buddy.

A. Yes, Buck would have taken Buddy out of the clutches of Miss—what's her name?

Q. Sophonsiba.

A. —Sophonsiba if he had won. And if that had happened then he would have taken Tomey's Turl back with him away from Tomey's Turl's girl, so if Buck lost, then Miss Sophonsiba would take Tomey's Turl's girl home with her. Tomey's Turl was playing for his sweetheart. Yes, that's what the story was, I think.

. . .

Q. I have another question about *The Bear*. In the final scene of *The Bear*, Boon is sitting under the tree with the squirrels, doing something with his shotgun. It's not clear to me whether he is destroying his shotgun or trying to put it back together.

A. It had jammed. He was trying to get a jammed shell out to make it fire, and he didn't want anybody else to shoot the squirrels. He was under the tree where the squirrels couldn't get out of it and he didn't want anybody else to shoot the squirrels until he could get his gun fixed.

. . .

Q. . . . *The Wild Palms* is so very interesting. I think the other, *Old Man,* is a bit of a struggle.

A. Well, you may be right. As I say, they all failed, and maybe it was a mistake to dovetail two of them together that way, but to me it seemed that it was necessary to counterpoint the story of Harry and Charlotte, which I did with the complete antithesis—a man that had a woman he didn't want and was going into infinite trouble even as far as going to jail to get rid of her.

Q. I have a couple of questions about the early Indian stories, about "Red Leaves." Did Doom in your mind, did he wreck the steamboat and maybe kill this man David Callicoat, whose name he took? Did he have some notion of getting that steamboat eventually which he finally picked up and transported twelve miles inland?

A. No, the steamboat simply got too far up the river and stayed too long and when the water fell in the late summer, it couldn't get out again, and so the owners of it just took the valuable machinery out and left the hulk there and Doom decided that would make a nice addition to his house and so he had his people drag it out of the river and across to the plantation.

Q. Did you ever hear of anyone's really ever doing that?
A. No.

Q. Were these Chickasaws ever known to be cannibals? There's some mention of how human flesh may have tasted between two of them once.

A. No, there's no record, but then it's—who's to say

8

whether at some time one of them might not have tried what it tasted like? Quite often young boys will try things that they are horrified to remember later just to see what it was like . . . . Maybe as children they may have found a dead man and cooked some of him to see what he tasted like. But they were not cannibals as far as I know.

Q. Do they exist just in memory now?

A. There are a few, there's a reservation, a remnant of Choctaws. The others, the Indians in my part of Mississippi have vanished into the two races—either the white race or the Negro race. You see traces of the features in the Negroes and a few of the old names in among white families, old white families.

Q. . . . There were Indians at one time in this area?

A. Oh yes. Yes, all the land records go back to the Indian patents, and our country's not very old, our land records are only a hundred fifty years old. That was frontier then.

Q. Sir, I'm curious about the occasional change in personality that some of your characters undergo between novels. For instance, Narcissa Benbow is fairly sympathetic in *Sartoris*, but by *Sanctuary* she's vicious. How do you account for this?

A. There again I am using the most available tool to tell what I'm trying to tell, and my idea is that no person is wholly good or wholly bad, that all people in my belief try to be better than they are and probably will be. And that if—when I need for a tool a particular quality in an individual I think that quality is there. It can be taken out, and for the moment it leaves the individual in an unhappy light, but in my opinion it hasn't destroyed or really harmed that individual.

Q. In other words, sir, she hasn't developed between novels. You're merely taking a different look at her, the same person.

A. That's right.

Q. Sir, to what extent were you trying to picture the South and Southern civilization as a whole, rather than just Mississippi—or were you?

9

A. Not at all. I was trying to talk about people, using the only tool I knew, which was the country that I knew. No, I wasn't trying to—wasn't writing sociology at all. I was just trying to write about people, which to me are the important thing. Just the human heart, it's not ideas. I don't know anything about ideas, don't have much confidence in them.

Q. In *The Bear,* Mr. Faulkner, once again, [at] the end of Part Three, Sam Fathers has died. Does he die in his own little cabin or does he ask Boon Hogganbeck and Ike to take him out and expose him on the four-cornered platform?

A. He knew that he was finished, he was tired of his life, and he—if he had been strong he could have done the deed himself. He couldn't. He asked Boon to, and I think Boon murdered him, because Sam told him to. It was the Greek gesture which Sam himself was too weak to do. He was done, finished. He told Boon to do it.

Q. And Ike knows this, and so tells the rest to let Boon alone?

A. That's right.

Session Two

February 15, 1957

PRESS CONFERENCE

... Q. Mr. Faulkner, is this your first visit to the University, by the way?

A. No sir, I was in Charlottesville years ago at a Spring literary festival. I came with Mr. Sherwood Anderson and Mr. Cabell was here then. I don't remember—Paul Green, I believe was here. What year that was I don't recall—about—

Q. '32 or so?

A. '32 or so, yes.

. . .

Q. Mr. Faulkner, could I ask you how important you think a college education is to a writer?

A. Well that's—is too much like trying to decide how important is a warm room to a writer. To some writers, some people, the college education might be of great importance, just like some of us couldn't work in a cold room. So that's a question I just wouldn't attempt to answer, and then I'm more or less out of bounds because I didn't have one myself.

Q. I was reading a book . . . yesterday which said that English teachers had gotten a body of American literature and stored it away in musty basements and had sort of stifled the creative impulse in America. . . . Do you think that's true?

A. No sir, I do not. I do not. I think that people read into the true meaning of college lots of things that are not there. I think that there's an importance in college that is—adumbrates a specialty like—of being a writer, that is, the

11

college is to produce first a human being, a humanitarian, and no man can write who is not first a humanitarian, and if the college can supply that to him, then the college is of infinite importance. If he has managed to acquire that outside of college, then he doesn't need the college. But you can't— I don't think you can say that the college makes or mars an artist.

Q. If he has it in him, it'll come out.

A. Yes. I would say that the college would help anyone, but it wouldn't make a writer that wouldn't have made himself—that is, I've never held with the mute inglorious Milton.

. . .

Q. . . . Just why did you accept [the invitation to come to University of Virginia]?

A. It was because I like your country. I like Virginia, and I like Virginians. Because Virginians are all snobs, and I like snobs. A snob has to spend so much time being a snob that he has little left to meddle with you, and so it's very pleasant here.

. . .

Q. Well, what contribution do you hope to make while you are here?

A. Well, I couldn't say that either, and that's why I hope that maybe there is one I can make. I think the contribution would come out of my experience as a writer, as a craftsman, in contact with the desire of young people to be writers, to be craftsmen, that maybe out of a hundred there may be one that will get something of value from the fact that I was in Charlottesville for a while. If there is one out of a hundred, I think that would be pretty good.

. . .

Q. Mr. Faulkner, could you tell me who you think is the most promising young writer in America?

A. I'm not familiar with young writers. Like most writers, as they get old they stop reading—that is, the reading they do is the things they loved when they were young men when they began to read, and so I haven't read a coeval book

12

in about fifteen years. I remember a book by a young man named William Styron that I thought showed promise.

Q. *Lie Down in Darkness?*
A. Yes.

. . .

Q. You aren't conscious of the critic having influenced you at any time? It raises the interesting question of the relationship between the critic and the artist.
A. If I ever listened to a critic I—he probably did influence me, because I think the artist takes everything that he needs from about any source, but I don't know that I ever listened to one, ever read one. But I'm sure that no writer is impervious to criticism. Sometimes he won't read it because he's afraid of what he might feel.

. . .

Q. Do you like to be where your subject-matter is?
A. Doesn't matter.

Q. Mr. Faulkner, what's your opinion of Tennessee Williams's work?
A. A play called *Camino Real* I think is the best. The others were not quite that good. I saw *Cat on a Hot Tin Roof* and that was about the wrong people—the problems of children are not worth three acts. The story was the old man, I thought, the father. That's all I know of Williams. *Camino Real* was—it touched a very fine high moment of poetry, I think.

. . .

Q. I suppose your grandson was an attractive fringe benefit of the second semester position, being near here.
A. Yes.

Q. What of the Southern tradition and heritage do you hope he will continue, and what do you hope won't . . .?
A. I hope of course that he will cope with his environment as it changes. And, I hope that his mother and father will try to raise him without bigotry as much as can be done. He can

13

have a Confederate battleflag if he wants it but he shouldn't take it too seriously.

. . .

Q. Mr. Faulkner, this is an odd question. I wonder whether you might have any comments on the Middle Eastern situation and how you think that's being handled? Just to get your— to get a writer's ideas on this.

A. Well, I think what we need now is not a golf player but a good poker player.

. . .

Q. Do you write with a particular reader in mind, Mr. Faulkner? Any audience?

A. No, I don't. I wrote for years before it occurred to me that strangers might read the stuff, and I've never broken that habit. I still write it because it worries me so much I've got to get rid of it, and so I put it on paper.

. . .

Q. Do you write with more ease now than you did when you started? Or do you write with more care, maybe I should say?

A. The fire is not as fierce as it was once. It's—probably I fumble less now than I did then, but I will put off sitting down to do the work more than I used to.

Q. How many more books do you feel that you are going to write? I mean, do you feel impelled to write—do you feel that you're going to write a great many more?

A. Probably, because I'm convinced I'll live to be about a hundred years old. I'll still be working on something then.

. . .

Q. . . . When did you begin [*The Town*]?

A. The last one—it took about a year.

Q. [*The Hamlet*]?

A. Oh no, I did that in nineteen-twenty—

Q. You did [*The Hamlet* in nineteen-twenty—?]—the publication date's 1940.

A. Well, I wrote it in the late twenties.

14

Q. Did you really? You wrote *The Hamlet* long before it was published?

A. It was mostly short stories. In 1940 I got it pulled together.

. . .

Q. What is literary about the creative impulse? What makes—what's the difference between being literary and not being?

A. There is a great difference. I don't know whether I could define it, but there's a great difference. There are literary people that have no impulse to create at all, that simply love the atmosphere in which books exist and are produced, that love to talk about books and about ideas.

Q. Excluding your own, Mr. Faulkner, what do you think is the single greatest book in American literature?

A. Probably *Moby-Dick*.

Q. Do you have any qualifications—you say probably—would there be any others that you might—?

A. There are others—*Huckleberry Finn*.

Q. Why do you give *Moby-Dick* the top position?

A. Well, I don't. I'm just naming ones that might be. I wouldn't give it the top position, but if I did, it would be for the reason that I rate Wolfe higher than Hemingway, that *Huckleberry Finn* is a complete controlled effort and *Moby-Dick* was still an attempt that didn't quite come off, it was bigger than one human being could do.

. . .

Q. Do you have a similar classification of poets as you do novelists?

A. No, I just know the poets whose work I like but I—

Q. Could you tell me whose you like?

A. Yes, *Leaves of Grass* is one of the good books, and I remember when I read more poetry I read Elinor Wylie, Conrad Aiken, E. A. Robinson, Frost.

. . .

Q. Mr. Faulkner, do you recall having read Henry James at any time?

A. Yes, without much pleasure. Henry James to me was a prig, except *The Turn of the Screw,* which was very fine *tour de force . . . .*

Session Three

February 20, 1957

UNDERGRADUATE COURSE IN AMERICAN LITERATURE

(Not recorded. Reconstructed from memory.)

[. . . Q. In connection with the character of Christ, did you make any conscious attempts in *The Sound and the Fury* to use Christian references, as a number of critics have suggested?

A. No. I was just trying to tell a story of Caddy, the little girl who had muddied her drawers and was climbing up to look in the window where her grandmother lay dead.

Q. But Benjy, for example, is thirty-three years old, the traditional age of Christ at death.

A. Yes. That was a ready-made axe to use, but it was just one of several tools.

. . .

Q. Your work has sometimes been compared with that of Hawthorne's tales with hard-hearted people like Jason. Do you think that one of the things that's wrong with the South is that there are too many characters like this, like Jason Compson, in it?

A. Yes, there are too many Jasons in the South who can be successful, just as there are too many Quentins in the South who are too sensitive to face its reality.

. . .

Q. In *The Sound and the Fury,* where Quentin sees the boys fishing, does his remark about the big fish have any symbolism? He says to them, I hope you don't catch that big fish, he deserves to be let alone.

A. Well, it doesn't have any meaning by itself, but Quentin knows he is going to die and he sees things much more clearly than he would otherwise. He sees things that are more important to him since he doesn't have to worry about them now, and when he wants the old fish to live, it may represent his unconscious desire for endurance, both for himself and for his people. It is just like when some people know they are going to die, and the dross is burned away and they know they can say things because in a while they won't be around to have to defend them.

Q. In the last part of Quentin's section, why do you begin to omit capitals on the names and on "I"?

A. Because Quentin is a dying man, he is already out of life, and those things that were important in life don't mean anything to him any more.

. . .

Q. What is the trouble with the Compsons?

A. They are still living in the attitudes of 1859 or '60.

Q. Why is it that Mrs. Compson refers to Benjy as having been sold into Egypt? Wasn't that Joseph in the Bible? Is the mistake yours or hers?

A. Is there anybody who knows the Bible here?

Q. I looked it up and Benjamin was held hostage for Joseph.

A. Yes, that's why I used them interchangeably. . . .]

18

Session Four

FEBRUARY 25, 1957

UNDERGRADUATE COURSE IN WRITING

. . . Q. I thought I might ask you, Mr. Faulkner, because somebody was speaking of it the other day to me, how you went about writing, how stories came to you. I have a friend, a writer, who has told me sometimes that she will think about her stories for quite a long time and then suddenly they'll be there, and they can be written down without perhaps a great deal of revision or fumbling, that they are there in the mind and they get down on paper that way. Do you have experience of that sort when you write or do you have different things happen?

A. That's sometimes true. I don't think you can make a hard and fast statement about the method of writing, of the conception of a story. It—of course the first thing, the writer's got to be demon-driven. He's got to have to write, he don't know why, and sometimes he will wish that he didn't have to, but he does. The story can come from an anecdote, it can come from a character. With me it never comes from an idea because I don't know too much about ideas and ain't really interested in ideas, I'm interested in people, so what I speak from my experience is probably a limited experience. But I'm interested primarily in people, in man in conflict with himself, with his fellow man, or with his time and place, his environment. So I think there's really no rule for how to begin to write.

. . .

Q. Mr. Faulkner, do you think that a writer can teach young writers?

19

A. I don't think anybody can teach anybody anything. I think that you learn it, but the young writer that is as I say demon-driven and wants to learn and has got to write he don't know why, he will learn from almost any source that he finds. He will learn from older people who are not writers, he will learn from writers, but he learns it—you can't teach it. Then I think too that the writer who's actually hot to say something hasn't got time to be taught. He's too busy learning—he knows what he wants—his instinct says to take this from this man or that from that man. That he's not—he hasn't got time to sit under a mentor and listen to try to learn.

Q. Mr. Faulkner, to get back to this business of style for just a minute. You mentioned in some class I attended that Dostoevsky and Conrad were two people you read a good deal when you were eighteen and nineteen years old. Would you say that you had got something in the way of arrangement of words from Conrad? Every now and then in your stories— I was thinking of a couple of passages in *The Bear,* passages here and there in other stories—there are arrangements of cadence, rhythm, which seem to me to be rather like Conrad. I'm thinking of a passage in "Youth," an arrangement of adjectives, "resplendent yet somber, full of danger, yet promising," the description of the East when that young boy comes upon it. There's something of the same kind of use of— kind of heavy arrangement of adjectives I've noticed in your writing. Does that seem a fair—?

A. Quite true. I got quite a lot from Conrad and I got quite a lot from a man that probably you gentlemen, young people, never heard of—a man called Thomas Beer. You probably know the name.

Q. I know the name Thomas Beer in connection with a critical work. Did he write *The Mauve Decade?*

A. . . . Yes, and I got quite a lot from him—was to me a good tool, a good method, a good usage of words, approach to incident. I think the writer, as I said before, is completely amoral. He takes whatever he needs, wherever he needs, and he does that openly and honestly because he himself hopes

20

that what he does will be good enough so that after him people will take from him, and they are welcome to take from him as he feels that he would be welcome by the best of his predecessors to take what they've done.

. . .

Q. Sir, speaking of symbolism, in your story "That Evening Sun," why did you name that fellow Jesus?

A. That was probably a deliberate intent to shock just a little. That's a—it's a valid name among Negroes in Mississippi—that is, you don't see it too often, but it's nothing unusual, it's not uncommon, but there may have been a little—not so much to shock but to emphasize the point I was making, which was that this Negro woman who had given devotion to the white family knew that when the crisis of her need came, the white family wouldn't be there.

. . .

Q. When did you first realize that you wanted to write, sir?

A. I think I had scribbled all my life, ever since I learned to read. I wrote poetry when I was a young man till I found that I—that it was bad poetry, would never be first-rate poetry. And I was in New Orleans, I worked for a bootlegger. This was in '21, '22, '23. I ran a launch from New Orleans across Pontchartrain down the Industrial Canal out into the Gulf where the schooner from Cuba would bring the raw alcohol and bury it on a sand-spit and we'd dig it up and bring it back to the bootlegger and his mother—she was an Italian, she was a nice little old lady, and she was the expert, she would turn it into Scotch with a little creosote, and bourbon. We had the labels, the bottles, everything—it was quite a business. And I met Sherwood Anderson. He was living there, and I liked him right off, and we would—got along fine together. We would meet in the evening, in the afternoons we'd walk and he'd talk and I'd listen, we'd meet in the evenings and we'd go to a drinking place and we'd sit around till one or two o'clock drinking, and still me listening to him talking. Then in the morning he would be in seclusion working, and the next time I'd see him, the same thing, we would spend the afternoon and evening together, the next morning he'd be working. And I thought then if that was the life it took to be a writer, that was the life for me. So I wrote a book and when I started I found that writing was fun, and I hadn't seen Mr. Anderson in some time till I met Mrs. Anderson on the street. She said, We haven't seen you in a long time. What's wrong? I said, I'm writing a book, and she said, Do you want Sherwood to look at it? And I said, No'm, it's not finished yet. I hadn't thought of anybody looking at it, it was fun to write the book. And I saw her later and she said, I told Sherwood you were writing a book and he said, Good God! Then he said that he will make a trade with you. If he don't have to read it, he will tell his publisher to take it. I said, Done. And so that was how I—my first book got published, and by that time I'd found that writing was fun, I liked it, that was my cup of tea and I've been at it ever since and will probably stick at it.

. . .

Q. Mr. Faulkner, from what viewpoint did you write the story from—I believe it was from *These Thirteen*—it was called "Carcassonne"?

A. That was—I was still writing about a young man in conflict with his environment. I—it seemed to me that fantasy was the best way to tell that story. To have told it in terms of simple realism would have lost something, in my opinion. To use fantasy was the best, and that's a piece that I've always liked because there was the poet again. I wanted to be a poet, and I think of myself now as a failed poet, not as a novelist at all but a failed poet who had to take up what he could do.

Q. Sir, in connection with that, there's an old French poem by the name of "Carcassonne"—I forget the author—and it has pretty much the general, the same sort of theme. I wonder if that was in your mind at the time.

A. I don't know the poem, though if I did know it and I had needed to steal from it, I'm sure I would—I wouldn't have hesitated.

Q. What do you mean, Mr. Faulkner, in your story "All the Dead Pilots," and I believe a story called "Honor," in which you give the impression that those people who fought in the war, after those experiences in the war will be dead the rest of their lives?

22

A. Well, in a way they were. That the ones that even continued to live very long were the exceptions, and the one among them that coped with the change of time or—you can count them on your thumbs almost—Rickenbacker's one but there're not too many others—Bishop, he finally drank himself to death, died last year, and others—Victor Yeates didn't live ten years. In a way they were dead, they had exhausted themselves psychically . . . anyway, they were unfitted for the world that they found afterward. Not that they rejected, they simply were unfitted, they had worn themselves out.

Q. You'd restrict that feeling to people who had been in aviation, not with people who had served in other branches of the armed services?

A. At that time, yes, because there was more concentration of being frightened to flying then than in infantry or ground troops. You just got scared worse quicker and more often flying than you did on the ground.

Q. You seem to distinguish between literary men and writing men. I was wondering if you wouldn't elaborate on that. Are not the two reconcilable? Cannot they be?

A. Yes, I think I said that some writing men are literary men, but I don't think that you have to be a literary man to be a writer. I think that to be a literary man infers a certain amount of—well, even formal education, and there are some writers that have never had formal education. Of course, you can be literary without the formal education, but I've got to talk in terms of what I know about Faulkner now, you see, and Sherwood Anderson—that we were not literary men in the sense that Edmund Wilson is a literary man or Malcolm Cowley, for instance.

Q. . . . . What short-story writers do you admire at the present time?

A. Now, that's a difficult question for me because I think not of writers but of the characters. I remember the characters they wrote about without being able to remember always just who wrote the piece. But when I was a young man this

Thomas Beer that I mentioned, he influenced me a lot. Chekhov. Can't think of some of the others.

Q. What about the present writers in your area of the country—a writer like Eudora Welty?

A. Well, I think again of the books rather than the writer. I think of a book of hers called *The Robber Bridegroom* which was quite different from any of the other things she has done, which to me was the worthwhile one . . . .

. . .

Q. . . . Do you feel a necessity to . . . tell all the truth about that character that you feel needs to be told regardless . . .?

A. No, I think that after about ten books, I had learned enough of judgment to where I could pick and choose the facet of the character which I needed at that particular time to move the story I was telling, so that I can take a facet of one character in one story and another facet of that character in another story. To me it's the same character, though sometimes to the reader it may seem as though the character had changed or had developed more—to me he hasn't. That I used my editorial prerogative of choosing what I needed from that particular character at that particular time.

. . .

Q. Mr. Faulkner, how much do you feel that the writer's being involved with people in his writings is dependent upon his being actively involved with real people in the real world?

A. I think that that has nothing to do with the writing. That he can be involved with people, he can be involved with alcohol, or with gambling or anything and it's not going to affect the writer. Now, I have no patience and I don't hold with the mute inglorious Miltons. I think that if he's demon-driven, with something to be said, then he's going to write it, he can blame his—the fact that he's not turning out the work on lots of things. I've heard lots of people say, Well, if I were not married and had children I would be a writer. I've heard people say, If I could just stop doing this I would be a writer. I don't agree with that. I think if you're going to write, you're going to write and nothing will stop you. If you can be involved, and probably the more you're involved, it may

24

be better for you. That maybe it's bad to crawl off into the ivory tower and stay there—maybe you do need to be involved, to get the edges beaten off of you a little every day—may be good for the writer.

Q. Mr. Faulkner, in the story "Red Leaves," the slave escapes from his Indian captors and goes and hides in the swamp and in order to avert his capture has the cottonmouth strike him in the arm. Then the Indians come and capture him anyway. And—why did this happen in the story? Is this to show that man can't escape his condition?

A. No, that was—the snake episode was to show that man when he knows he's going to die thinks that he can accept death, but he doesn't—he doesn't, really. The Negro at the time, he said, I'm already dead, it doesn't matter, the snake can bite me because I'm already dead, but yet at the end he still wanted to put off—that man will cling to life, that in preference—between grief and nothing, man will take grief always.

. . .

Q. Many writers beginning to write, usually in their first work make one of their characters, usually the hero, an image of himself. Now, I don't find this true in your writing at all. But may I ask you, do you ever find yourself identifying with one of your characters, and have to resist—for instance someone like Gavin Stevens or just [?] the old man in the last pages of *A Fable* who comes out of the crowd?

A. I don't know whether anyone could say—any writer could say just how much he identifies himself with his characters. Quite often the young man will write about himself simply because himself is what he knows best. That he is using himself as the standard of measure, and to simplify things, he writes about himself as—perhaps as he presumes himself to be, maybe he hopes himself to be, or maybe as he hates himself for being. Though after that, the more you write, the more you see you have to write, the more you have learned by writing, and probably you don't really have time to identify yourself with a character except at certain moments when the character is in a position to express truthfully things

25

which you yourself believe to be true. Then you'll put your own ideas in his mouth, but they—when you do that they'll become his. I think that you're not trying to preach through the character, that you're too busy writing about people. It just happens that this man agrees with you on this particular point and so he says it.

Q. Mr. Faulkner, you seem to say that a writer should write out of the heart and I am assuming that also—this is an assumption—that you believe that a writer should write from the heart. Now as opposd to writing from the—out of the heart, there's writing out of the glands, which you mentioned before. May a writer successfully write from the glands rather than from the heart?

A. He can successfully do it, like what's his name? Spillane and the toughs theme [?], but it's not good writing, it's not worth doing, in my opinion. It's successful but it ain't worth doing. I—what I meant, to write from the heart is—it's the heart that has the desire to be better than man is, the up here can know the distinction between good and evil, but it's the heart that makes you want to be better than you are. That's what I mean by to write from the heart. That it's the heart that makes you want to be brave when you are afraid that you might be a coward, that wants you to be generous, or wants you to be compassionate when you think that maybe you won't. I think that the intellect, it might say, Well, which is the most profitable—shall I be compassionate or shall I be uncompassionate? Which is most profitable? Which is the most profitable—shall I be brave or not? But the heart wants always to be better than man is.

Q. Was the "Rose for Emily" an idea or a character? Just how did you go about it?

A. That came from a picture of the strand of hair on the pillow. It was a ghost story. Simply a picture of a strand of hair on the pillow in the abandoned house.

. . .

Q. Mr. Faulkner, you say you're interested in and have been throughout your writing in people rather than ideas.

I was just wondering, as you were saying that, about, for example a book like the *Fable*, at what point did the allegory—did you become conscious of it? Obviously you didn't take the idea and impose it, I gather from what you say. What got you into the *Fable*, what—.

A. That was *tour de force*. The notion occurred to me one day in 1942 shortly after Pearl Harbor and the beginning of the last great war, Suppose—who might that unknown soldier be? Suppose that had been Christ again, under that fine big cenotaph with the eternal flame burning on it? That He would naturally have got crucified again, and I had to—then it became *tour de force,* because I had to invent enough stuff to carry this notion.

Q. You were writing from an idea then?

A. That's right, that was an idea and a hope, an unexpressed thought that Christ had appeared twice, had been crucified twice, and maybe we'd have only one more chance . . . .

Session Five

MARCH 7, 1957

THE ENGLISH CLUB

Q. [The people in *The Hamlet* don't seem to have much contact with the outside world. I was wondering about what time the stories take place. Is it the 1890's, or the next decade?]

A. Well, when you go to the trouble to invent a private domain of your own, then you're the master of time, too. I have the right, I think, to shift these things around wherever it sounds best, and I can move them about in time and, if necessary, change their names. This would be 1906 or 07 this happened. That is, the more you write, the more you've got to compromise with such facts as time and place. And so I've got to agree with Mr. Gwynn and establish this somewhere in time, so it's about 1907.

Q. Mr. Faulkner, have you ever seen such an auction [like that in "Spotted Horses"] taking place?

A. Yes'm. I bought one of these horses once. They appeared in our country, every summer somebody would come in with another batch of them. They were Western range-bred ponies, pintos—had never had a bridle on them, had never seen shelled corn before, and they'd be brought into our town and auctioned off for prices from three or four dollars up to six or seven. And I bought this one for $4.75. I was, oh I reckon, ten years old. My father, at that time, ran a livery stable, and there was a big man, he was six feet and a half tall, he weighed two hundred pounds, but mentally he was about ten years old, too. And I wanted one of those horses,

29

and my father said, Well, if you and Buster can buy one for what money you've saved, you can have it. And so we went to the auction and we bought one for $4.75. We got it home, we were going to gentle it, we had a two-wheeled cart made out of the front axle of a buggy, with shafts on it, and we fooled with that critter—it was a wild animal, it was a wild beast, it wasn't a domestic animal at all. And finally Buster said that it was about ready, so we had the cart in a shed—Estelle probably remembers this—we put a croker-sack over the horse's head and backed it into the cart with two Negroes to fasten it in, to buckle traces and toggles and things, and me and Buster got in the seat and Buster said, All right boys, let him go, and they snatched the sack off the horse's head. He went across the lot—there was a big gate, the lane, it turned it at a sharp angle—it hung the inside wheel on the gatepost as it turned, we were down on one hub then, and about that time Buster caught me by the back of the neck and threw me just like that and then he jumped out. And the cart was scattered up that lane, and we found the horse a mile away, run into a dead-end street. All he had left on him was just the hames—the harness gone.[1] But that was a pleasant experience. But we kept that horse and gentled him to where I finally rode him. But I loved that horse because that was my own horse. I bought that with my own money.

. . .

Q. Mr. Faulkner, do you feel that the gap between the people and the law that exists in "Spotted Horses" has closed any since then? . . .

A. Will you explain a little more what that means?

Q. Well, it's so inappropriate, and we feel that in the end it's so ridiculous, really. It's so far from the people and the way they live, and it doesn't seem to apply to them. I just wondered if you felt that it were more appropriate now.

Q. You mean that Mrs. Armstid doesn't get her money back in court?

[1] This episode appears in Part 3 of *The Bear* as Ike McCaslin's recollection of his debt to Boon Hogganbeck.

30

Q. Yes.

A. Oh well, that's one of the natural occupational hazards of breathing, is conflict with the law, with police. I think that all people have to face that and accept it, and do the best they can with it. That's—if she had got her money back, it would have been bad on me because my story would have blown up.

. . .

Q. Mr. Faulkner, Eula Varner seems to be the sort of character who in some ways seems almost larger than life and seems to be invested with a meaning that's almost symbolic. When you conceived this character, did she seem to represent, let us say, some of the best aspects of the Varners?

A. No, you're quite right, she was larger than life. That she was an anachronism, she had no place there, that that little hamlet couldn't have held her, and when she moved on to Jefferson, that couldn't hold her either. But then that'll be in the next book, the one that'll be out next month. You're quite right, she was larger than life, she was too big for this world.

Q. You had said previously that *The Sound and the Fury* came from the impression of a little girl up in a tree, and I wondered how you built it from that, and whether you just, as you said, let the story develop itself?

A. Well, impression is the wrong word. It's more an image, a very moving image to me was of the children. 'Course, we didn't know at that time that one was an idiot, but they were three boys, one was a girl and the girl was the only one that was brave enough to climb that tree to look in the forbidden window to see what was going on. And that's what the book —and it took the rest of the four hundred pages to explain why she was brave enough to climb the tree to look in the window. It was an image, a picture to me, a very moving one, which was symbolized by the muddy bottom of her drawers as her brothers looked up into the apple tree that she had climbed to look in the window. And the symbolism of the muddy bottom of the drawers became the lost Caddy,

31

which had caused one brother to commit suicide and the other brother had misused her money that she'd send back to the child, the daughter. It was, I thought, a short story, something that could be done in about two pages, a thousand words, I found out it couldn't. I finished it the first time, and it wasn't right, so I wrote it again, and that was Quentin, that wasn't right. I wrote it again, that was Jason, that wasn't right, then I tried to let Faulkner do it, that still was wrong.

Q. Mr. Faulkner, one thing that we sometimes seem to see with acquisitive people like the Snopeses is that after they have made the gains which they want very much to make, respectability seems to set in and start to work on them too. Do you see any signs of that happening in that clan?

A. No, only that the rapacious people—if they're not careful—they are seduced away and decide that what they've got to have is respectability, which destroys one, almost anybody. That is, nobody seems to be brave enough anymore to be an out-and-out blackguard or rascal, that sooner or later he's got to be respectable, and that finishes it.

Q. Why aren't they blackguards anymore?

A. They ain't brave and strong and tough like they used to be.

Q. Why not?

A. It's the curse of the times maybe, and maybe there's a— three-or-four-color printing of advertisements have been too seductive or a picture of a fine big car in two colors with a handsome young woman by it so that you almost think the woman comes with the new car to make the installment payments and one is—there's so much pressure to conform, to be respectable.

Q. More than in the Victorians.

A. I think so, yes. In the Victorian they tried to force you to be respectable to save your soul. Now they compel you to be respectable to be rich.

Q. Were these people blackguards to save their souls? I'm not quite sure I understand the connection.

A. Well, I think that possibly the Old Adam in man suggests to him to be a blackguard if he can get away with it, and when there's a great deal of pressure to be respectable, if there is a great enough reward for the respectability, he will choose that in preference to the pleasure of being a scoundrel and a blackguard. That people don't have enough verve and zest anymore, which is not the fault of man so much as the fault of the time that we live in, to where he—there's too much pressure against being an individualist, and a good first-rate scoundrel is an individualist. He don't really belong to a gang. Once he's got to join a gang, he becomes a second-rate scoundrel. But a first-rate scoundrel, like a first-rate artist, he's an individualist, and the pressure's all against being an individualist—you've got to belong to a group. It don't matter much what group, but you've got to belong to it, or there's no place for you in the culture or the economy. Maybe to belong to a gang, you might escape the atom bomb.

Q. Are you saying that he has to be a scoundrel to be an individualist?

A. No sir, I say a scoundrel, to be a good one, must be an individualist, that only an individualist can be a first-rate scoundrel. Only an individualist can be a first-rate artist. He can't belong to a group or a school and be a first-rate writer.

Q. You could have some grudging admiration for Flem Snopes, who pretty well sticks to his character.

A. Well, until he was bitten by the bug to be respectable, and then he let me down . . . .

Q. Are there any good Snopeses? That boy of Eck's [Wall Street Panic] seems like a nice little fellow. Is he going to get depraved too?

A. No no. He turned into, in his way, a pretty good boy. He wanted no more of Snopes. He tried to remove himself from the aura and orbit of Snopes.

. . .

Q. Mr. Faulkner, you said before that it was your belief that man would prevail. Well, in the light of this book *The Hamlet* and several others that we've discussed recently, what type of man do you think will prevail, what kind—the scoundrel?

A. No no, the scoundrel in time is seduced away by the desire to be respectable, so he's finished. There's a—what quality in man that prevails, it's difficult to be specific about, but somehow man does prevail, there's always someone that will never stop trying to cope with Snopes, that will never stop trying to get rid of Snopes.

Q. . . . A remnant?

A. No, the impulse to eradicate Snopes is in my opinion so strong that it selects its champions when the crisis comes. When the battle comes it always produces a Roland. It doesn't mean that they will get rid of Snopes or the impulse which produces Snopes, but always there's something in man that don't like Snopes and objects to Snopes and if necessary will step in to keep Snopes from doing some irreparable harm. Whatever it is that keeps us still trying to paint the pictures, to make the music, to write the books—there's a great deal of pressure not to do that, because certainly the artist has no place in nature and almost no place at all in our American culture and economy, but yet people still try to write books, still try to paint pictures. They still go to a lot of trouble to produce the music, and a few people will always go to hear the music, which still has nothing to do with the number of people that will produce the Cadillac cars or the economy which will give everybody a chance to buy a Cadillac car on the installment plan, or the deep freezes. That is, all that's advertised, it has to be advertised, in order to keep people buying it, but the books, the music, that's not advertised, yet still there are people that will pay for it, will buy the pictures. It's a slow process but yet it apparently goes on. That we will even outlast atom and hydrogen bombs—I don't know right now how we will do it but my bet is we will.

. . .

Q. Mr. Faulkner, along this respectability-scoundrel line, how do you explain Colonel Sutpen, who sweeps into Jefferson and grimly sets himself up and at long last decides he'll have respectability . . . ? Does he really lose his individuality or isn't this respectability just another notch in his rifle, so to speak?

A. He wanted more than that. He wanted revenge as he saw it, but also he wanted to establish the fact that man is immortal, that man, if he is man, cannot be inferior to another man through artificial standards or circumstances. What he was trying to do—when he was a boy, he had gone to the front door of a big house and somebody, a servant, said, Go around to the back door. He said, I'm going to be the one that lives in the big house, I'm going to establish a dynasty, I don't care how, and he violated all the rules of decency and honor and pity and compassion, and the fates took revenge on him. That's what that story was. But he was trying to say in his blundering way that, Why should a man be better than me because he's richer than me, that if I had had the chance I might be just as good as he thinks he is, so I'll make myself as good as he thinks he is by getting the same outward trappings which he has, which was a big house and servants in it. He didn't say, I'm going to be braver or more compassionate or more honest than he—he just said, I'm going to be as rich as he was, as big as he was on the outside.

Q. And he never really attained this respectability?

A. No, he was—the Greeks destroyed him, the old Greek concept of tragedy. He wanted a son which symbolized this ideal, and he got too many sons—his sons destroyed one another and then him. He was left with—the only son he had left was a Negro.

Q. Mr. Faulkner, you have said that you regarded respectability as one of the prime enemies of individualism. Do you regard love as an enemy of individualism?

A. No no. What's love got to do with respectability? No sir, I do not. Respectability is an artificial standard which comes from up here. That is, respectability is not your concept or my concept. It's what we think is Jones's concept of respectability.

Q. I don't mean to defend respectability in love or out. What I mean to do is—Quiet, please!—what I mean to ask is this. Isn't there a basic dichotomy between the kind of individualism which you are praising and the attitude of love?

A. If you will substitute decency for respectability I would agree with you. I don't quite follow you between respectability and love, decency and love. That's an interesting point. Has anybody else got a thought on that?

. . .

Q. Mr. Faulkner, do you regard *Pylon* as a serious novel, and what were you driving at in that novel?

A. To me they were a fantastic and bizarre phenomenon on the face of a contemporary scene, of our culture at a particular time. I wrote that book because I'd got in trouble with *Absalom, Absalom!* and I had to get away from it for a while so I thought a good way to get away from it was to write another book, so I wrote *Pylon*. They were ephemera and phenomena on the face of a contemporary scene. That is, there was really no place for them in the culture, in the economy, yet they were there, at that time, and everyone knew that they wouldn't last very long, which they didn't. That time of those frantic little aeroplanes which dashed around the country and people wanted just enough money to live, to get to the next place to race again. Something frenetic and in a way almost immoral about it. That they were outside the range of God, not only of respectability, of love, but of God too. That they had escaped the compulsion of accepting a past and a future, that they were—they had no past. They were as ephemeral as the butterfly that's born this morning with no stomach and will be gone tomorrow. It seemed to me interesting enough to make a story about, but that was just to get away from a book that wasn't going too well, till I could get back at it.

Q. I think that perhaps we've taken enough of Mr. Faulkner's energy, unless, sir, you feel the wish to carry on a bit more . . . .

A. Well, I've told you, this is a dreadful habit to get into, where you can stand up in front of people and talk and nobody can say, Shut up and sit down.

Session Six

MARCH 9, 1957

UNDERGRADUATE COURSE IN CONTEMPORARY LITERATURE

Q. Sir, a fyce plays a minor part in "Was" and in a few more of your stories, I believe. Well, is a fyce just a mongrel or is he an out-of-the-ordinary mongrel that you might equate with the primitive?

A. He is—in our Mississippi jargon, he is any small dog, usually—he was a fox or rat terrier at one time that has gotten mixed up with hound, with bird-dog, everything else, but any small dog in my country is called a fyce.

Q. Can we look upon him as representing the primitive, such as the bear and the forest?

A. No, he's the—in a way, the antithesis of the bear. The bear represented the obsolete primitive. The fyce represents the creature who has coped with environment and is still on top of it, you might say. That he has—instead of sticking to his breeding and becoming a decadent degenerate creature, he has mixed himself up with the good stock where he picked and chose. And he's quite smart, he's quite brave. All's against him is his size. But I never knew a fyce yet that realized that he wasn't big as anything else he ever saw, even a bear.

Q. Mr. Faulkner, into what strata would these people fit— Mr. Hubert and—

A. They were the aristocracy of provincial Mississippi at that time. It was still frontier. In Natchez they had the fine Empire furniture, people had—they spent their money on ob-

37

jets d'art from Europe, furnishings and fine clothes. In the country, these people, they were aristocracy, but they were still frontier, they were still the tall man with the long rifle, in a way. That even their splendor was a little on the slovenly side, that they went through the motions of living like dukes and princes but their life wasn't too different from the man who lived in a mud-floored hovel. No, they represented the aristocracy, they were the wealthy, the men of power, the owners of slaves.

Q. Could you explain the significance of the title "Was"?

A. Yes, this was the first chapter in a book which was composed of short stories. It covered a great deal of time. The central character in the book was a man named Isaac McCaslin who was old at the time of the book. But this background which produced Isaac McCaslin had to be told by somebody, and so this is Isaac McCaslin's uncle, this Cass here is not old Ike, this is Ike's uncle. And "Was" simply because Ike is saying to the reader, I'm not telling this, this was my uncle, my great-uncle that told it. That's the only reason for "Was"— that this was the old time. But it's part of him too.

Q. Sir, does the presentation of the ribbon to Uncle Buddy have any significance from medieval tales or anything?

A. Yes, that was Miss Sophonsiba with that belief of hers and her brother too that they were the rightful heirs to the Earldom of Warwick, and Miss Sophonsiba lived on Walter Scott, probably, and she had nothing to do, and she would read the fine flamboyant tales of chivalry where the maiden cast the veil to the knight in the tournament and that was all that was.

Q. Sir, a more general question, not limited to this story. The role of fate seems very strong in your work. Do you believe in free will for your characters?

A. I would think I do, yes. But I think that man's free will functions against a Greek background of fate, that he has the free will to choose and the courage, the fortitude to die for his choice, is my conception of man, is why I believe that man will endure. That fate—sometimes fate lets him

38

alone. But he can never depend on that. But he has always the right to free will and we hope the courage to die for his choice.

Q. Sir, do you look at your humor as a—with the same inspiration as you do a serious thing or is it more a relaxing kind of work?

A. No, no, it's a part of man too, it's a part of life. That people are—there's not too fine a distinction between humor and tragedy, that even tragedy is in a way walking a tightrope between the ridiculous—between the bizarre and the terrible. That it's—possibly the writer uses humor as a tool, that he's still trying to write about people, to write about man, about the human heart in some moving way, and so he uses whatever tool that he thinks will do most to finish the picture which at the moment he is trying to paint, of man. That he will use humor, tragedy, just as he uses violence. They are tools, but an ineradicable parts of life, that humor is.

Q. What is the significance of the title, "Red Leaves"?

A. Well, that was probably symbolism. The red leaves referred to the Indian. It was the deciduation of Nature which no one could stop that had suffocated, smothered, destroyed the Negro. That the red leaves had nothing against him when they suffocated him and destroyed him. They had nothing against him, they probably liked him, but it was normal deciduation which the red leaves, whether they regretted it or not, had nothing more to say in.

Q. Sir, you use hunting terms all through "Was" when they're chasing Tomey's Turl. Is there any significance to this—I mean, do they think that perhaps this colored man is not about—well, say he's on the same plane as the fox?

A. At that time he was, at the very time that these twin brothers had believed that there was something outrageous and wrong in slavery and they had done what they could. In fact, they had given up their father's fine mansion to let the slaves live in it and they had built a two-room log cabin that they lived in. That they by instinct knew that slavery was wrong, but they didn't know quite what to do about it. And in the heat of the pursuit—well, in daily life, they would use the

39

terms in which the Negro was on a level with the dog or the animal they ran. And especially in the heat of a race, which—though this was more of a deadlier purpose than simple pleasure, in the heat of running this man the man became quarry that would have received the same respect that the bear or the deer would—that is, the bear or the deer would have had his chance for his life. They wouldn't have betrayed him, tricked him, they wouldn't have built a deadfall for him. They would have run him all fair with the dogs and if he could escape, could kill the dogs and get away, good for him. If he couldn't, it was too bad.

Q. Sir, never having been fox-hunting, what do you mean by "going to earth," as far as Tomey's Turl was concerned?

A. That's when the quarry finds a hole in the ground, a den, and runs into it. The fox before the dogs, he will try first to trick the dogs, and if he can't, then he gets into something that the dogs can't follow him into. He goes—finds an old fox den or something that he knows, that the dogs are too big to follow, he gets in there, he's gone to earth.

Q. Sir, did Tomey's Turl stack the deck, and if so—?

A. Oh yes, because he wanted Tennie and he wanted to go back home and take Tennie with him.

Q. Well, I understood that in the last thing it says that if he—if Mr. Hubert didn't call Uncle Buddy, then everything would stay just the way it was, and that Tomey's Turl would go back with Uncle Buddy and Uncle Buck and that Tennie would stay with Mr. Hubert and leave it just the way it was before.

A. No no, if Uncle Buddy saved Uncle Buck from Miss Sophonsiba, then Uncle Buddy would have to buy Tennie. That was the way the bet was settled, and so Tomey's Turl, he didn't care whether Uncle Buck was safe from Miss Sophonsiba or not, but he wanted Tennie to go back home with him, and so he hunted around, found that last deuce for Uncle Buddy. He was playing for Tennie, Uncle Buddy was playing for his brother, to save his brother. Their aims were the same though the end was slightly different.

40

Q. Sir, in another one of your stories, "Percy Grimm," do you think that the type of person that is exemplified there is prevalent in the South today, perhaps in the White Citizens Councils?

A. I wouldn't say prevalent, he exists everywhere, I wrote that book in 1932 before I'd ever heard of Hitler's Storm Troopers, what he was was a Nazi Storm Trooper, but then I'd never heard of one then, and he's not prevalent but he's everywhere. I wouldn't say that there are more of him in the South, but I would say that there are probably more of him in the White Citizens Council than anywhere else in the South, but I think you find him everywhere, in all countries, in all people.

Q. Sir, was Percy Grimm ever punished for his crime?

A. I think in time that every Storm Trooper suffers for it. He don't suffer any retribution, any stroke of lightning from the gods, but he's got to live with himself, and there comes a time when you've got to live with that, when you're too old and the fire which enables you to get a certain amount of hysterical adrenalic pleasure out of things like that is gone, and all you have left is to remember what you did and you probably wonder why in God's name you did things like that, and you have to live with it, and I think that quite often unexplained suicides go back to some man who has done something like that and he gets old, and he's got to live with it, and decides it's not worth living with it.

Q. You spoke a little while ago of Greek themes. I was wondering if you think that modern literature or twentieth-century literature, so to speak, could feature the truly tragic hero that you would find in Greek times, or do you think the characters should be meaner or more simple? . . .

A. That's a difficult question to answer. I think the writer has got to write in terms of his environment, and his environment consists not only in the immediate scene, but his readers are part of that environment too, and maybe nobody can write forever without expecting to be read, and probably a writer, whether he intends to or not, or knows it or not, is going to shape what he writes in the terms of who will read it. So maybe when there are fine listeners, there will be fine poets again, that maybe the writing that is not too good is not just the writer's fault, it may be because of the environment, a part of which is the general effluvium of the readers, the people who will read it. That does something to the air they all breathe together, that compels the shape of the book. It would be fine if people could write in the old simple clear Hellenic tradition, but then maybe that would be now obsolete, that there was a time for that, the time for that is not now, it may come back, if life does go in cycles.

Q. Sir, in your excerpt from *The Unvanquished*, "An Odor of Verbena," why is that sprig of verbena left on Bayard's pillow right at the very end, when she leaves, she says she's going to abjure verbena for ever and ever, and then he goes off, he walks into town and he meets Mr. Redmond, I believe it is, and then without any gun or anything, and then comes back and the sprig of verbena is left on his pillow.

A. That—of course, the verbena was associated with Drusilla, with that woman, and she had wanted him to take a pistol and avenge his father's death. He went to the man who had shot his father, unarmed, and instead of killing the man, by that gesture he drove the man out of town, and although that had violated Drusilla's traditions of an eye for an eye, she—the sprig of verbena meant that she realized that that took courage too and maybe more moral courage than to have drawn blood, or to have taken another step in a endless feud of an eye for an eye.

Q. But then why did she leave?

A. Because she was at that time too old, she was still too involved in it to accept that morally. I mean accept it physically, that her husband had not been avenged by his own son. That is, her intellect said, This was a brave thing, but the Eve in her said, My husband, my lover has not been avenged. And she could say, You were brave, but she—this is not for me, that I—that sort of bravery is not for me.

Q. Sir, is there any reason for the Southern—the blossoming of Southern writing, that is, are there any circumstances in the Southern environment that would bring about the blossoming of great authors as it has?

A. I don't know. That's a literary question and I wouldn't undertake to answer it. I might say that when that so-called blossoming of Southern writers came along, it was at a time when nobody in the South had much money, they couldn't travel, and they had to invent a world a little different from the shabby one they lived in so they took to writing, which is cheaper—than that is, a ream of paper and a pencil is cheaper than a railroad ticket.

Q. Sir, why, in the beginning of your book about—you mention Ikkemotubbe, why does Ikkemotubbe cease to own the land as soon as he realizes that it is saleable, and do the people like the Compsons who have bought the land, do they ever belong to the land in the sense that Ikkemotubbe previously had?

A. No, I don't think they do. I think the ghost of that ravishment lingers in the land, that the land is inimical to the white man because of the unjust way in which it was taken from Ikkemotubbe and his people. That happened by treaty, which President Jackson established with the Chickasaws and the Choctaws, in which they would take land in Oklahoma in exchange for their Mississippi land, and they were paid for it, but they were compelled to leave it, either to leave on—to follow a chimera in the West or to stay there in a condition even worse than the Negro slave, in isolation. There are a few of them still in Mississippi, but they are a good deal like animals in a zoo: they have no place in the culture, in the economy, unless they become white men, and they have in some cases mixed with white people and their own conditions have vanished, or they have mixed with Negroes and they have descended into the Negroes' condition of semi-peonage.

Q. And even the aristocracy, the original aristocracy was tainted. They never owned the land. The land was never theirs.

A. That's right. The Indians held the land communally,

43

a few of them that were wise enough to see which way the wind was blowing would get government patents for the land. There was one of them, a Choctaw chief, was one of the wealthiest men in Mississippi, Greenwood Leflore, he was wise enough to get a patented deed to his land and to take up the white man's ways, he was a cotton planter, he'd built a tremendous mansion and imported the furnishings from France, and he was quite wealthy. And then when in '61 he declined to accept the Confederacy and Confederate troops were sent in there and his stables were set on fire, the story is that when they demanded that he accept an oath to the Confederacy, he went into the house and got a United States flag and wrapped it around himself and came out and walked into that burning barn and died there, but that's—we don't know whether that's so or not, but that's the legend. But the house is still there, it's a museum now, and his descendants, they are two great-great-nieces. They're mostly white now. They own the place.

Session Seven

March 11, 1957

UNDERGRADUATE COURSE IN CONTEMPORARY LITERATURE

Q. This is a question about *Light in August.* Could you tell me your purpose in placing the chapter about Hightower's early life in the end of the novel, that is, rather than when Hightower first appears?

A. It may be this. Unless a book follows a simple direct line such as a story of adventure, it becomes a series of pieces. It's a good deal like dressing a showcase window. It takes a certain amount of judgment and taste to arrange the different pieces in the most effective place in juxtaposition to one another. That was the reason. It seemed to me that was the most effective place to put that, to underline the tragedy of Christmas's story by the tragedy of his antithesis, a man who— Hightower was a man who wanted to be better than he was afraid he would. He had failed his wife. Here was another chance he had, and he failed his Christian oath as a man of God, and he escaped into his past where some member of his family was brave enough to match the moment. But it was put at that point in the book, I think, because I thought that was the most effective place for it.

Q. Sir, do you find it easier to create a female character in literature or a male character?

A. It's much more fun to try to write about women because I think women are marvelous, they're wonderful, and I know very little about them, and so I just—it's much more fun to try to write about women than about men—more difficult, yes.

Q. Sir, in "Delta Autumn," in the thoughts of Ike McCaslin, when he's talking to the colored girl, you write, "Maybe in a thousand or two thousand years in America, but not now, not now." I was wondering how you might apply that to the present-day conditions that have happened since the writing of the story, with the Supreme Court decision and what not.

A. He used "a thousand or two thousand years" in his despair. He had seen a condition which was intolerable, which shouldn't be but it was, and he was saying in effect that this must be changed, this cannot go on, but I'm too old to do anything about it, that maybe in a thousand years somebody will be young enough and strong enough to do something about it. That was all he meant by the numbers. But I think that he saw, as everybody that thinks, that a condition like that is intolerable, not so much intolerable to man's sense of justice, but maybe intolerable to the condition, that any country has reached the point where if it is to endure, it must have no inner conflicts based on a wrong, a basic human wrong.

. . .

Q. Sir, in "Was" you tell us how Uncle Buck successfully foiled an attempt by Mr. Hubert Beauchamp to get him to marry Sophonsiba. Well, eventually they do get married, and I wonder if you could give us any idea as to whether she eventually caught him.

A. Oh, I think that women are much stronger, much more determined than men, and just because these men had wasted an evening over a deck of cards, that hadn't changed Miss Sophonsiba's intentions at all and probably Uncle Buck finally just gave up. That was his fate and he might just as well quit struggling.

Q. Sir, can you tell us where Sutpen acquired his money in "Wedding in the Rain"? First he came back with the architect and all his—all the Negroes or sort of creatures that he had, and built his house, and then later on came back with the furniture.

A. He very likely looted his Caribbean father-in-law's plantation when he married the daughter. I don't know that I ever decided myself just how he did it but very likely he

46

looted and wrecked the whole place, took the girl because he didn't want her especially, he wanted a son, he wanted to establish his dynasty. And I imagine that he got that money to the States and then had to hide it here and there. There were no banks in those days, no safe place to put it. Probably was gold, something that was intrinsic of itself, and he would go off wherever he had buried it and dig up a little more when he needed it.

Q. Sir, in your story *The Bear,* why did Boon kill Sam Fathers?

A. Because Sam asked him to. Sam's life had finished then. He was an old man, he was sick, and Sam at that point represented his whole race. The white man had dispossessed the whole race, they had nothing left, and Sam was old, he was weak and sick. That was the Greek conception, and Sam knew that Boon and this little boy who was too young to have used the knife or whatever it was, would defend Sam's right to die, and would approve of the fact that Boon, the instrument, was willing to kill Sam, but Sam was done with life, and he wanted that done, and Boon was the servant that did it.

Q. Sir, in "A Rose for Emily" is it possible to take Homer Barron and Emily and sort of show that one represents the South and the North? Is there anything on your part there trying to show the North and the South in sort of a battle, maybe Miss Emily representing the South coming out victorious in the rather odd way that she did?

A. That would be only incidental. I think that the writer is too busy trying to create flesh-and-blood people that will stand up and cast a shadow to have time to be conscious of all the symbolism that he may put into what he does or what people may read into it. That if he had time to—that is, if one individual could write the authentic, credible, flesh-and-blood character and at the same time deliver the message, maybe he would, but I don't believe any writer is capable of doing both, that he's got to choose one of the two: either he is delivering a message or he's trying to create flesh-and-blood, living, suffering, anguishing human beings. And as any man works out of his past, since any man—no man is himself, he's the sum of his past, and in a way, if you can accept the term, of his future too. And this struggle between the South and the North could have been a part of my background, my experience, without me knowing it.

Q. Sir, why is it, in "Death Drag," Jock left despite Captain Warren's plea to stay there or accept the raincoat or accept any sort of job? Was it anything besides pride that made him leave, fly off in that old crate?

A. Yes, it was—pride was about what it was. The—it's—'course is probably true of all flying people, but I do know that the flying people out of that war, most of them would have been better off if they had died on the eleventh of November, that few of them were any good to try to take up the burden of peace, and this man was lost and doomed. Of course, Warren was different. He had managed to cope with 1919, but this other man would never cope with 1919. He was hopeless, he was doomed.

Q. Sir, in your novels, you said in one of the other classes that you begin with a character in mind or more than one character. In your short stories, do they—do you conceive of them the same way? Do you start with a person or do you—?

A. Sometimes with a person, sometimes with an anecdote, but the short story is conceived in the same terms that the book is. The first job the craftsman faces is to tell this as quickly and as simply as I can, and if he's good, if he's of the first water, like Chekhov, he can do it every time in two or three thousand words, but if he's not that good, sometimes it takes him eighty thousand words. But they are similar, and he is simply trying to tell something which was true and moving in the shortest time he can, and then if he has sense enough stop. That is, I don't believe the man or the woman sits down and says, Now I'm going to write a short story, or Now I'm going to write a novel. It's an idea that begins with the thought, the image of a character, or with an anecdote, and even in the same breath, almost like lightning,

48

it begins to take a shape that he can see whether it's going to be a short story or a novel. Sometimes, not always. Sometimes he thinks it'll be a short story and finds that he can't. Sometimes it looks like it's to be novel and then after he works on it, he sees that it's not, that he can tell it in two thousand or five thousand words. No rule to it.

. . .

Q. Do you have any trouble remembering, say, a short story that you might have written in 1925 or something like that?

A. I remember the people, but I can't remember what story they're in nor always what they did. I have to go back and look at it to unravel what the person was doing. I remember the character, though.

. . .

Q. Do you ever jump up in the middle of the night and write something down?

A. Oh, yes. Yes, lots of times. I've never had any order. I have heard of people that can set aside so many hours a day and—or to write so many words a day, but that has never been for me. I like to write when it's hot and then I quit and rest and then I get at it again. And sometimes, fourteen or sixteen hours a day, and then sometimes I won't write a word for fourteen or sixteen days.

. . .

Q. Sir, I understand *Sanctuary,* you've said that it was written for the sensational value. Would you say, now, for a young writer who might be trying to break into it, do you think that he should devote his time and talents, if any, towards a sensational type of work, or do you think that he should try to write more or less from the soul, you might say, or write as he feels rather than what he feels might be accepted?

A. I would say, if he is creating characters which are flesh-and-blood people, are believable, and are honest and true, then he can use sensationalism if he thinks that's an effective way to tell his story. But if he's writing just for sensationalism, then he has betrayed his vocation, and he deserves to suffer from it. That is, sensationalism is in a way an incidental tool, that he might use sensationalism as the carpenter picks up

49

another hammer to drive a nail. But he doesn't—the carpenter don't build a house just to drive nails. He drives nails to build a house.

. . .

Q. When you read these books you've read before, Mr. Faulkner, do you find new things in them constantly?

A. In the sense that you find new things in old friends. That is, there's some reason that you like to go back and spend an hour or two with an old friend. It may not be for anything new, unless the evocation with a little more experience on your own part will throw a new light onto something that you thought you knew before and you find now you didn't, that you maybe know a little more about truth, that what the good writers say to the young man, he knows instinctively are true things. Later on, as he knows a little more, he knows why they're true, and in that sense it is something new, yes.

Q. Could you give us some of the titles of these books, Mr. Faulkner?

A. Yes'm. I read *Don Quixote* every year. I read the Old Testament. I read some of Dickens every year, and I've got a portable Shakespeare, one-volume Shakespeare, that I carry along with me. Conrad, *Moby-Dick*, Chekhov, *Madame Bovary*, some of Balzac almost every year, Tolstoy. I haven't thought of Artzybashev in years. I think I'll get him out and read him again—Artzybashev. Gogol. Most of the Frenchmen of the nineteenth century I read in every year.

. . .

Q. Sir, of the new books you say you occasionally read, have you found any in the last few years that you regard as superior books, superior writing?

A. I remember one about a destroyer in the Pacific by—I believe he was a Virginia man, Eyster? That was, I thought, a pretty good book. There's a young man, a Mississippian, Shelby Foote, that shows promise, if he'll just stop trying to write Faulkner and will write some Shelby Foote. Yes, I've seen a few books, but I don't remember titles nor writers too well. I remember characters and incidents that seem to me to be true, which is the test . . . .

50

Q. What about the Greek tragedies? Do you ever enjoy reading those?

A. When I was young, yes. I haven't read any of the Greek tragedies in a long time, but when I was young, yes.
. . .

Q. Sir, what do you think of Aristotle's theories about tragedy? Do you—there's a lot of dispute about that now, *The Death of a Salesman.* Do you think he's right or—

A. What theory is this?

Q. That a tragedy must—the hero must be a man of high place so that he can fall all the further.

A. Well, I don't think Aristotle meant by high place what it sounds like. I think he meant a man of integrity, more than a man of aristocracy, unless—is that what you meant by high place?

Q. Well, I'm—that's what I say, I believe he does mean money-wise and society-wise rather than integrity. I'm not an authority, but that's—

A. Well, I think that was because he used the high place, the money, the riches, the title as symbols, that a king must be brave, a queen must be chaste, as simple symbols, as puppets. But tragedy, as Aristotle saw it, it's—I would say, is the same conception of tragedy that all writers have: it's man wishing to be braver than he is, in combat with his heart or with his fellows or with the environment, and how he fails, that the splendor, the courage of his failure, and the trappings of royalty, of kingship, are simply trappings to make him more splendid so that he was worthy of being selected by the gods, by Olympus, as an opponent, that man couldn't cope with him so it would take a god to do it, to cast him down.
. . .

Q. ... Was your imagination ... circumscribed in a different way in the *Fable* from the way in which it ordinarily works where you didn't have, presumably, the specific historical pattern in mind?

A. I think that whenever my imaginaton and the bounds of that pattern conflicted, it was the pattern that bulged ...

that gave. When something had to give it wasn't the imagination, the pattern shifted and gave. That may be the reason that a man has to rewrite and rewrite—to reconcile imagination and pattern. Of course, any work of art in its conception when it reaches a point where the man can begin to work has got to have some shape, and the problem then is to make imagination and the pattern conform, meet, be amicable, we'll say. And when one has to give, I believe it's always the pattern that has to give. And so he's got to rewrite, to create a new pattern with a bulge that will take this bulge of the imagination which insists that it's true, it must be.

. . .

Q. Mr. Faulkner, did you ever find yourself surprised at repeating yourself and say, By Jove, I did that thing better twenty-five years ago, or, By Jove, this is better than it was twenty-five years ago?

A. No, because to me there ain't any better. It's either good or it's nothing, and it's—what I did twenty-five years ago didn't suit me and so I forgot that. I'm working on another one, I hope that this one is going to be the right one. Of course, I know it ain't but the one twenty-five years ago is under the bridge. It's too bad, but there's nothing I can do about it anymore, except write a new one.

Q. Mr. Faulkner, do you think an author has his prerogative to create his own language? In other words, to go against what the people create, vernacular? Do you think an author has the right to create his own—I believe Joyce and Eliot have done it—have tried to create, they found that language was not—did not suit their purposes, so they had to go beyond and make a—

A. He has the right to do that provided he don't insist on anyone understanding it. That is—what I'm trying to say is—that I believe I'm paraphrasing Whitman, didn't he say, "To have good poets we must have good readers, too," something like that? Who knows?

Q. Whitman, "great audiences."

A. Well, the writer, actually, that's an obligation that he

assumes with his vocation, that he's going to write it in a way that people can understand it. He doesn't have to write it in the way that every idiot can understand it—every imbecile in the third grade can understand it, but he's got to use a language which is accepted and in which the words have specific meanings that everybody agrees on. I think that *Finnegans Wake* and *Ulysses* were justified, but then it's hard to say on what terms they were justified. That was a case of a genius who was electrocuted by the divine fire.

Q. Mr. Faulkner, it's often been said about great novels or great short stories that they wouldn't pass muster in a freshman English composition course. Now I was wondering, since this is your first stay at a university, if you had any comments on the traditional or the apparently traditional conflict between the creative writer and the schoolman.

A. Well, as an old veteran sixth-grader, that question is I think outside of my province, because I never got to freshman English. I don't know how much it would conflict. Maybe before I've left the University I will be able to pass freshman English.

Q. Mr. Faulkner, with more and more capable Negroes coming to the fore in all facets of public life, do you believe that half a dozen capable Negro fiction writers could do a world of good for the segregation problem?

A. I do, yes.

Q. Well, out of seventeen million people and some of them becoming very adequate physicians and lawyers, don't you believe that they can develop some writers of stature also?

A. I do, yes. I think that people like Armstrong and Dr. Ralph Bunche and George Washington Carver have done much more for the Negro race than all the N.A.A.C.P. leaders, much more, and there's no reason at all why the Negro shouldn't produce good writers. He has got to have—he's got to be freed of the curse of his color. He's got to have equality in terms that he can get used to it and forget that he is a Negro while he's writing, just like the white man hasn't got

53

time to remember whether he's a Gentile or a Catholic while he's writing, and the Negro has got to reach that stage and the white man has got to help him because he can't do it by himself under these conditions.

Q. He's in the best position to write sympathetically about his own conditions?

A. He should be, yes. But you can't write sympathetically about a condition when it's constant outrage to you, you see. You've got to be objective about it.

Q. Mr. Faulkner, do you look on Ike McCaslin as having fulfilled his destiny, the things that he learned from Sam Fathers and from the other men as in his—when he was twelve to sixteen? Do you feel that they stood him in good stead all the way through his life?

A. I do, yes. They didn't give him success but they gave him something a lot more important, even in this country. They gave him serenity, they gave him what would pass for wisdom —I mean wisdom as contradistinct from the schoolman's wisdom of education. They gave him that.

Q. And was—did he ever have any children? Was he able to pass on this—

A. No, no children.

Q. —that had been transmitted to him?

A. In a way, every little eight- or ten-year-old boy was his son, his child, the ones that he taught how to hunt. He had passed on what he had. He was not trying to tell them how to slay animals, he was trying to teach them what he knew of respect for whatever your lot in life is, that if your lot is to be a hunter, to slay animals, you slay the animals with the nearest approach you can to dignity and to decency.

. . .

Q. Do you often find that you can't improve on what you've originally put down?

A. Oh yes, yes. I think any writer keeps at it until he knows that that's the best he can do. It may not be good enough, but when he realizes that's the best he can do, then he moves on to the next sentence or the next paragraph.

54

Q. That's not exactly what I meant. I mean, you say you write as fast as you can to get it out, and then you go back and build up the constructions in there and—

A. No, no. I didn't mean that. I mean that I don't like to —the mechanics of putting the stuff on paper, and I'll try to get it in shape in my mind before I take the—do the work. I didn't mean that I scribbled and then went back over it and edited, no. It's done as much as possible mentally until it begins to sound right. Then I put it down.

Q. Sir, in your writing you try to get very close to people and draw people as you think they are. What do you think of the approach of men like Mencken and Shaw, who really— well, possibly I'm wrong, but I don't think they try to give the public the picture of people, they rather try and slap them in the face a little bit and paint an extreme?

A. Well, they were using the tools of their trade as they believed they were the best tools. I think that Shaw was trying to write about human beings in the light of his own intelligence and his own wit and his own distaste for certain conditions. I think that Mencken was still a constantly angry, indignant man more—he was first that. He was only second a critic, a sociologist, he was mainly just a mad man. Shaw, of course, wasn't. Shaw was an artist.

Q. You mentioned a while ago, in noting some of the books that you liked particularly, *Madame Bovary* and also Tolstoy. I take it from what you also said that the things you admire about these two very different artists would be the fact that they both hit the truth, Flaubert in his extremely precise . . . way, Tolstoy in his almost shapeless way. Would you say something about your own preferences or attitudes toward the different extremes of craftsmanship in *War and Peace* as opposed to *Bovary?*

A. Well, in *Bovary* I saw, or thought I saw, a man who wasted nothing, who was—whose approach toward his language was almost the lapidary's, that he was, whether he had the leisure—I don't know exactly what the term I want—that is, a man who elected to do one book perfectly, in the characters, and in the method, in the style, as against a man who was so busy writing about people that he didn't have much time to bother about style and when he did attain style, he was just as astonished as anybody else. Though that comparison I grant you is better between Flaubert and Balzac, maybe. Well, I think of the man that wrote *Salammbo* and *La Tentation de St. Antoine* and *Madame Bovary* was a stylist who was also—had enough talent to write about people too. But everybody can't do that, everybody can't do both, you have to choose maybe, What shall I do, shall I try to tell the truth about people or shall I try to tell the truth in a chalice.

Q. Does the luxuriance of the foliage in *War and Peace* offend your sense of craftsmanship?

A. No. No, nothing—I'm not enough of a conscious craftsman to remember that I have ever been offended by any style or method. I think that the moment in the book, the story, demands its own style and seems to me just as natural as the moment in the year produces the leaves. That when Melville becomes Old Testament, Biblical, that seems natural to me. When he becomes Gothic, that seems natural to me, too, and I hadn't, really hadn't stopped to think, Now where does one change and become another? Though with the *Bovary* it's as though you know from the very first as soon as you see what he's going to do that he will never disappoint you, that it'll be as absolute as mathematics.

Session Eight

March 13, 1958

UNDERGRADUATE COURSE IN CONTEMPORARY LITERATURE

Q. Mr. Faulkner. This is sort of a question of motivation for the writer. Many of the best Southern writers write about the degeneration of the old aristocracy and the determination to live and to think according to the old traditions and standards. Now do you think that this continued determination on the part of those around him causes the writer to revolt against this system, and accordingly is it a—does this attitude —does it furnish a motivation for writing?

A. It does, in that that is a condition of environment. It's something that is handed to the writer. He is writing about people in the terms that he's most familiar with. That is, it could have sociological implications, but he's not too interested in that. He's writing about people. He is using the material which he knows, the tools which are at hand, and so he uses the instinct or the desire or whatever you will call it of the old people to be reactionary and tory, to stick to the old ways. It's simply a condition, and since it is a condition it lives and breathes, and it is valid as material.

Q. Sir, I believe you were in Europe in 1923 at the same time Anderson and Hemingway and others [were]. At that time, did you associate with them, and if not, was there any specific reason why you were not thrown together, and do you think the group was influenced or influenced each other in any way from their association?

A. They may have. I think the artist is influenced by all in his environment. He's maybe more sensitive to it because he

57

has got to get the materials, the lumber that he's going to build his edifice. I—at that time I didn't think of myself as a writer, I was a tramp then, and I didn't—I wasn't interested in literature nor literary people. They were—I was—there at the same time, I knew Joyce, I knew of Joyce, and I would go to some effort to go to the café that he inhabited to look at him. But that was the only literary man that I remember seeing in Europe in those days.

. . .

Q. Sir, it has been argued that "A Rose for Emily" is a criticism of the North, and others have argued saying that it is a criticism of the South. Now, could this story, shall we say, be more properly classified as a criticism of the times?

A. Now that I don't know, because I was simply trying to write about people. The writer uses environment—what he knows—and if there's a symbolism in which the lover represented the North and the woman who murdered him represents the South, I don't say that's not valid and not there, but it was no intention of the writer to say, Now let's see, I'm going to write a piece in which I will use a symbolism for the North and another symbol for the South, that he was simply writing about people, a story which he thought was tragic and true, because it came out of the human heart, the human aspiration, the human—the conflict of conscience with glands, with the Old Adam. It was a conflict not between the North and the South so much as between, well you might say, God and Satan.

Q. Sir, just a little more on that thing. You say it's a conflict between God and Satan. Well, I don't quite understand what you mean. Who is—did one represent the—

A. The conflict was in Miss Emily, that she knew that you do not murder people. She had been trained that you do not take a lover. You marry, you don't take a lover. She had broken all the laws of her tradition, her background, and she had finally broken the law of God too, which says you do not take human life. And she knew she was doing wrong, and that's why her own life was wrecked. Instead of murdering one lover, and then to go on and take another and when she used him up to murder him, she was expiating her crime.

58

Q. . . . She did do all the things that she had been taught not to do, and being a sensitive sort of a woman, it was sure to have told on her, but do you think it's fair to feel pity for her, because in a way she made her adjustment, and it seems to have wound up in a happy sort of a way—certainly tragic, but maybe it suited her just fine.

A. Yes, it may have, but then I don't think that one should withhold pity simply because the subject of the pity, object of pity, is pleased and satisfied. I think the pity is in the human striving against its own nature, against its own conscience. That's what deserves the pity. It's not the state of the individual, it's man in conflict with his heart, or with his fellows, or with his environment—that's what deserves the pity. It's not that the man suffered, or that he fell off the house, or was run over by the train. It's that he was—that man is trying to do the best he can with his desires and impulses against his own moral conscience, and the conscience of, the social conscience of his time and his place—the little town he must live in, the family he's a part of.

. . .

Q. In *The Bear,* Mr. Faulkner, was there a dog, a real Lion?

A. Yes, there was. I can remember that dog—I was about the age of that little boy—and he belonged to our pack of bear and deer dogs, and he was a complete individualist. He didn't love anybody. The other dogs were all afraid of him, he was a savage, but he did love to run the bear. Yes, I remember him quite well. He was mostly airedale, he had some hound and Lord only knows what else might have been in him. He was a tremendous big brute—stood about that high, must have weighed seventy-five or eighty pounds.

Q. In any bear hunt that Lion participated in, did he ever perform a heroic action like the one in the story?

A. No, not really. There's a case of the sorry, shabby world that don't quite please you, so you create one of your own, so you make Lion a little braver than he was, and you make the bear a little more of a bear than he actually was. I am sure that Lion could have done that and would have done it, and it may be at times when I wasn't there to record the action, he did do things like that.

Q. This question is also concerned with *The Bear*. In conclusion of the story, Ike McCaslin finds Boon destroying his rifle. Now I was wondering if this incident just showed that Boon could not, shall we say, compete with the mechanical age, or whether this was showing the end of an order, the fact that Lion and old Ben were dead, that the hunters weren't returning to the cabin any more, and the land had been sold to a lumber company.

A. A little of both. It was that Boon, with the mentality of a child, a boy of sixteen or seventeen, couldn't cope not only with the mechanical age but he couldn't cope with any time. Also, to me it underlined the heroic tragedy of the bear and the dog by the last survivor being reduced to the sort of petty comedy of someone trying to patch up a gun in order to shoot a squirrel. That made the tragedy of the dog and the bear a little more poignant to me. That's the sort of *tour de force* that I think the writer's entitled to use.

. . .

Q. I know that you stated that you don't read the critics regarding your own work. However, I wonder what ideas you have regarding the aims or the proper function of a literary critic, not only of your works, but shall we say of others as well.

A. I would say he has a valid function, a very important function, but to me he's a good deal like the minister—you don't need to listen to him unless you need him, and I in my own case, I know, I have already decided about the value of my work. There's nothing anybody can tell me I don't know about it, and the critic, nor I either, can improve it any by that time and the only way to improve it is to write one that will be better next time, and so I'm at that and I probably just don't have time to read the critics.

. . .

Q. What would you have done if they had asked you to make changes [in your first novel]?

A. Well, I don't know, because I had lost my bootlegging job of the—I believe the Federal people finally caught him, and I had a job as an ordinary seaman in a freighter then. I spent the next year or two in ships, and by that time I was working on another book, and so I got out of touch with this one. I don't—I reckon I would have changed it probably if the publisher had said, If you make a few changes, we'll print it. I probably would.

Q. Sir, I think you said that you haven't yet achieved your own personal goal as a writer. What is that goal and is it likely that you will succeed in achieving it?

A. That's difficult to say. It's when I have done something that, to use Hemingway's phrase, makes me feel good, that is completely satisfactory, maybe that will be the goal, and I hope just a little that I'll never quite do that because if I do there won't be any reason to go on writing, and I'm too old to take up another hobby. It's—I think that a writer wants to make something that he knows that a hundred or two hundred or five hundred, a thousand years later will make people feel what they feel when they read Homer, or read Dickens or Balzac, Tolstoy, that that's probably his goal. I don't think that he bothers until he gets old like this and has a right to spend a lot of time talking about it to put that into actual words. But probably that's what he wants, that really the writer doesn't want success, that he knows he has a short span of life, that the day will come when he must pass through the wall of oblivion, and he wants to leave a scratch on that wall—Kilroy was here—that somebody a hundred, a thousand years later will see.

Q. Sir, why do you regard *The Sound and the Fury* as your best work?

A. It was the best failure. It was the one that I anguished the most over, that I worked the hardest at, that even when I knew I couldn't bring it off, I still worked at it. It's like the parent feels toward the unfortunate child, maybe. The others that have been easier to write than that, and in ways are better books than that, but I don't have the feeling toward any of them that I do toward that one, because that was the most gallant, the most magnificent failure.

61

Q. Mr. Faulkner, you said that even though you did not bring it off, you worked hardest at it. How do you feel that you failed to bring *The Sound and the Fury* off?

A. It don't make me feel good enough, to use Hemingway's phrase. That's a condition that probably I can't put into words, but if I ever do strike it, I will know it. I think that that's true of any writer.

Q. Well, aren't there parts of it that make you feel good enough?

A. Well, that's not enough—parts of it are not enough, it must be all, you see. You can't compromise, you know, it's either good or it ain't, there's no degrees of goodness. It's either all right or it's not all right.

. . .

Q. Can you make any comment on the part that the Old General plays in *A Fable*, who seemed to me to take two distinct, different parts if not more, in the theme of Passion Week, including the Three Temptations? Would you care to elaborate at all on that character?

A. Well, to me he was the dark, splendid, fallen angel. The good shining cherubim to me are not very interesting, it's the dark, gallant, fallen one that is moving to me. He was an implement, really. What I was writing about was the trilogy of man's conscience represented by the young British Pilot Officer, the Runner, and the Quartermaster General. The one that said, This is dreadful, terrible, and I won't face it even at the cost of my life—that was the British aviator. The Old General who said, This is terrible but we can bear it. The third one, the battalion Runner who said, This is dreadful, I won't stand it, I'll do something about it. The Old General was Satan, who had been cast out of heaven, and—because God Himself feared him.

Q. Well, what—the thing that has puzzled me was that, going back, as far as I could gather, he also had been the father of the Corporal.

A. Yes, that's right.

Q. And that is what has somewhat puzzled me in the allegorical—

A. That was a part of Satan's fearsomeness, that he could usurp the legend of God. That was what made him so fearsome and so powerful, that he could usurp the legend of God and then discard God. That's why God feared him.

Q. Mr. Faulkner, would you care to say anything about the allegorical function of the horse in *A Fable?* He seems to have some very complex and interesting characteristics.

A. Not to me, no. That was simply another struggle between man and his conscience and his environment. The horse was simply a tool—that is, that foul and filthy Cockney hostler was still capable of love for something. That maybe if he'd had a better childhood, a better background, he might have been capable of better love, of something more worthy than a horse. But he was capable of love for one thing, that he could sacrifice to and could defend, even though it was only a horse.

Q. In the story "Red Leaves," in the Indian burial ritual, would it have brought disgrace to that . . . whole ritual had the man-servant committed suicide during the chase, before they caught him?

A. No, they could still have brought his body back and immolated that. No, they were simply cleaning house, that was what the rule said—When the chief went back to the earth, his body servant and his dogs and his horse went with him. No, it would have been no disgrace. In fact, if he had done that quicker, they would have been pleased because it would have saved them all the trouble of tracking him back and forth through that swamp, which they didn't want to do. They were a lazy indolent people, and there wasn't any use of anyone causing all that trouble when he couldn't get away.

Q. What is your purpose in writing into the first section of *The Sound and the Fury* passages that seem disjointed in themselves if the idea is not connected with one another?

A. That was part of the failure. It seemed to me that the book approached nearer the dream if the groundwork of it

was laid by the idiot, who was incapable of relevancy. That's
—I agree with you too, that's a bad method, but to me it
seemed the best way to do it, that I shifted those sections back
and forth to see where they went best, but my final decision
was that though that was not right, that was the best to
do it, that was simply the groundwork of that story, as that
idiot child saw it. He himself didn't know what he was seeing.
That the only thing that held him into any sort of reality,
into the world at all, was the trust that he had for his sister,
that he knew that she loved him and would defend him, and
so she was the whole world to him, and these things were
flashes that were reflected on her as in a mirror. He didn't
know what they meant.

Q. You spoke a minute ago of the writer seeking to leave
some degree of his mark on posterity. I was wondering if you
think that the effect on the artist is better today when he can
somehow achieve his immortality during his lifetime because
of the communications being so much wider and greater than
formerly when perhaps the writer's fame came to him long
after his death and maybe he was the only one during his lifetime that was satisfied with his work?

A. I don't think so. I believe the writer takes a longer view
than that. He ain't too interested in what the contemporary
world thinks about him. He has a longer view, that he is aimed
not at Jones of 1957 but of Jones of 2057 or 4057.

Q. Well, do you think that you would have been just as
satisfied if your work say had never been discovered until
4057?

A. I think so, sure, yes. Of course when they began to
bring in a little money, that was nice, I liked the money, but
the glory, the rest of it's not very valuable.

Q. Well, then thinking that this period doesn't matter too
much, do you go back over the things, and do you still have
a lot of time left to work over the ones that you've already
written? Do you go back and worry about them and wish you
had done them differently?

A. I wish I had done them better, but I don't have time to

64

worry about it too much. That's just a constant thought or belief that I would like to be able to do them over again— that is, not to go back and take one single book and write another version of it, but if I could go back and take one single book and write another version of it, but if I could go back to say 1920 when I started, that I could do a better job. Of course I wouldn't, but that's an idle thought that occurs only when I haven't got anything better to do. The best thing is to write another book and do it, because it takes only one book to do it. It's not the sum of a lot of scribbling, it's one perfect book, you see. It's one single urn or shape that you want to do.

. . .

Q. When you do write about people that way—well, of course, you don't have to put up with the critics, but I've noticed particularly when a new book comes out, all the Freudian implications are pulled out and all sorts of undercurrents rather than just the simple Here's what happened and—of course, there's always more to it than that, but all kinds of weird things are just pulled out of the hat and thrown around. Would that bother you, does it disturb you to have everything sort of misconstrued?

A. I can't say because I'm not aware of it. I don't read the critics. I don't know any literary people. The people I know are other farmers and horse people and hunters, and we talk about horses and dogs and guns and what to do about this hay crop or this cotton crop, not about literature. I think— I'm convinced, though, that that sort of criticism whether it's nonsensical or not is valid because it is a symptom of change, of motion, which is life, and also it's a proof that literature— art—is a living quantity in our social condition. If it were not, then there'd be no reason for people to delve and find all sorts of symbolisms and psychological strains and currents in it. And I'm quite sure that there are some writers to whom that criticism is good, that it could help them find themselves. I don't know that the critic could teach the writer anything because I'm inclined to think that nobody really can teach anybody anything, that you offer it and it's there and if it is your will or urge to learn it you do, and the writer that does need the criticism can get quite a lot of benefit from it.

. . .

Q. Sir, what are the Spotted Horses symbolic of, if anything?

A. As spotted horses, I don't know. That may be symbolical, but as horses, that was—they symbolized the hope, the aspiration of the masculine part of society that is capable of doing, of committing puerile folly for some gewgaw that has drawn him, as juxtaposed to the cold practicality of the women whose spokesman Mrs. Littlejohn was when she said "Them men!" or "What fools men are!" That the man even in a society where there's a constant pressure to conform can still be taken off by the chance to buy a horse for three dollars. Which to me is a good sign, I think. I hope that man can always be tolled off that way, to buy a horse for three dollars.

Q. Mr. Faulkner, what sort of reading do you best enjoy? Do you have much time for the work of your contemporary novelists?

A. No, I don't. I haven't read a contemporary book in twenty-odd years, unless someone says, This is a good book, I think you would like it, and so I will get that book and read it, but I've got out of the habit of keeping up with contemporaries because I never was a literary man in the sense of needing to keep abreast of the establishment of literature. To me, reading is like writing—I do it for fun. I'm not too interested in what anybody else has done, that I read books because it's fun.

. . .

Q. Sir, could you suggest any books that one read first, in order to get a clearer and more comprehensive picture of your complete works, and if there are any, why these specific choices?

A. There are none. I think the best way to read—no, I can't say the best way, this is the way I read—I take the book and I can tell within two or three pages if I want to read that book now. If I don't, I put that down and I take another. I would say to take Faulkner that same way, and read a page or two until you find one that you want to read another page. It would be difficult for anyone except an expert to plot out a schedule for you. I would do it that way, I think.

Q. Sir, do you have any solution for a man to find peace if he cannot write, as you?

A. Well, I don't think the writer finds peace. If he did, he would quit writing. Maybe man is incapable of peace. Maybe that is what differentiates man from a vegetable. Though maybe the vegetable don't even find peace. Maybe there's no such thing as peace, that it is a negative quality.

Q. I am speaking of peace in his own heart.

A. Yes, well, I'm inclined to think that the only peace man knows is—he says, Why good gracious, yesterday I was happy. That at the moment he's too busy. That maybe peace is only a condition in retrospect, when the subconscious has got rid of the gnats and the tacks and the broken glass in experience and has left only the peaceful pleasant things—that was peace. Maybe peace is not is, but was.

Q. Do you enjoy reading Shakespeare? I heard you speak of Homer. I was just wondering how you felt—

A. Yes'm, I still read Shakespeare. I have a one-volume Shakespeare that I have just about worn out carrying around with me.

Q. Mr. Faulkner, I think you told somebody once that if you had a—were writing something, and had something to get up to every morning and go to work on, you'd never have to be afraid of anything in the world any more. And I wonder what you meant by that.

A. I mean by that, that fear, like so many evil things, comes mainly out of idleness, that if you have something to get up to tomorrow morning, you're too busy to pay much attention to fear. Of course, you have the fears, but you have—you don't have time to take them too seriously if you have something to get up to do tomorrow. It don't matter too much what it is, and if it's something that you yourself believe is valid, in the sense that the artist believes what he's doing is valid in that it may do something to uplift man's heart, not to make man any more successful, but to temporarily make him feel better than he felt before, to uplift his heart for a moment.

Q. In *The Bear*, Mr. Faulkner, is the possession and destruction of the wilderness a symbolic indication of any sort of corruption in the South, and if this is true, what sort of prognostication does this have for the future and for the South or the country as a whole?

A. Well, of course the destruction of the wilderness is not a phenomenon of the South, you know. That is a change that's going on everywhere, and I think that man progresses mechanically and technically much faster than he does spiritually, that there may be something he could substitute for the ruined wilderness, but he hasn't found that. He spends more time ruining the wilderness than he does finding something to replace it, just like he spends more time producing more people than something good to do with the people or to make better people out of them. That that's to me is a sad and tragic thing for the old days, the old times, to go, providing you have the sort of background which a country boy like me had when that was a part of my life. That I don't want it to change, but then that's true of everyone as he grows old. He thinks that the old times were the best times, and he don't want it to change.

Q. Is the short story "Death Drag" based on an actual event or experience in your life?

A. Not too much. They were—I did a little, what they call barnstorming in the early days after the War, when aeroplanes were not too usual and people would pay a hundred dollars to be taken for a short ride in one, but I don't remember anything that was specifically like this. This was again a human being in conflict with his environment and his time. This man who hated flying, but that was what he had to do, simply because he wanted to make a little money.

Q. What symbolic meaning did you give to the dates of *The Sound and the Fury?*

A. Now there's a matter of hunting around in the carpenter's shop to find a tool that will make a better chicken-house. And probably—I'm sure it was quite instinctive that I picked out Easter, that I wasn't writing any symbolism of the Passion Week at all. I just—that was a tool that was good for the particular corner I was going to turn in my chicken-house and so I used it.

68

Q. Sir, you mentioned some of the Russian authors before. What do you think of Dostoevsky? Do you consider him one of the best?

A. He is one who has not only influenced me a lot, but that I have got a great deal of pleasure out of reading, and I still read him again every year or so. As a craftsman, as well as his insight into people, his capacity for compassion, he was one of the ones that any writer wants to match if he can, that he was one who wrote a good Kilroy Was Here.

Q. There's a line in "Was" that—I wonder if you would explain something about it. That Tomey's Turl says to Cass, "Anytime you wants to get something done, from hoeing out a crop to getting married, just get the women-folks to working at it. That all you needs to do—then all you needs to do is set down and wait." Well, that's good advice, but does he use it in this story? Does Tomey's Turl get the women folks to work for him?

A. Well, I'm sure he would if he'd had time, but people were running him with dogs so much and harrying and harrassing from pillar to post he didn't have time, but if he could have got the men to stop long enough, then Miss Sophonsiba would have settled that whole thing. She would have taken Uncle Buck home, then Tomey's Turl and Tennie could have gotten married and things would have been settled. It was the men that kept things stirred up, probably Tomey's Turl knew that soon as the dust settled, no matter what was the outcome of that poker game, Miss Sophonsiba and Uncle Buck would get married and that then he and Tennie would be let alone.

. . .

Q. Mr. Faulkner, I wonder if you could comment on who you think in say two hundred years from now will be the biggest Kilroys Were Here of this century, which writers will leave the biggest Kilroy, if any?

A. I don't want to answer that question because I'm too unfamiliar with contemporary writers. I haven't read any contemporaries since the three or four of my time, and so often a remark like that in simple talk, it gets out, and someone's feelings have been hurt that the man that spoke it had no intention of hurting because he didn't even know he existed, and so for that reason I wouldn't answer that question at all. I would say that I think that Sherwood Anderson has not received the recognition that he deserves and some day will have.

Q. What about Hemingway?

A. Hemingway, now he's alive, and that's where I'd better stay out of trouble by saying nothing, you see.

Q. Would you say anything about your own writings . . . or would you hurt your own feelings?

A. No, I still haven't done it, but I intend to live to be about a hundred years old, so I've got forty more years yet. By that time I'll answer your question if you're still around.

Session Nine

APRIL 13, 1957

GRADUATE COURSE IN AMERICAN FICTION

UNDERGRADUATE COURSE IN THE NOVEL

... Q. Who is the central character of *Absalom, Absalom!?* It seems so obviously to be Sutpen, yet it's been said that it's also the story of Quentin, and I was wondering just who is the central character?

A. The central character is Sutpen, yes. The story of a man who wanted a son and got too many, got so many that they destroyed him. It's incidentally the story of Quentin Compson's hatred of the bad qualities in the country he loves. But the central character is Sutpen, the story of a man who wanted sons.

Q. Sir, in the same book I was wondering what is supposed to be the reader's attitude toward Mr. Coldfield, the father of Ellen?

A. Well, my attitude is that he was a pretty poor man. I don't know what the reader's attitude might be, but I still felt compassion and pity for him, but he was a poor man in my opinion.

Q. Sir, what sort of a deal was made between Goodhue Coldfield and Sutpen in reference to the bill of lading? They pulled some sort of deal.

A. I don't remember. That book is so long ago to me, but Coldfield was a petty, grasping man and Sutpen was a bold, ruthless man, and Sutpen used Coldfield's pettiness for his, Sutpen's, ends, but I don't remember exactly what it was.

71

Q. Sir, in *Light in August* the central character Joe Christmas had most of his troubles and persecutions and in his search to find himself was based on his belief that he was part Negro and yet it's never made really clear that he is. Was he supposed to be part Negro, or was this supposed to add to the tragic irony of the story?

A. I think that was his tragedy—he didn't know what he was, and so he was nothing. He deliberately evicted himself from the human race because he didn't know which he was. That was his tragedy, that to me was the tragic, central idea of the story—that he didn't know what he was, and there was no way possible in life for him to find out. Which to me is the most tragic condition a man could find himself in—not to know what he is and to know that he will never know.

Q. Sir, if he is not—does not definitely have Negro blood, well, what is the significance of Gavin Stevens's surmise there at the end when he explains that there's a conflict of blood? That is only a guess that stands for a guess and not a final knowledge of—?

A. Yes, that is an assumption, a rationalization which Stevens made. That is, the people that destroyed him made rationalizations about what he was. They decided what he was. But Christmas himself didn't know and he evicted himself from mankind.

. . .

Q. Mr. Faulkner, in working out the situation of Joe Christmas, did you deliberately have in mind a correspondence between his situation and Oedipus, for example, as has recently been brought out in an essay published in the *Virginia Quarterly* magazine?

A. No, not deliberately and not consciously. That's another matter of the writer reaching back into the lumber room of his memory for whatever he needs to create the character or the situation, and the similarity is there but it was not by deliberate intent. It was by coincidence—not accident but by coincidence.

. . .

Q. Mr. Faulkner, in *Wild Palms* there is a passage strongly

72

reminiscent of the Grand Inquisitor in Dostoevsky's *Brothers Karamazov* the import of which seems to condemn not Christ but organized religion. In *Light in August,* much of the action seems to stem from almost fanatical Calvinism. Would it be true to surmise that you favor strongly individual rather than an organized religion?

A. I do, always.

Q. Then you think perhaps that man must work out his own salvation from within rather than without?

A. I do, yes.

. . .

Q. In another class you stated that you seldom have the plot of your novels worked out before you begin to write, but that they simply develop from a character or an incident. I was wondering if you remember what character or what incident caused you to write *Absalom, Absalom!?*

A. Sutpen.

Q. You thought of that character and then—

A. Yes, the idea of a man who wanted sons and got sons who destroyed him. The other characters I had to get out of the attic to tell the story of Sutpen.

. . .

Q. I've been looking for Sutpen's—the reason for Sutpen's downfall, Mr. Faulkner, and it seems to me that the Civil War played a part in it. Is that true?

A. Yes.

Q. But that's not the main reason?

A. No, I used the Civil War to—for my own ends there. Sutpen's country was wrecked by the Civil War, but that didn't stop Sutpen, he was still trying to get the son, still trying to establish a dynasty. He was still trying to get even with that man who in his youth had said, Go to the back door.

Q. Sir, in *Light in August* much of the action comes back to the theme or the picture of a column of yellow smoke coming up from Joanna Burden's cabin. I was wondering—you had said that in *The Sound and the Fury* you got the idea of the

73

story from seeing a little girl like Caddy in a tree. I was wondering whether that happened with *Light in August*. Perhaps that was a theme that you had seen and that you started from in that story.

A. No, that story began with Lena Grove, the idea of the young girl with nothing, pregnant, determined to find her sweetheart. It was—that was out of my admiration for women, for the courage and endurance of women. As I told that story I had to get more and more into it, but that was mainly the story of Lena Grove.

. . .

Q. In *Sanctuary,* Mr. Faulkner, is the character of Popeye emblematic of evil in a materialistic society? What would he stand for?

A. No, he was to me another lost human being. He became a symbol of evil in modern society only by coincidence but I was still writing about people, not about ideas, not about symbols.

Q. Sir, I've been told that the title *Light in August* came from a colloquialism for the completion of a pregnancy. Is that true?

A. No, I used it because in my country in August there's a peculiar quality to light and that's what that title means. It has in a sense nothing to do with the book at all, the story at all.

Q. How do you pronounce the name of your mythical county?

A. If you break it down into syllables, it's simple. Y-o-k, n-a, p-a, t-a-w, p-h-a, YOK[Yock]-na-pa-TAW-pha. It's a Chickasaw Indian word meaning water runs slow through flat land.

Q. Mr. Faulkner, what was the particular significance of having Wash Jones, a very humble man, be the instrument through which Sutpen met his death? Does that relate back to the social stratum from which Sutpen himself came and have there a sort of ironic effect? Just what was the idea of that?

74

A. In a sense. In another sense Wash Jones represented the man who survived the Civil War. The aristocrat in the columned house was ruined but Wash Jones survived it unchanged. He had been Wash Jones before 1861 and after 1865 he was still Wash Jones and Sutpen finally collided with him.

. . .

Q. In *Light in August* do you feel that Rev. Hightower dies feeling that he has achieved a certain kind of salvation—some sort of salvation?

A. He didn't die. He had wrecked his life. He had failed his wife. He had failed himself, but there was one thing that he still had—which was the brave grandfather that galloped into the town to burn the Yankee stores, and at least he had that. Everything else was gone, but since he had been a man of God he still tried to be a man of God and he could not destroy himself. But he had destroyed himself but he still couldn't take his own life. He had to endure, to live, but that was one thing that was pure and fine that he had—was the memory of his grandfather, who had been brave.

Q. How much of the story of *Absalom, Absalom!* is reconstructed by Shreve and Quentin? How does the reader know which to accept as objective truth and which to consider just a [reflection] of their personalities?

A. Well, the story was told by Quentin to Shreve. Shreve was the commentator that held the thing to something of reality. If Quentin had been let alone to tell it, it would have become completely unreal. It had to have a solvent to keep it real, keep it believable, creditable, otherwise it would have vanished into smoke and fury.

Q. Sir, along that same line, you mentioned at the English Club that you had had to lay aside *Absalom* at one point, to resume it later on. I wonder if it might not have been the point where toward the end of Miss Rosa's section—where you might have felt that she was running away with you, because right after that Shreve comes in. Is that in your memory at all, sir?

A. I can't say just where it was that I had to put it down,

75

that I decided that I didn't know enough at that time maybe or my feeling toward it wasn't passionate enough or pure enough, but I don't remember at what point I put it down. Though when I took it up again I almost rewrote the whole thing. I think that what I put down were inchoate fragments that wouldn't coalesce and then when I took it up again, as I remember, I rewrote it.

. . .

Q. Mr. Faulkner, I would like to ask you to identify a quality for me. I am thinking of a sentence toward the end of *The Bear*. I am going to read part of the sentence so that you will understand what I am asking about. "There was a boy who wished to learn humility and pride in order to become skillful and worthy in the woods. He suddenly found himself becoming so skillful so rapidly that he feared that he would never become worthy because he had not learned humility." Then finally—it goes on—". . . until an old man who could not have defined either had led him as though by the hand to that point where an old bear and a little mongrel of a dog showed him that by possessing one thing other he would possess them both." What is that "one thing other"?

A. Courage.

Q. . . . I wondered if it was pity or truth, Mr. Faulkner.

A. Courage, it was. A little dog that never saw a bear bigger than he was.

Q. Is the title of *Absalom, Absalom!* taken from the passage in the Bible found in Second Samuel?

A. Yes.

Q. Did you write the novel with this episode in your mind or did you first write the novel and then realizing the similarity in the name—?

A. They were simultaneous. As soon as I thought of the idea of the man who wanted sons and the sons destroyed him, then I thought of the title.

. . .

Q. Mr. Faulkner, what do you consider your best book?

76

A. The one that failed the most tragically and the most spendidly. That was *The Sound and the Fury*—the one that I worked at the longest, the hardest, that was to me the most passionate and moving idea, and made the most splendid failure. That's the one that's my—I consider the best, not— well, best is the wrong word—that's the one that I love the most.

. . .

Q. Mr. Faulkner, most people are very struck by your change in style in *Light in August*. For example, you use the present tense to tell the story rather than the past. Did you mean something by that or were you just using a new form for dramatic import?

A. No, that just seemed to me the best way to tell the story. It wasn't a deliberate change of style. I don't know anything about style. I don't—I think a writer with a lot to—pushing inside him to get out hasn't got time to bother with style. If he just likes to write and hasn't got anything urging him, then he can become a stylist, but the ones with a great deal pushing to get out don't have time to be anything but clumsy, like Balzac, for instance.

Q. Mr. Faulkner, in *Absalom, Absalom!* when Shreve and Quentin are reconstructing the story for each other, they set up a lawyer who was directing the campaign of Charles's mother to gain revenge against Sutpen. Was there really a lawyer, do you think, or is it just a product of their imagination as they reconstructed the story?

A. I'm sorry, I don't remember that.

Q. They speak about the man who was counseling Charles's mother in trying to get back at Sutpen.

A. There probably was a lawyer. I don't remember that book, but yes, yes, there was a lawyer. That sounds too logical in Mississippi terms. Yes, he was—there was a little lawyer there.

. . .

Q. Sir, how good a judge of his own work do you think any writer can be?

A. He is—can judge only in whether it's good enough to suit him or not, otherwise, he's probably a rotten judge of it, because he gets involved personally and he refuses to recognize the bad sometimes and he insists that the mediocre is first rate, because he is involved personally.

Q. And conversely, may fail to appreciate?
A. That's right.

Q. Mr. Faulkner, is there any purpose in the repetition on the same sets of characters throughout your writing?
A. No, only that I have led a—all of my life has been lived in a little Mississippi town and there's not much variety there. A writer writes from his experience, his background, in the terms of his imagination and his observation. That would be the explanation, I think.

Q. Sir, in line with that, some of your novels pick up characters where you left them off in other novels you had written a good number of years before. For example, most of the incidents involving the Snopes, as I understand it, were written from 1929 on and yet you've come out with a book this year about the Snopes. Do you find it difficult to, over a period of years, pick up those characters and carry their personalities through along the same vein?
A. No, no. Those characters to me are quite real and quite constant. They are in my mind all the time. I don't have any trouble at all going back to pick up one. I forget what they did, but the character I don't forget, and when the book is finished, that character is not done, he still is going on at some new devilment that sooner or later I will find out about and write about.

Q. It's been said that you write about the secret of the human heart. Is there one major truth of the human heart?
A. Well, that's a question almost metaphysical. I would say if there is one truth of the human heart, it would be to believe in itself, believe in its capacity to aspire, to be better than it is, might be. That it does exist in all people.

78

. . .

Q. I was wondering whether Charles Bon in *Absalom, Absalom!* ever had suspicions of who his father was. . . .

A. I think he knew. I don't know whether he—his mother probably told him. I think he knew.

Q. Was it a conscious knowledge, would you say, or unconscious knowledge?

A. Probably it was a conscious knowledge in the sense that his mother had told him who his father was. It may be that he didn't believe it, or didn't know or didn't care. I think—I don't believe that he felt any affinity with Sutpen as father and son, but probably his mother had told him and—that she had been deserted and if anything, if he did believe it, he hated Sutpen, of course.

Q. Sir, do you—according to Nathaniel Hawthorne the greatest sin was the violation of the human heart. Would you say that you think along those lines as far as what the greatest sin could be or the greatest crime or characteristic of sin? Would you agree with that statement?

A. Yes, yes, I agree with that.

Q. Sir, did you feel any connection between the servant Nancy in *Requiem for a Nun* and the servant Nancy in "That Evening Sun"?

A. She is the same person, actually.

Q. They both have that incident about Mr. Stovall in the street.

A. Yes. She is the same person actually. These people I figure belong to me and I have the right to move them about in time when I need them.

Q. Mr. Faulkner, throughout your work there seems to be a theme that there's a curse upon the South. I was wondering if you could explain what this curse is and if there is any chance of the South to escape.

A. The curse is slavery, which is an intolerable condition—no man shall be enslaved—and the South has got to work that curse out and it will, if it's let alone. It can't be compelled to do it. It must do it of its own will and desire, which I believe it will do if it's let alone.

. . .

Q. Was the reaction of the people to Sutpen's second marriage—when no one showed up at [the wedding] . . . —was that reaction caused by the people's dislike of his life or his social errors or because of their not being told why—where he got his money?

A. Oh, he had violated the local mores. They feared him and they hated him because of his ruthlessness. He made no pretense to be anything else except what he was, and so he violated the local mores and they ostracized him. Not in revenge at all, but simply because they wanted no part of Sutpen.

Q. Sir, you say that you feel that there is hope for the South, yet the Snopeses have taken over Frenchman's Bend, Flem is president of the bank in Jefferson. Are those the men that are going to lead the South out of darkness?

A. They are the men that can cope with the new industrial age, but there will be something left—as this—we mentioned a while ago—of the old cavalier spirit that will appear, that does appear. By cavalier spirit, I mean people who believe in simple honor for the sake of honor, and honesty for the sake of honesty.

Q. Do you think people will band together, or how do you think they will accomplish this feat? Don't you feel that there is a curse and that it should be removed . . .?

A. They won't band together. I doubt if people accomplish very much by banding together. People accomplish things by individual protest.

Q. Is Sutpen meant to be a completely depraved character, something like Claggart in *Billy Budd* or Iago in *Othello,* or is he meant to be pitied?

A. To me he is to be pitied. He was not a depraved—he was amoral, he was ruthless, completely self-centered. To me he is to be pitied, as anyone who ignores man is to be pitied, who does not believe that he belongs as a member of a human family, of the human family, is to be pitied. Sutpen didn't

80

believe that. He was Sutpen. He was going to take what he wanted because he was big enough and strong enough, and I think that people like that are destroyed sooner or later, because one has got to belong to the human family, and to take a responsible part in the human family. . . .

Session Ten

April 15, 1957

. . . Q. Sir, why do you sometimes satirize the South, and at other times very strenuously satirize it? I mean, what is your general feeling for the South, I mean the deep South?

A. It's my country, my native land and I love it. I'm not trying to satirize it, I'm trying—that is, I'm not expressing my own ideas in the stories I tell, I'm telling about people, and these people express ideas which sometimes are mine, sometimes are not mine, but I myself am not trying to satirize my country, I love it, and it has its faults and I will try to correct them, but I will not try to correct them when I am writing a story, because I'm talking about people then.

. . .

Q. What would you say would be the relation of the rather charming story you just read ["Shingles for the Lord"] to the —what kind of lumber did you take from fact to build this story? . . . How did you shape it to make it different from what you might have done . . .?

A. Well, these people that I know, they are my people and I love them. They might well have done this. I just got to it before they did.

. . .

Q. Can a writer write about people without ever passing judgment on them?

A. Well, he—I doubt if you can know anybody, an imaginary character or living person without passing judgment on them. That's a little too God-like. You've got to pass judg-

83

ment, you've got to love, you've got to hate even, the character that you have created yourself.

Q. Mr. Faulkner, what is your objective in using long sentences over short sentences? Do you feel—is that a stream-of-consciousness effect or do you feel you can convey your thoughts easier by them?

A. That is a matter of the carpenter trying to find the hammer or the axe that he thinks will do the best job. Another thing is, everyone has a foreknowledge of death that is, he will have only a very short time comparatively to do the work and he is trying to put the whole history of the human heart on the head of a pin, you might say. Also, to me, no man is himself, he is the sum of his past. There is no such thing really as was because the past is. It is a part of every man, every woman, and every moment. All of his and her ancestry, background, is all a part of himself and herself at any moment. And so a man, a character in a story at any moment of action is not just himself as he is then, he is all that made him, and the long sentence is an attempt to get his past and possibly his future into the instant in which he does something. . . .
. . .

Q. Well, this is more or less a question of fact. In *The Sound and the Fury* was Jason Compson, was he a bastard?

A. No. Not an actual one—only in behavior.
. . .

Q. In that connection, did you write it in the order in which it was published?

A. Yes. . . . I wrote the Benjy part first. That wasn't good enough so I wrote the Quentin part. That still wasn't good enough. I let Jason try it. That still wasn't enough. I let Faulkner try it and that still wasn't enough, and so about twenty years afterward I wrote an appendix still trying to make that book what—match the dream.

Q. Mr. Faulkner, are you conscious of any way or theme, any attempt that you have more frequently . . . something that turned out to be a dead-end or a blind alley . . . and then you put that in terms—some other way?

A. Yes sir, that's a matter of—as much of that as possible is done up here. I have written three manuscripts that never did quite please me and I burned them up. But it's—you try and you try and you try to do the best you can to make something which to you was passionate and moving, so passionate and moving that it wouldn't let you alone you had to write it, and then you do the best you can to make it as passionate and moving to anyone who reads it as it was to you, because it seems worth while, worth doing.

Q. Why did you suppose that it didn't work out in those three books?

A. It could be that I didn't know enough. It could be that the people were not good enough people. That they never did —that the books, the manuscripts, were never good enough for me to pass them so I just put them in the fire and got rid of them.

. . .

Q. Sir, do you think that man is getting better and better every day in every way?

A. I think that man tries to be better than he thinks he will be. I think that that is his immortality, that he wants to be better, he wants to be braver, he wants to be more honest than he thinks he will be and sometimes he's not, but then suddenly to his own astonishment he is.

. . .

Q. Then may I ask if all of these characters in *The Sound and the Fury*—that you would call them "good people"?

A. I would call them tragic people. The good people, Dilsey, the Negro woman, she was a good human being. That she held that family together for not the hope of reward but just because it was the decent and proper thing to do.

. . .

Q. Sir, you indicated before that *A Fable* was a departure in that—insofar that it was the only book that was written from an absolute idea with regular city limits to it. But I find—at least, *I* find—that the basic crucifixion image in *A Fable* occurs over and over again in your books. It occurs in *Light in August*. It happens in a kind of way even in *Sanctu-*

ary. It happens in *Requiem for a Nun* especially, with Nancy. Isn't *A Fable* simply a more positive way of approaching the problem?

A. As a result, it might be. Remember, the writer must write out of his background. He must write out of what he knows and the Christian legend is part of any Christian's background, especailly the background of a country boy, a Southern country boy. My life was passed, my childhood, in a very small Mississippi town, and that was a part of my background. I grew up with that. I assimilated that, took that in without even knowing it. It's just there. It has nothing to do with how much of it I might believe or disbelieve—it's just there.

. . .

Q. Conrad Aiken once said that after he had written a story, the story then seemed perhaps more real than the things which had happened, and that as he thought back on it he felt that the thing he had written was that had happened in his life as it had as opposed to the actual fact. Do you find that so or not?

A. No, I don't. That's Mr. Aiken's own point of view. That's not mine too much. That my people are no more real than the actual world, but no less real. That is, they have their place in life too, to me.

. . .

Q. Man, in trying to be better than he is in this way—do you feel that he can pretty much do this on his own? . . .

A. Not always. Sometimes he needs help. Not always.

Q. Can he rely on a power outside beyond himself?

A. Sometimes, yes, but the world to be better than he is is in himself. He may not be able to do it without help from outside, or from a greater power than he, but the desire to be better than he is afraid he might be is inside him, inside his conscience —unless he is an idiot, of course.

Q. Mr. Faulkner, the book of yours which troubles me most, is—puzzles me most, doesn't trouble me at all—is *As I Lay Dying*. Somebody once suggested to me that—I think there's thirteen characters—constitute really the separate parts of just one man. Is this so?

A. No. They were—I was writing about people again. I took these people, and—that's a simple *tour de force*. I took this family and subjected them to the two greatest catastrophes which man can suffer—flood and fire, that's all. That was simple *tour de force*. That was written in six weeks without changing a word because I knew from the first where that was going.

. . .

Q. Mr. Faulkner, in reference to *The Sound and the Fury* again is the "tale told by an idiot, full of sound and fury, signifying nothing" applicable to Benjy as is generally thought, or perhaps to Jason?

A. The title, of course, came from the first section, which was Benjy. I thought the story was told in Benjy's section, and the title came there. So it—in that sense it does apply to Benjy rather than to anybody else, though the more I had to work on the book, the more elastic the title became, until it covered the whole family.

. . .

Q. I'd like to ask if your people are derived principally from an area or region of Mississippi . . . .

A. I don't think that people are that different. I think there is not a great deal of difference between Southerners and Northerners, and Americans and Russians and Chinese. That I'm simply using the background, the color, the smells, the sounds that I am familiar with, but the people in my opinion are not that different. They could be anywhere. Of course they would wear different clothes, and their behavior might be a little awry from what it is in North Mississippi, but the behavior would be the same, they would have the same anguishes, the same hopes, and they—Russians or Chinese—would still want to be better than they are afraid they might be, and they would try to be better.

. . .

Q. What is the meaning of the title "A Rose For Emily"?

A. Oh, it's simply the poor woman had had no life at all.

Her father had kept her more or less locked up and then she had a lover who was about to quit her, she had to murder him. It was just "A Rose for Emily"—that's all.

. . .

Q. And you said earlier the style is not as important as the feelings of a writer . . .?

A. No, I think what I said was that anyone who is busy writing about people hasn't got time enough to bother with style. I don't say that style is not important, there are people to whom style is very important—Walter Pater, for instance. Style is very important. Mr. Cabell, style was very important. But there are other people that are too busy writing about men and women, human beings, the human heart in conflict with its self, with its fellows, or with its environment, to have time to bother with style. I wish that that were not so. I wish that I did have a good, lucid, simple method of telling stories.

. . .

Q. Mr. Faulkner, do you always write one story at a time, and finish that before you go to the other one? That is, do you ever have two or three stories going at once or one story at a time?

A. I'd rather write one at a time, but sometimes two of them are so urgent that they won't let me alone, I have to do two at once, but I'd much rather one would let me alone and let me finish it.

Session Eleven

April 25, 1957

MARY WASHINGTON COLLEGE

Q. Do you want to ask Mr. Faulkner anything?

A. And let them be anything. I think that if you try to rehearse the question first, it's not too good. Whether it seems frivolous to you or not, ask it. We'll take the gloves off.

Q. Mr. Faulkner, when you were in Japan and talked to the young Japanese writer did you find that their problems were the same as the young American writers?

A. I'm sure they were, but it was—I never did touch the Japanese. They all spoke English, but it was like two people running at top speed on opposite sides of a plate-glass window. You could see the mouth move, you could see the human features, the gestures, but there was no communication. And then suddenly the paths parted and one went this way, that was all. There was no communication. I'm sure their problems were the same problems but their country is so different. It's a culture of the intellectual process, the result doesn't matter, it's the—the wheels click properly, which is completely alien to me, to any Occidental, but I never did touch the Japanese. But I'm quite sure their problems were the same as mine and that if we could have spoken to one another we would have benefitted both of us, but we simply couldn't.

. . .

Q. What I want to ask you, do you get any reaction from readers of your translated works, where the North American reader is difficult, or he distorts the meaning of American words? [?]

89

A. The only language I read with any ease is French and the French translations I've read have been very fine, I thought. . . .

. . .

Q. Mr. Faulkner, if you do read them, how seriously do you take your critics—that is, those people who write in the literary magazines, *Hudson Review,* and so forth. Do you think it's particularly rewarding for students to read the critics of your work?

A. I should think so. I don't read [them] . . . I'm too busy. But I should think it might be valuable for students to read that. I'm sure it would be valuable, but the writer, if he's as busy as I am and has got as much that he needs to say as I have and knows he never will live long enough to say it all, he ain't got time to read what anybody else says about his work because he already knows what it is—it ain't good enough, that's why he's writing another.

. . .

Q. You have a new novel coming out soon which is a continuation of *The Hamlet.* Have you had that—did you have that in mind a long time?

A. Yes, I thought of the whole story at once like a bolt of lightning lights up a landscape and you see everything but it takes time to write it, and this story I had in my mind for about thirty years, and the one which I will do next—it happened at that same moment, thirty years ago when I thought of it, of getting at it.

Q. Mr. Faulkner, you're sometimes quoted as saying that *Sanctuary* was a pot-boiler. Will you repudiate that idea? I would like for you—I would like to repudiate it for you if you—

A. Well, that book was basely conceived. I had written and had never made much money, and I—when I was footloose I could do things to make money—I could run a bootlegging boat, I was a commercial airplane pilot—things like that— then I got married and I couldn't do things like that anymore, and so I thought I would make a little money writing a book. And I thought of the most horrific idea I could think of and

90

wrote it. I sent it to the publisher, and he wrote me back and said, Good Lord, if we print this, we'll both be in jail. That was about 192- —about 1930, I think, when you couldn't say things in print like you can now. So I forgot it, I wrote two more books, they were published, and then one day I got the galleys for *Sanctuary* and I read it and—probably it was because I didn't need money so badly then, but anyway I saw what a base thing it was in concept, what a shabby thing it was and so I wrote the publisher and said, Let's throw it away. He didn't have much money at the time and he said, We can't do that because I've had plates made and that costs something. And I said, Well, I'll just have to rewrite it. And he said, All right, you rewrite it and I'll pay half of the new plates and you pay half of the new plates. So I rewrote it, did the best I could with it. I got a job passing coal to earn the $270 to pay my half for the plates to print the book and then the publisher went bankrupt. I didn't get any money at all. So I did the best I could with the book. It was in a way already in the public domain, I couldn't throw it away and I rewrote it and did the best I could with it. . . .

Session Twelve

April 27, 1957

GRADUATE COURSE IN AMERICAN FICTION

UNDERGRADUATE COURSE IN THE NOVEL

...Q. Mr. Faulkner, is your opinion of Tennyson in *Light in August,* as expressed by Hightower's remark that reading Tennyson is "like listening in a cathedral to a eunuch chanting in a language he does not even need to not understand," is that your opinion of Tennyson?

A. No sir, that was Hightower's opinion, and I'm not responsible for his opinion. I have a different opinion of Tennyson myself, that when I was younger, I read Tennyson with a great deal of pleasure. I can't read him at all now.

Q. In *Absalom, Absalom!,* which you said you didn't remember very well last time, do you happen to remember when Charles Bon realizes that Sutpen is his father? Is it before or after he leaves New Orleans to go to the university?

A. I should think that his mother dinned that into him as soon as he was big enough to remember, and that he came deliberately to hunt out his father, not for justice for himself, but for revenge for his abandoned mother. He must have known that, that must have been in his—the background of his childhood, that this abandoned woman never let him forget that.

Q. Does the New Orleans lawyer have personal gain in mind in helping Bon and his mother?

A. Possibly, yes. Yes, when he located Sutpen, knew that Sutpen was a wealthy man in his time, yes, he thought there

93

would be gain, but Bon didn't want gain, he wanted revenge, for his mother.

. . .

Q. How far do you think the relationship between Charles Bon and Sutpen parallels what you consider the general racial situation in the South?

A. It was a manifestation of a general racial system in the South which was condensed and concentrated as the writer has got to do with any incident or any character he takes, for the reason that he hasn't got sixty years. He has got to do his job in—between the covers of a book, but—that is, epitomize a constant general condition in the South, yes.

. . .

Q. There are so many parallels of violence in your writings which suggest the actions of the Ku Klux Klan that I am curious to know why you have never mentioned it directly that I know of.

A. The spirit that moves a man to put on a sheet and burn sticks in your yard is pretty prevalent in Mississippi, but not all Mississippians wear the sheet and burn the sticks. That they scorn and hate and look with contempt on the people that do, but the same spirit, the same impulse is in them too, but they are going to use a different method from wearing a night-shirt and burning sticks. The Ku Klux Klan is the dull dreary minority. There's nothing dramatic enough in the Ku Klux Klan for me to have needed to use that in a story, though I can't say that some day I won't need to use it.

. . .

Q. Mr. Faulkner, in *The Sound and the Fury,* can you tell me exactly why some of that is written in italics? What does that denote?

A. I had to use some method to indicate to the reader that this idiot had no sense of time. That what happened to him ten years ago was just yesterday. The way I wanted to do it was to use different colored inks, but that would have cost so much, the publisher couldn't undertake it.

Q. Doesn't that go on with Quentin, too?

A. Yes, because he was about half way between madness

and sanity. It wasn't as much as in Benjy's part, because Quentin was only half way between Benjy and Jason. Jason didn't need italics because he was quite sane.

Q. And another thing I noticed, you don't advise that people have to have a subject and predicate for verbs and all those things.

A. Well, that—I think that's really not a fair question. I was trying to tell this story as it seemed to me that idiot child saw it. And that idiot child to me didn't know what a question, what an interrogation was. He didn't know too much about grammar, he spoke only through his senses.

Q. I'm referring mostly to Quentin and he certainly—he attended Harvard, he should have known.

A. Well, Quentin was an educated half-madman and so he dispensed with grammar. Because it was all clear to his half-mad brain and it seemed to him it would be clear to anybody else's brain, that what he saw was quite logical, quite clear.

. . .

Q. Sir, this is another naive question. In trying to get out a meaning that ties all the characters together in *Light in August,* it seems that all of them in one way or another have been deprived of love in one form or another and are trying to find something. Did it have some sort of meaning like that to you?

A. That's possible. Of course I didn't think of that at the time. I was simply writing about people, but that's possible, that's valid. But that too was coincidental with the writer.

Q. Well, they were all put into difficult circumstances, more or less—cut off, sort of.

A. Well, yes, but then so many people are. So many people are seeking something and quite often it is love—it don't have to be love between man and woman, it's to be one with some universal force, power that goes through life, through the world. It could take the form of—the object of it could be a man or woman, because that is a part of man's or woman's instinctive nature to have an object, an immediate object to project that seeking for love on.

. . .

Q. Mr. Faulkner, I think a student's natural reaction after writing a paper or something at least to hand in at school is to hand it to his roommate or someone close to him and have him read it and give an opinion on it. Do you do this after you've written a story or novel? Is there anybody in your family or close friends that you give it to and just say, What do you think of this?

A. No, because I have more confidence in my own judgment than anybody else's and I know that it don't suit me yet, so I have never thought of showing it to anybody else because I don't really care what they think, it hasn't suited me yet. Probably if I do do something that does suit me, I will worry and harass everybody to death to look at it.

. . .

Q. Mr. Faulkner, when you revived Temple Drake and Gowan Stevens in *Requiem for a Nun,* I take it that was a later process. It wasn't like *The Hamlet* and *The Town* and *The Mansion* where you conceived of the whole thing at once?

A. Yes, that's right, it was—I began to think what would be the future of that girl? and then I thought, What could a marriage come to which was founded on the vanity of a weak man? What would be the outcome of that? And suddenly that seemed to me dramatic and worthwhile, but that was—you're quite right—I hadn't thought of that when I wrote *Sanctuary.*

Q. Mr. Faulkner, from your remarks, I would say that you have a belief that in developing the characters in the story that the writer also develops, may be. Did I gather that that's correct?

A. I'm sure he does. That the writer is learning all the time he writes and he learns from his own people, once he has conceived them truthfully and has stuck to the verities of human conduct, human behavior, human aspirations, then he learns—yes, they teach him, they surprise him, they teach him things that he didn't know, they do things and suddenly he says to himself, Why yes, that is true, that is so.

Q. Referring to an earlier question, did you say that *Light in August* argues . . . for the acceptance of an inevitably tragic view of life?

96

A. I wouldn't think so. That the only person in that book that accepted a tragic view of life was Christmas because he didn't know what he was and so he deliberately repudiated man. He didn't belong to man any longer, he deliberately repudiated man. The others seemed to me to have had a very fine belief in life, in the basic possibility for happiness and goodness—Byron Bunch and Lena Grove, to have gone to all that trouble.

Q. This genealogy with all these people that were connected with each other, McCaslins and everybody—was that made up before the books were written or as each one was written?

A. No, that came along as these people appeared. I would think of one character to write a story about and suddenly he would drag in a lot of people I never saw or heard of before, and so the genealogy developed itself.

Q. Some of your names in your books are very suggestive, very highly suggestive. I wonder if that was pure coincidence or did you intend to make names like Gail Hightower, Joanna Burden . . . ?

A. Well, that is out of the tradition of the pre-Elizabethans, who named their characters according to what they looked like or what they did. . . . Of course, it seems to me that those people named themselves, but I can see where that came from—it came from the—my memory of the old miracle plays, the morality plays in early English literature. Chaucer.

Q. Sir, are you conscious of any similarity between Thomas Sutpen and Flem Snopes? They are—I don't suppose there's any comedy in *Absalom* anywhere, and there's a great deal of course in *The Hamlet* and *The Town,* but both of them are—have a grand design and are unscrupulous about getting in—they use people.

A. Well, only Sutpen had a grand design. Snopes's design was pretty base—he just wanted to get rich, he didn't care how. Sutpen wanted to get rich only incidentally. He wanted to take revenge for all the redneck people against the aristocrat who told him to go around to the back door. He wanted to show that he could establish a dynasty too—he could make himself a king and raise a line of princes.

Q. It seems as if Flem had something of the same thing in mind. He wants respectability even more than money, doesn't he?

A. No, no, he only found out when he thought [it] was almost too late that he'd have to have respectability, he didn't want it until he found out he had to have it. He would have done without it if he could, but he suddenly had to have it.

. . .

Q. This callous attitude of Sutpen and Flem Snopes, this ability to use people without realizing they're people, sort of dehumanizing them, it seems to gradually get worse as they go from country into town and cities. Is that a definite, is that a conscious thing ?

A. It didn't get worse because they came into cities. They had to come into cities to find more people to use. But it got worse because of the contempt which the ability to use people develops in anyone. There are very few people that have enough grandeur of soul to be able to use people and not develop contempt for [them]. And that—the contempt for people came not because they moved to the city but out of success.

. . .

Q. I would like to ask you on this business of the Old South and the New South—in *The Bear,* where the young boy returns as a man and sees the forest cut down, I would like to know, do you like the Old South or the New South better?

A. Well, the New South has got too many people in it and it is changing the country too much. It's—has—it gets rid of the part of Mississippi that I liked when I was young, which was the forest. Though it's foolish to be against progress because everyone is a part of progress and he'll have no other chance except this one so he—it's silly not to cope with it, to compromise with it, cope with it. Probably anyone remembers with something of nostalgia the—his young years. He forgets the unpleasant, the unhappy things that happened, he remembers only the nice things, and so maybe the Northerner feels the same way about the Old North and the New North that the Southerner feels about the Old South and the New South.

. . .

Q. . . . I think in a recent *Life* magazine there was an article about your governor and his citing the progress being made in Mississippi as far as the schools were concerned—how the governor will, just as you said, he will stand by segregation until his last dying breath, but he will do all that he can to improve the colored folk.

A. This one is a better man than anybody in Mississippi expected. I imagine if they had known his true sentiments, they would never have elected him. And he is—I have had some correspondence with him since he was elected, and every now and then he sends me copies of letters he writes to his legislature and every now and then he quotes me, things that I have said on the subject of segregation. And he is someone that realizes, that sees that this is an obsolesence that simply ain't going to work any longer, something must be done about it. But he has got to represent his state too, and he cannot come out for a sudden abolishment of segregation, but he knows that something must be done and he thinks that, as a lot of people in Mississippi do, that all the Negro wants is equality, is educational, economic equality, that he don't want to mix with white people any more than white people want to mix with him, and the governor says that if he has decent schools, as good schools as he could get anywhere, if he has the right to go where he wants to into white churches, if he wants to go there, into the white stores as he can do, that that will solve the question. As someone has said, apparently the difficulty is the Mississippian don't want the Negro to sit down with him. They can stand up, that's all right, they can ride in the same elevator, but they can't sit in the same church. Maybe if everybody stood up in church, the Negro could come in too. . . .

Session Thirteen

April 30, 1957

THE JEFFERSON SOCIETY

Q. . . . Sir, . . . the story you just read, "The Waifs" [last chapter of *The Town*], . . . does it have any other meaning other than just being a tall story?

A. No. To me it was just funny, funny and a little terrible, too, those waif children with absolutely no future. I—it was funny, yes, as a—yes, that's right, a tall story, but with the tragic implications, assuming that any infant human is of some value, should be of some value in any culture.

Q. Sir, could you give us some of the points you had for combating Communism . . . ?

A. Well, I think the first one would be to believe in "me," in "I," rather than "we," to be oneself, to resist the pressure to relinquish individuality. That's the first thing and maybe that's all anyone has to do to combat Communism. That is, I think that it can be combated, must be combated, and conquered, if it is to be conquered, not by people forming mass meetings in groups but by individuals. That if the—we who would try to proselytize our fellows into resisting Communism, I think that's all we have to teach them—the importance of me, of I, myself. That the individual is more important than any mass or group he belongs to. That the individual is always more important than any state that he belongs to. That the state must never be the master of the individual, it is the servant of the individual. That the individual—and to retain that superiority over the state, the individual must be independent of the state, he mustn't accept gratuity from the state. He

100

musn't let the state buy him by pensions or relief or dole or grant of any sort.

. . .

Q. Sir, along these lines is that how you take the position of the artist in the South, in the deep South, compares with the artist in, say, the North or in Europe?

A. Well, I would say that in our culture there is really no place for the artist. In Europe, the old culture, there is a definite place—the artist quite often, because he is a good artist, he suddenly finds himself a power in politics, which never happens in this country because he is a good artist, a good writer or a good painter or a good philosopher. He becomes a power in politics in our culture so far because he has been successful. It doesn't matter what he was successful in. That's because we still haven't quite exhausted the natural resources to where we have got to use the best in people. When we reach the point where we have exhausted natural resources and all we have left will be people, then the artist, I think, will find a place for himself in the fabric of the culture. So far he hasn't.

. . .

Q. Sir, you state that in order to be an artist one has to be individualistic, and then you said that in order to combat Communism one must foster the spirit of individualism. Now, I was wondering if there was a contradiction between this in the case of the Soviet artists, if we can call them artists. Do they have individualism, or if they have, are they Communists?

A. The ones that we know about, whose work we see, are not individualists. They have been compressed, repressed into the mass. I am convinced that the heirs to Dostoevsky, Gogol, Tolstoy are still writing the good books. They are hidden in out-houses, under floors, in Russia, because they don't dare let the government find them. That some day they will appear, and those people are the ones who insist on being individualists even in a totalitarian condition like Russia. I think that no condition, no government can destroy the will among a few to be individualists.

Q. Sir, your theory to combat such a political and social

101

theory as Communism by being an individual sounds very good but is it possible to achieve today in our society, for an individual to do that without isolating himself from our society? If it is possible, what means would you . . . . ?

A. Well, I will use an analogy. There's some people who are writers who believed they had talent, they believed in the dream of perfection, they get offers to go to Hollywood where they can make a lot of money, they begin to acquire junk swimming pools and imported cars, and they can't quit their jobs because they have got to continue to own that swimming pool and the imported cars. There are others with the same dream of perfection, the same belief that maybe they can match it, that go there and they resist the money. They don't own the swimming pools, the imported cars. They will do enough work to get what they need of the money without becoming a slave to it, and that, in that sense, it is as you say, it is going to be difficult to go completely against the grain or the current of a culture. But you can compromise without selling your individuality completely to it. You've got to compromise because it makes things easier.

Q. In social legislation how can you combat something like that such as pensions or social security? What can an individual do about that?

A. Well, you probably can't. But you can insist on yourself keeping free of it.

Q. That still would mean paying taxes, wouldn't it?

A. Sure, you would have to pay taxes, but then we haven't quite reached the stage where one has got to accept social benefits. You can do work. You can join a union. Of course, you have got to acquiesce to an extent to a mass if you join a union but you don't have to accept the social benefits. You can still be an individualist, and belong to a union and work, and there probably is somewhere in the country still ways that man can earn a living without having to belong to a union.

. . .

Q. Sir, a few minutes ago you mentioned that people in your home town were looking into your books for familiar

102

characters. Realizing that you've got a rich legacy in your experiences, but it seems to me that nowadays the modern novelist is writing merely thinly disguised autobiography. Which do you think is really more valuable from the sense of the artist, the disguised autobiography, or making it up from whole cloth, as it were?

A. I would say that the writer has three sources, imagination, observation, and experience. He himself doesn't know how much of which he uses at any given moment because each of the sources themselves are not too important to him. That he is writing about people, and he uses his material from the three sources as the carpenter reaches into his lumber room and finds a board that fits the particular corner he's building. Of course, any writer, to begin with, is writing his own biography because he has discovered the world and then suddenly discovered that the world is important enough or moving enough or tragic enough to put down on paper or in music or on canvas, and at that time all he knows is what has happened to him because he has not developed his capacity to perceive, to draw conclusions, to have an insight into people. His only insight in it is into himself, and it's a biography because that's the only gauge he has to measure—is what he has experienced himself. As he gets older and works more, imagination is like any muscle, it improves with use. Imagination develops, his observation gets shrewder as he gets older, as he writes, so that when he reaches his peak, his best years, when his work is best, he himself doesn't know and doesn't have time to bother and doesn't really care how much of what comes from each of these sources, that then he is writing about people, writing about the aspirations, the troubles, the anguishes, the courage, and the cowardice, the baseness and the splendor of man, of the human heart.

Q. Mr. Faulkner, do you think a writer writes better when he is young, or writes better when he's old?

A. Well, that's something you can't say. Some write best when they are young, write themselves out. Some never reach their top speed until late in life. That's—you just can't say. That no man knows when he will reach—do his best and very few have the courage to say, I have done my best and now is the time to break the pencil and quit. Very few can do that. It is a lack of courage, but probably more a lack of judgment. That the artist is trying to match a dream of perfection and he still believes as long as he can breathe that he will do it, even though his judgment might tell him that he has failed, that his work is going downhill. That's difficult to face when you have given—dedicated your life to something like that and then before life is over to find out that you picked the wrong racket, you might say, when it's too late.

Q. Well, do you think you've reached your peak . . . ?

A. No, I intend to live to be at least a hundred and I'll probably still be writing. That's my thought now. I may change tomorrow, but right now that's my thought.

. . .

Q. . . . In one of your recent lectures, I asked you whether you thought the artist in the United States was part of the society in which he lives, or whether he was an outsider looking in on—looking out at society. Now, is the American artist a part of his society today? Do you still feel that? If, he—it is hard to be an individualist in the United States, then how can the artist who is obviously an individualist be part of a society strictly anti-individualistic?

A. Because, with few exceptions, the artist in America is something else, too. Like me, he's a farmer, or he's a lawyer like Edgar Masters, or a doctor like William Carlos Williams. The exceptions are the people who are literary and nothing else and they have no place in the culture until they are successful and make money at it, at their own trade. In that sense the man can be an individualist and be an artist. Also a lawyer can be a lawyer, can be a member of the profession of law or medicine and still be an individualist in his own philosophy of living. I meant only that in the old countries a man that obtains renown as an artist, before he knows it he becomes a part of the philosophy of his culture. He has a place in his government quite often. In this country that don't happen. If he ever turns up with a place in the American government, it's because he was also a successful farmer or successful doctor or builder

104

of motor cars, not because he was a successful philosopher or successful artist.

Q. . . . He has to have the joint occupation, in other words.

A. That's right. To be perfectly at home anywhere in the American culture, yes.

Q. And if he doesn't have a joint occupation, then he's no longer a part of [that culture]. Is that correct?

A. That's right. He's recognized only by his fellows, by his fellow craftsmen.

Q. And not by his society?

A. That's right. Yes, I doubt if Mr. Charles E. Wilson, for instance, knows who Edmund Wilson is—ever heard of him.

Session Fourteen

May 6, 1957

Q. I don't know if this will please you or not, but in *The New York Times* review of *The Town* yesterday, the reviewer said that he thought you were tired of Yoknapatawpha County chronicle. Do you have any comment on that?

A. I don't think that I am, though of course the last thing any writer will admit to himself is that he has scraped the bottom of the barrel and that he should quit. I don't quite believe that's true yet. But it's probably not tiredness, it's the fact that you shouldn't put off too long writing something which you think is worth writing, and this I have had in mind for thirty years now. So maybe it could be a little stale to me, though I don't think that's true, either. It was not a novel. I think that anything that can't be told in one standardized book is not a novel. That is, it can't follow the fairly rigid rules which—in which a novel has got to be compressed to be a novel. This is really a chronicle that seemed to me amusing enough or true enough to be put down no matter what rules of integrity it had to violate, so in that sense it's not a novel, it's a chronicle, and I don't think that fatigue had anything to do with it—that is, fatigue with the county, the background. It may have been a staleness because I had thought of it, had remembered it, and planned to write it so long before I got to it.

Q. Why did you wait so long, sir, before writing this book?

A. There were so many other things that got in the way of it. I would write a little on it and then I would think of something else that seemed more urgent, that did fit into the more or less rigid pattern which a novel has got to conform to and this was too loose to fit into that form to give the pleasure which doing a complete job within the rules of the craft demand. That it's more fun doing a single piece which has the unity and coherence, the proper emphasis and integration, which a long chronicle doesn't have. That was the reason. Though it had to be done before I did stop writing.

Q. Mr. Faulkner, do you plan to write any more short stories?

A. Well, I can't say. The writer writes because he has fun doing it, and he expects to have fun doing that as long as he lives. Just like the man that likes to ride a bicycle or likes to ride horses or likes to fish. He expects to have fun fishing as long as he can walk around and find a place to fish or ride the bicycle, and I'm sure that as long as I live I will still try to write, and so I wouldn't say what form that writing will take.

Q. Mr. Faulkner, do you mean that some of the writing in *The Town* is thirty years old, or did you not rewrite it or anything of the sort?

A. Some of it is thirty years old, yes.

Q. Mr. Faulkner, do you still think of people in *The Town* as people and not as symbols?

A. Yes. Yes, to me they are people, and they have grown older as I have grown older, and probably they have changed a little—my concept of them has changed a little, as they themselves have changed and I changed. That they have grown. I know more about people than I knew when I first thought of them, and they have become more definite to me as people and that may be what seems like staleness gets into it.

Q. Mr. Faulkner, does Flem Snopes understand the woman he is married to at all?

A. I think he did. He had to teach himself a certain shrewdness about people in order to make the money which he believed was the end of existence. Just as he had to teach himself something about respectability when he found out that he would need respectability, that just greed, rapacity, wasn't enough. He probably understood all of his life that he ever needed to understand.

Q. Is there any particular reason, Mr. Faulkner, why *As I Lay Dying* is published along with *The Sound and the Fury?*

A. Yes, a very good reason. The two of them together made exactly enough pages to make a proper-sized book that the publisher could charge the regulation price on.

. . .

Q. Mr. Faulkner, in *As I Lay Dying,* did Jewel purchase the horse as a substitute for his mother?

A. Well, now that's something for the psychologist. He bought that horse because he wanted that horse. Now there was the need to use symbolism which I dug around, scratched around in my lumber room, and dragged out. That was an indication, a simple quick way to show that he did not belong to that family. That he was the alien there. Now just exactly what the connection is between the desire to buy a dangerous untamed horse and to be a country preacher I don't know, but that was the reason for the horse—to show quickly that he did not belong to the rest of the family.

Q. Can we attach any significance to his letting his father sell the horse later on in the story?

A. Only that people want to do better than they can do. That this man who loved nothing but that horse would never have believed that he would have sacrificed that horse for anything, yet when the crisis came he did behave better than he thought he would behave. He sacrificed the only thing he loved for someone else's good.

Q. Mr. Faulkner, does Jewel actually know or did he just sense that he is illegitimate?

A. He don't know and he probably don't care, but his mother knew, and whether she ever—no, she probably never told him. To him it made no difference.

Q. In the same book, was Darl out of his mind all through the book? Or did that come as a result of things happening during the book?

A. Darl was mad from the first. He got progressively madder because he didn't have the capacity—not so much of sanity but of inertness to resist all the catastrophes that happened to the family. Jewel resisted because he was sane and he was the toughest. The others resisted through probably simple inertia, but Darl couldn't resist it and so he went completely off his rocker. But he was mad all the time.

Q. Is that why he speaks more beautifully than anybody else?

A. Yes.

Q. Mr. Faulkner, was Darl's motive in burning the barn—is that simply an indication of his madness or was he motivated by his desire to make of no consequence Jewel's sacrifice of his horse in order to get his mother's body to Jefferson?

A. Probably in Darl's mind that was a violation of some concept, some shape of beauty, to drag that dead putrefying body around any further, and he did the only thing his mad brain could conceive to rid the earth of something which should have been under ground days ago.

Q. Mr. Faulkner, why did Vardaman say "My mother is a fish"?

A. That was the child, nobody had paid any attention to him. He saw things that baffled and puzzled him, and nobody —none of the adults would stop long enough to show him any tenderness, any affection, and he was groping and that occurred to him that because of the—now, that's another book I should have read, I don't remember exactly what happened, except when he brought the fish home, something that happened from the outside got the fish confused with the fact that he knew his mother's body was in a room and that she was no longer his mother. She couldn't talk or—anyway, suddenly her position in the mosaic of the household was vacant.

Q. Then Vardaman was really—well, he was sane too, it

110

was really just his inability to distinguish illusion and reality that—

A. That's right. He was a child trying to cope with this adult's world which to him was, and to any sane person, completely mad. That these people would want to drag that body over the country and go to all that trouble, and he was baffled and puzzled. He didn't know what to do about it.

Q. Would you say that Vardaman's love for his mother was the most sincere?

A. Well, it was because of the child's dependence on his mother, and probably to that child nobody else except the mother paid any attention to him. She was something stable, and his love for her was clinging to something that was stable in his world.

Q. In the end of the story, sir, Anse marries a woman whose name is already Bundren. Could you explain this?

A. No no, her name wasn't Bundren, but he heard the gramophone and as soon as he got his first wife buried he got a wedding license and two dollars and went back and married the one with the gramophone. Her name was Bundren when his family saw her, but it hadn't been until then. They were married then.

. . .

Q. Mr. Faulkner, I recently read an author who indicated a writer's life is a lonely one due to the number of hours that are spent in his self-imposed solitary confinement. And I wondered if you ever shared his feelings, if you have the same feelings that it's a lonely life while you are writing.

A. No, not to me. It's a solitary—the writing is a solitary job—that is, nobody can help you with it, but there's nothing lonely about it. I have always been too busy, too immersed in what I was doing, either mad at it or laughing at it to have time to wonder whether I was lonely or not lonely, it's simply solitary. I think there is a difference between loneliness and solitude.

Q. In your novel *As I Lay Dying,* Mr. Faulkner, if there

has to be a villain in the story could I be wrong in saying that he was Anse?

A. I'm not too sure there has to be a villain in the story. If there is a villain in that story it's the convention in which people have to live, in which in that case insisted that because this woman had said, I want to be buried twenty miles away, that people would go to any trouble and anguish to get her there. The simplest thing would have been to bury her where she was in any pleasant place. If they wanted to be sentimental about it they could have buried her in some place that she would like to go and sit by herself for a while. Or if they wanted to be practical they could have taken her out to the back yard and burned her. So if there was a villain it was the convention which gave them no out except to carry her through fire and flood twenty miles in order to follow the dying wish, which by that time to her meant nothing.

. . .

Q. Mr. Faulkner, what are some of these other things which create the hostility in Addie Bundren besides the attitude she seems to inherit from her father about life?

A. Well, it could be her New England tradition,[1] abolitionist tradition, set down in that land where abolition had failed, where there was still the same condition which her father had believed was of the first importance to change and alter, and she couldn't change and alter it, or maybe she had begun to assume the attitude of so many Southern people that it couldn't be changed and altered because the Negro would be incapable of change, and she may have hated herself for having gone against the tradition, the beliefs, of her father. At the same time she had learned that his beliefs were impractical. And that's another book that I will have to read again. I will say that that might have had something to do with it.

. . .

Q. What is the feeling that Dewey Dell in *As I Lay Dying* —what is the feeling that Dewey Dell has towards her brother Darl?

---

[1]Mr. Faulkner here confuses Addie Bundren in *As I Lay Dying* with Joanna Burden in *Light in August*.

112

A. She knows without being able to phrase it that he is different somehow from the others through his madness. That maybe he is more perceptive. That he could be more tolerant of her—that is, she knows by instinct that if he found out that she was pregnant it wouldn't make a great deal of difference, but if Jewel found out she was pregnant he would go out and find somebody to kill, and for that reason she knows that Darl is capable of a sympathy, a sensitivity, that won't react in violence to serve an empty and to a woman foolish and silly code, and he is the only one in the family that she could say, I'm pregnant, I'm in trouble, and would get—well, maybe not too much sympathy, but no violent reaction that would merely add more trouble to what she already had.

Q. Mr. Faulkner, as long as we are on Darl, how is it that he could give such detailed description to his mother's death while he is out cutting wood some place else?

A. Who can say how much of the good poetry in the world has come out of madness, and who can say just how much of super-perceptivity the—a mad person might not have? It may not be so, but it's nice to think that there is some compensation for madness. That maybe the madman does see more than the sane man. That the world is more moving to him. That he is more perceptive. He has something of clairvoyance, maybe, a capacity for telepathy. Anyway, nobody can dispute it and that was a very good way, I thought, a very effective way to tell what was happening back there at home—well, call it a change of pace. A trick, but since the whole book was a *tour de force,* I think that is a permissible trick.

Q. Sir, Dr. Peabody—I think his name is—is he put in just to afford a sort of comic relief or a definite purpose, because of his size and difficulty in getting up the mountain and so forth?

A. Mainly it was to give for the moment what may be called a nudge of credibility to a condition which was getting close to the realm of unbelief. That is, he is brought in from comparatively the metropolitan outland for a moment which says, Well, if he comes out there and sees these people, well then maybe they do exist. Up to that time they were functioning in this bizarre fashion almost inside a vacuum, and pretty soon you wouldn't have believed it until some stranger came in as a witness. Another trick.

Q. Mr. Faulkner, Whitfield appears to be a pretty hypocritical man in *As I Lay Dying?* By the time we see him as an older man in "Barn Burning" he seems to be a pretty delightful person. Has anything that we don't know about happened to him in between?

A. No, I wouldn't say he was a hypocritical man. He had to live a hypocritical life. That is, he had to live in public the life which the ignorant fanatic people of the isolated and rural South demand of a man of God, when actually he was just a man like any of them. I don't mean that all rural preachers are capable of behaving in private like he did, but they themselves are doing the best they can for a reason. They believe that man is doomed to sin, that he must struggle always against the Devil, and if he sins then he confesses and tries to do better, and tries to earn salvation still even if he does sin. That he was the victim of his environment also, of land in which there wasn't much relief from the arduous hard work for very little of the time, there was nothing to please the spirit—no music, no pictures, most of them couldn't read and when they could, the books were not available, and so they took what relief they could, knowing that they were committing sin but they would try to do better tomorrow.

Q. Mr. Faulkner, . . . [in] *As I Lay Dying,* Addie says, when she finds she is going to have Cash, "that living was terrible, and that this was the answer to it." Does this mean that this is the confirmation to the fact that living is terrible, or does this mean that she is wrong, that it isn't terrible?

A. She had probably married Anse because of pressure from her people, but she probably saw through him that he was no good. She was ambitious probably and she married him against her inclination and she saw nothing ahead of her but a dull and dreary life as a slave without—just a slave, no pay, no compensation—then suddenly she found that there was something in motherhood that didn't, maybe didn't compensate for it but alleviated it. That there was some reason for

114

the suffering and the anguish that people, all people, seem to have to go through with. Cash was the first child, and she said to herself, For the sake of this helpless child I can endure. That's what is meant by that, I think.

Q. Did you consciously or unconsciously parallel *As I Lay Dying* with *The Scarlet Letter?*

A. No, a writer don't have to consciously parallel because he robs and steals from everything he ever wrote or read or saw. I was simply writing a *tour de force* and as every writer does, I took whatever I needed wherever I could find it, without any compunction and with no sense of violating any ethics or hurting anyone's feelings because any writer feels that anyone after him is perfectly welcome to take any trick he has learned or any plot that he has used. Of course we don't know just who Hawthorne took his from. Which he probably did because there are so few plots to write about.

Q. Mr. Faulkner, I think that the *Times* said that you take some of your names of caricatures of Southern politicians and so forth, such as Vardaman, and I just wondered where you got, if that was true, and if so, where did you get the rest of your names like Darl? They seem sort of unusual.

A. Darl was of course the rural Mississippi pronunciation of Darrell. They would call it Darl. Vardaman, Bilbo—they are very popular with country people in Mississippi to name their children after governors and senators and the politicians that come out and shake their hands and say, I'm one of you all, even if I do have a white shirt every day. I'm just—you're just as good as I am and I'm one of you, and so they name their children after the successful politicians.

Q. Eula seems changed from *The Hamlet* to *The Town*. She becomes more unselfish and more perceptive, almost philosophical. I wonder what the reason for this is.

A. Well, I would like to think the reason is because she is older. I would like to think that all people learn a little more. Also, she had that child. I like to think that the claim that the child, the helpless child which didn't ask to be brought into the world makes on anyone, no matter how selfish they might

115

have been up to that time. It was because she suddenly realized that this child was growing up and had to be protected and without trying to learn more about people or to become more philosophical, she did that because she knew that this child must be defended and protected. That it already had two strikes on it anyway and nobody was going to do anything for it except her.

. . .

Q. What is your reason for using Charles Mallison as your narrator in *The Town,* or rather, in certain sections of *The Town?* Why have him tell part of the story?

A. I thought it would be more amusing as told through the innocence of a child that knew what he was seeing but had no particular judgment about it. That something told by some-one that don't know he is telling something funny is sometimes much more amusing than when it's told by a professional wit who is hunting around for laughs. Also, to have it told partly by a child, partly by a grown man. It's to hold the object up and look at it from both sides, from two points of view.

Q. Mr. Faulkner, does the writer collect a number of events and situations like a newspaper reporter and then derive a story from these events, or does he conceive of the problem or situation that he wants to present to the world and then think up the story which will present these to the world, or both of these ideas at once?

A. Of course, he collects his material all his life from every-thing he reads, from everyting he listens to, everything he sees, and he stores that away in sort of a filing cabinet. I be-lieve that he thinks either of an anecdote concerning people or character which is moving enough to be worth writing about and then when he begins to write, the character demands that he be shown in certain lights so the writer simply hunts around in his filing case—in my case it's not anything near as neat as a filing case, it's more like a junk box—and he digs out some-thing that he has read or seen to throw the flashlight on the particular moment. But he don't get out and do any research. I think if he does that he is not really a fiction writer. He be-comes something else.

116

Q. What does the young writer without the store-box of experience start out with?

A. When did you learn to read? How many years ago?

Q. Do you just take it from what you read?

A. Sure, you can get a lot of it. That's a very good way to learn the craft of writing—from reading. Just like a very good way to be a carpenter is from watching a seasoned carpenter do it. So you have been gaining experience all your life, and you will gain more as you get older. But you should have a pretty good size filing case or junk box of your own by now. You've been reading twelve, fifteen years—that's the main source, because there are so few plots and what you read—the plot has not changed too much, only the people involved in it have changed, and to see this same plot repeated time after time with different people motivated by it or trying to cope with it, you can learn about people that way, to match against your own experience with living people. So that you can remember things that you read when you were twelve, fourteen years old that you've forgotten. Suddenly at twenty-one you say, Why yes, that's so, because I saw that yesterday. That was so.

Q. Mr. Faulkner, did you intend any Christ symbolism in *Light in August* in Joe Christmas?

A. No, that's a matter of reaching into the lumber room to get out something which seems to the writer the most effective way to tell what he is trying to tell. And that comes back to the notion that there are so few plots to use that sooner or later any writer is going to use something that has been used. And that Christ story is one of the best stories that man has invented, assuming that he did invent that story, and of course it will recur. Everyone that has had the story of Christ and the Passion as a part of his Christian background will in time draw from that. There was no deliberate intent to repeat it. That the people to me come first. The symbolism comes second.

Q. Well, I was just wondering why [for] such a sort of bad man as Joe Christmas you would use Christ, whether. . . .

117

A. Well, Joe Christmas—I think that you really can't say that any man is good or bad. I grant you there are some exceptions, but man is the victim of himself, or his fellows, or his own nature, or his environment, but no man is good or bad either. He tries to do the best he can within his rights. Now with Christmas, for instance, he didn't know what he was. He knew that he would never know what he was, and his only salvation in order to live with himself was to repudiate mankind, to live outside the human race. And he tried to do that but nobody would let him, the human race itself wouldn't let him. And I don't think he was bad, I think he was tragic. And his tragedy was that he didn't know what he was and would never know, and that to me is the most tragic condition that an individual can have—to not know who he was.

. . .

Q. Did you ever put yourself in a story like Hemingway does?

A. No, and I don't think that Hemingway does it, either. I think that any writer worth his salt is convinced that he can create much better people than God can. That he is too busy changing Hemingway and Faulkner, though he certainly can't say just how much of Hemingway or Faulkner he put in because that to him too is not too important. That the important thing is the figure that he is putting on paper—trying to make stand up on its hind legs and cast a shadow.

Q. Mr. Faulkner, but every now and then you can't help but putting into the mouth of somebody your own thoughts.

A. Well, that's when the bloke agrees with me, surely.

Q. Mr. Faulkner, in *The Town* when Eula Varner Snopes comes to Gavin Stevens's office at night, is it out of sheer sympathy for his plight?

A. Yes. By that time she had learned something of compassion for people through her determination to protect that girl, and to see someone that anguished over the need for a particular woman to her seemed foolish. That hers was more of a Hellenic attitude. That wasn't important enough to be frustrated about, and if that was going to make him feel any better she was perfectly willing to help him.

118

Q. What ever happened to her first lover, Hoake Mc-Carron?

A. We don't know, but we were done with him by that time so we don't know.

Q. A few generations back, was the de Spain blood or lineage the best in the county?

A. It represented aristocracy, yes.

Q. Was it better, do you think, than that of the Compson or the Sartoris family?

A. It was stronger, it was less prone to the aberrations, to the degeneracy into semi-madness which the Compsons reached. It didn't degenerate into the moral weakness of the Sartorises, it was tougher blood. It may be it wasn't quite as exalted as theirs was at one time, that it by instinct—it kept a certain leaven of a stronger stock by instinctive choice. It was simply stronger—not better but stronger.

Q. Mr. Faulkner, could you tell me in your writing which character is most nearly perfectly tragic?

A. It would be between Sutpen and Christmas, Dilsey. I don't think I have a choice. It would probably be between those three.

Q. Mr. Faulkner, in the middle of *The Town* you seem to change your feeling toward Flem Snopes. He's a comical, vicious, rapacious, rather pitiable character, and then toward the end you create sympathy for him, and the reader feels sorry for him almost. Probably circumstances. Is this deliberate or—

A. Well, I didn't. I still don't feel sorry for him. He simply—to gain what he wanted, he had to assume all sorts of things that had never occurred to him in his wildest dream that he would have to. Like respectability, for instance. That he still clung to his undeviating aim, but he had to take on all sorts of what he considered foolishness and extra baggage in order to stick to it. That he was using—he came from nothing with no equipment. He was bent on being president of that bank. He himself didn't know how to get there. All he knew was that he must get there, and he used whatever came to his hand, he coped with any situation that came up to get what he wanted. I never did feel sorry for him any more than one feels sorry for anyone who is ridden with an ambition or demon as base as simple vanity and rapacity and greed. I think that you can be ridden by a demon, but let it be a good demon, let it be a splendid demon, even if it is a demon, and his was a petty demon. So I don't feel sorry for Flem for that reason.

Q. Sir, Flem Snopes has been moved from the hamlet to the town. Can we expect him to go to the city?

A. No, the next is his mansion. He has got the outside symbol of what he has believed he wanted all the time.

Q. Sir, how is [Flem] going to be able to exist in the same town with his terribly good [cousin] Wall Street Panic?

A. Well now, that's going to cost me four dollars to answer that question because you won't buy the next book, you see.

Q. Mr. Faulkner, if men are to a certain extent victims of their environment, I wonder if when you write how much you feel that the writer—or you—are the creator of what you are writing or if it ever gets away from you? Do you feel that you are an instrument of an idea . . .?

A. Well, the feeling is not really quite that exalted. Once these people come to life, they begin—they take off and so the writer is going at a dead run behind them trying to put down what they say and do in time. Well, he's—well, in that sense he's an instrument. They have taken charge of the story. They tell it from then on. The writer has just got to keep up with them and put it down, and to give it some order, to follow the rules of composition, but I think he himself never knows just what they might do and say next. It's got to fit in with his concept of what is true before he will put it down.

Q. The material that you wrote thirty years ago in *The Town*, was that reworked or does that stand as it was?

A. It has been reworked around the joints, you might say, the suture, to make it join and not show a rough place, but the material is practically as it was written thirty years ago.

120

Q. Mr. Faulkner, I pull you back for a moment to that junk box that you mention. Were you speaking figuratively there or do you really, like so many authors, have a box in which you—

A. No, no. It's up here.

. . .

Q. Mr. Faulkner, which one of your novels required the least rewriting?

A. *As I Lay Dying.*

. . .

Q. According to your answer to my earlier question, I suppose you connect no—make no connection at all between the family relationships in *The Sound and the Fury* and those of *As I Lay Dying.*

A. Well, there would be certain similarities because of simple geography. That is, there are certain similarities in family relationships between a family of planters and a family of tenant farmers. The superficial differences could be vast and varied, but basically the same relationship is there because it's based on the need for solidarity in a country which not too long ago was still frontier. It's all because of the influence of a violent form of the Protestant religion, on politics, something on the economy of the country. So the relationships would be in that sense basically similar.

Q. Then you couldn't go so far as to say, for example, that Darl is the Quentin of the Bundrens and that Cash is the Jason of the Bundrens.

A. Well, you could if that is any pleasure to you. I mean by that that some people get a certain amount of pleasure in hunting around in a writer's work for reasons, for symbols, for similarities, and of course they are very likely all there, but the writer himself is too busy simply writing about people in conflict with themselves and one another and their background to wonder or even care whether he repeats himself or whether he uses symbols or not. He would use a symbol at the drop of a hat if that was the simplest way to throw the light on the particular incident he's telling about, and it's perfectly valid, I think, for anyone to seek for those symbols. That

121

there's a pleasure in doing that just like the reason for reading a book is—it's a pleasure.

Q. Mr. Faulkner, I wonder, since we are discussing reasons, if you have any particular reason for the rather unusual structure of *Requiem for a Nun*. Was that work meant to be a dramatic presentation, or is it experiment in form, or did you feel that it was necessary to the story that you were telling?

A. I felt that that was the best way to tell that story. That the story of those people fell into the hard simple give-and-take of dialogue. The longer—I don't know what you would call those interludes, the prefaces, preambles, whatever they are—was necessary to give it the contrapuntal effect which comes in orchestration, that the hard give-and-take of the dialogue was played against something that was a little mystical, made it sharper, more effective, in my opinion. It was not experimentation, it was simply because to me that seemed the most effective way to tell that story.

. . .

Q. Sir, even though you love people, have you ever gotten so mad at them that you were going to write something like one of Mencken's articles, sort of slapping people in the face?

A. Well, I don't think I love people. I would like to think that I think that people are marvelous, and I have a great compassion for people and man's mistakes and the anguish, his condition, but I don't think that I love people. But I think that you have got to have a hatred of man's condition and a frustration toward it to write as Mencken wrote. That one can hate man's condition and believe that man wants to change it, and can try to change it, and possibly will change it, still not get in a rage at man because he doesn't change his condition over night—which seems to have been Mencken's trouble. That Mencken, in a way, he gave up. He quit. He said that man stinks and always will stink. I don't agree with that.

. . . .

Q. Mr. Faulkner, you say you get your characters and ideas and so forth by observing. Well, I just wondered if while you were here these few months if you have observed any new characters, or—can we expect to find ourselves perhaps in one of your later books?

122

A. I think I said that the characters come from observation, experience, and imagination—all three, and I said also that the writer gains—does his research with every breath he draws, and I also said that he has no morals, no morality about what he will use, so you needn't be surprised to find anything that I've seen in Virginia in what I write next. But also remember that I'm convinced I can improve on the Lord and so you won't quite recognize yourself if you do. You'll be changed.

Session Fifteen

May 7, 1957

UNIVERSITY RADIO

ENGLISH DEPARTMENT LANGUAGE PROGRAM

. . . Q. . . . By the way, Mr. Faulkner, how many different types of dialect do you try to distinguish? Now I notice, of course, the difference between the speech of the Negroes and the poor white trash. Are there any other distinctions that you try to make?

A. I would say there are three. The dialect, the diction, of the educated semi-metropolitan white Southerner, the dialect of the hill backward Southerner, and the dialect of the Negro —four, the dialect of the Negro who has been influenced by the Northern cities, who has been to Chicago and Detroit.

Q. Four different dialects?

A. Four.

Q. Do you find that your characters change their dialect as they improve in financial status?

A. Not always. Sometimes. The ones that are—that take up snobbery easily, yes, they will change their dialect, and young people have an aptitude for changing their dialect like the comedian does.

. . .

Q. Mr. Faulkner, I had—have down here on a list several words that I would like to ask you about. One is the word *pussel-gutted*. You spoke about Jewel calling his horse *pussel-gutted* and that was in mock affection. And then in another place Peabody—this is by the way in *As I Lay Dying*—Peabody has *pussel-gutted* himself eating cold greens. I suppose that means make yourself flabby.

A. Bloated. Yes.

Q. That's a Georgia term. I know that term.

Q. Is there a plant that you're—that is behind that figure of speech, *pussel*?

A. No.

Q. There's a plant in Virginia called pursley and I thought maybe it was the same thing. It's a hideous plant, an ugly plant, it gets full of water.

A. It could derive from that. I don't know. I've heard it all my life. It means someone that is bloated, that has a tremendous belly that he shouldn't have.

. . .

Q. May I ask you about another word that I noticed, and that's the word *peakling*. You said about Jewel, or rather in connection with Jewel it was said, "I told them that's why Ma always whipped him and petted him more. Because he was *peakling* around the house. . . ."

A. That's probably a corruption or contraction between *puny* and *weakly*. That's like the contraction or corruption between *mist* and *drizzle* becomes *mizzle*.

Q. Mr. Faulkner, I noticed that Vernon and Uncle Billy, in *As I Lay Dying,* often say *aye* for *yes.* I wondered if that was common or whether it was just characteristic of the older generation.

A. That is common among the older people whose ancestry was Scottish. They came to the mountains of North Carolina, then they came to the mountains of Virginia, then they came to the hills of Mississippi and they kept their old ways. They would say *to red up a room,* just as you hear in Scotland—means to clean a room, to make the beds, sweep.

. . .

Q. Mr. Faulkner, may I ask you if I—if there's something here in Mississippi folklore that I miss, not having grown up in Mississippi. Cora says, "His face looked like one of these

126

here Christmas masts that had done been buried a while and then dug up." What is a Christmas *mast?*

A. Oh, the toy mask, the comic faces that children buy in the stores for Halloween and Christmas time.

Q. And *mast* is really for *mask?*
A. Mast, yes.

Q. Just like *dust* for *dusk?*
A. Yes. That's right.
. . .

Q. What does this mean, Mr. Faulkner? Let's see, "They all piled over the crest of the hill just in time to see Tomey's Turl a way out across the flat almost to the woods and the dogs streaking down the hill and out onto the flat. They just *tongued* once and when they came boiling up around Tomey's Turl they looked like they were going to jump up and lick him in the face."

A. Another verb made from a noun. They *gave tongue* once.
. . .

Q. Mr. Faulkner, some days ago I remember your saying that you thought you could move, say, to a Maine village, a fishing village or a lumbering village, and it wouldn't be long before you would be writing about people there, yet I remember yesterday you said that it was the inflection, the sound of the words and the dialect that was very much a part of the people that you write about. Don't you think that though you could see stories quickly in the lives of this imagined Maine group of people, it would take you a long time to get on to their talk, their pronunciation, and so forth?

A. I've had no trouble yet when I have been in New England. I would have to listen to it and get into the habit of remembering to use their own terms, their own diction, but there was no difficulty about understanding what they meant. . . .

Session Sixteen

May 8, 1957

ENGINEERING STUDENTS

Q. Mr. Faulkner, were you playing a kind of fugue on the theme of races here? Were you having a lot of fun with that?

A. I had a lot of fun with it, I wasn't playing a fugue on the theme of races, I was writing about people in what I—what to me was amusing terms, and I hoped it would be amusing terms to the reader. No, it was primarily about people, about people who had got into a predicament and solved it with the only tools they had.

Q. Mr. Faulkner, this is a little bit off the theme of literature, but I'd like to—if you wouldn't mind telling us a little about your trip to Greece? I would like to hear a little about that if that's not getting too far off the subject—too far away from it.

A. It was a strange experience in that that was the only country that looked exactly like we had—I mean, the background, the educational background of the Anglo-Saxon had taught him to expect it to look. And sure enough there was the Hellenic light that I had heard of, had read about. And I saw Homer's wine-dark sea too. And there was a—the only place I was in where there was a sense of a very distant past but there was nothing inimical in it. In the other parts of the Old World there is a sense of the past but there is something Gothic and in a sense a little terrifying. . . . The people seem to function against that past that for all its remoteness in time it was still inherent in the light, the resurgence of spring, you didn't expect to see the ghost of the old Greeks, or expect to see the actual figures of the gods, but you had a sense that they were near and they were still powerful, not inimical, just powerful. That they themselves had reached and were enjoying a kind of a nirvana, they existed, but they were free of man's folly and trouble, of having to involve themselves in man's problem. That they at last had the time to watch what man did without having to be involved in it. Yes, it was very interesting. I think that two weeks is not only too short, it's an insult to that country, that one should go with no limit to his visit. That there's no end to what you can see, and then sure enough you see something which is exactly like what you imagined. There will be the plain and across it suddenly there is Parnassus with snow on it, and the old ruins, they look ancient but there's a sense as though it happened only yesterday. That whether Agamemnon ever lived, ever was an actual man or not, there he was, because he had to be. It was necessary. That he was in the literary history of man's spirit, so therefore he must have existed at one time as a flesh and blood man.

Q. Mr. Faulkner, in your new book, *The Town,* you have Flem Snopes assuming the mask of respectability And I was wondering, since you, I think, are going to write a trilogy, that I was wondering what type of character would Flem Snopes assume, say, in your next book?

A. He had never heard of respectability. He didn't even know it existed, until suddenly he found that he needed it. And so he assumed it, and as soon as he doesn't need respectability any longer, he will cast it away. That he had a certain aim which he intended to attain. He would use whatever tools necessary with complete ruthlessness to gain that end, and if he had to use respectability, he would use that. If he had to use religious observance, he would use that. If he has to destroy his wife, he will do that. If he has to trick a child, a girl child, into being his tool, he will do that with no compunction whatever. That respectability to him was just a tool.

. . .

Q. . . . What was the germ of that story ["Was"], do you recall it perhaps?

130

A. The germ of the story was one of the three oldest ideas that man can write about, which is love, sex. And to me it was comic, of the man that had got himself involved in an engagement, and he himself couldn't extricate himself and his—he had to call on his brother, and his brother used the only tools he had, which was his ability to play poker. Which to me what was funny. Also it was—it had a certain sociological importance in—to show my country as it really was in those days. The elegance of the colonial plantation didn't exist in my country. My country was still frontier. The plantation, the columned porticos, that was Charleston and Natchez. But my country was still frontier. People lived from day to day, with a bluff and crude hardiness, but with a certain simplicity. Which to me is very interesting because the common picture of the South is all magnolias and crinoline and Grecian portals and things like that, which was true only around the fringes of the South. Not in the interior, the back wood.

. . .

Q. Have you enjoyed your stay here at the University?

A. Yes sir, very much.

Q. We were interested in your comment of coming to Virginia because you liked snobs, I wonder. . . .

A. Well, that was—I thought that we were more or less informal then and I didn't really mean that as a serious observation. Let me define what I mean by—a snob is someone who is so complete in himself and so satisfied with what he has that he needs nothing from anybody. That when a stranger comes up, he can accept that stranger on the stranger's terms provided only the stranger observe only a few amenities of civilization. And to me that's what the people, what Virginians do. They never push at me. They want nothing of me. They will offer me their hospitality and they will accept me. All I have to do is just to behave decently.

. . .

Q. Then could I ask you what Ike Snopes is supposed to be in *The Hamlet*? What were you creating then? Is he someone like someone whom you knew or what?

A. No no. No writer is satisfied with the folks that God

131

creates. He's convinced that he can do much better than that. To me Ike Snopes was simply an interesting human being with man's natural, normal failings, his—the baseness which man fights against, the honor which he hopes that he can always match. The honesty, the courage which he hopes that he can always match. And at times he fails. And then he is pitiable. But he is still human, and he still believes that man can be better than he is, and that is what the writer is trying to do, is interested in—to show man as he is in conflict with his problems, with his nature, with his own heart, with his fellows, and with his environment. That's all, in my opinion, any book or story is about. Of course it has mutations. The problems fall into the categories of money or sex or death. But the basic story is man in conflict with his own heart, with his fellows, or with his environment.

. . .

Q. Sir, you say that your characters are—as much as possible, anyway—just people. And yet I sort of got the idea that Flem Snopes is sort of a practically inhuman character and sort of symbolic himself. Does that ever—did that enter when you wrote that, or—?

A. Well, it would depend on what he is symbolic of. You see people who are inhuman people. I think that I didn't invent an inhuman—the inhuman type which Flem is a manifestation of. I think that Jason Compson in another book of mine is completely inhuman. But in a way he is, I hope, a living man. I have known people in actual life who were hopeless, who in the terms of the humanities, in the terms of the verities of man's condition, compassion and pity and courage, unselfishness, he was inhuman, but he was still a living man. He was not created to be a symbol of anything. He was simply created because suddenly he had a place in that particular scene that I was writing about, in that particular problem of human beings that I was writing about. Not to symbolize anything at all.

. . .

Q. Most of us here tonight, I think, are rather young men in the field of Engineering. A lot of us hope to be getting out this year. I wonder if you have—this may be an off-beat question—I wonder if you have any advice to young men getting ready to go out in the light, you might say, from the point of view of someone who has studied human beings and people as much as you have.

A. There was a very wise man said to me once, "I never give anybody advice because they might take it." And at first I didn't understand what he meant by that but now I think I do. Actually nobody can bathe for you, you know. You've got to do that yourself, and the experience, the advice you get, I think, is not by asking for it, you get that by some form of osmosis. You will get it from the books you read, from your experiences in college. Every man has got to stand on his own feet and I think now that I wouldn't accept anyone's advice. That I would rather make my own mistakes than to accept advice which might save me because I know now that mistakes don't hurt you.

Q. Well, that's good advice in itself.

A. Thank you.

. . .

Q. Someone who talked to you gave a list of virtues. I've heard you mention some of them tonight. Do you have that ready? I think that courage and honesty were among your list of virtues.

A. Well, let's use a little better word to me than virtues— they're the verities of the human heart. They are courage, honor, pride, compassion, pity. That they are not virtues, or one doesn't try to practice them, in my opinion, simply because they are good. One practices—tries to practice them simply because they are the edifice on which the whole history of man has [been] founded and by means of which his—as a race he has endured this long. That without those verities he would have vanished, just like the mastodon and the other ephemeral phenomena of nature have come and gone in the history of the world. Man has endured despite his frailty because he accepts and believes in those verities. That one must be honest not because it's virtuous but because that's the only way to get along. That if people lied constantly to one another you would never know where you were, you would never know

133

what was going on. That if people didn't practice compassion there would be nothing to defend the weak until they got enough strength to stand for themselves. If one didn't practice something of pride, one would have nothing to be proud about, to have said, I did well, I did nothing that I was ashamed of, I can lie down with myself and sleep. That is, they are the verities to be practiced not because they are virtue but because that's the best way to live in peace with yourself and your fellows. . . .

Session Seventeen

May 13, 1957

GRADUATE COURSE IN THE NOVEL

... Q. It's been both stated and denied that Sir Walter Scott has greatly influenced Southern people, especially during the—not the recent unpleasantness but the less recent unpleasantness, the mid-nineteenth century war, the War Between the States. I notice you named one of your characters Quentin, as a rather romantic-minded individual. Seems to me you suggest by that name that he is the type of Southerner who was influenced by the kind of thing that Walter Scott—

A. Not necessarily. I think that Scott was read more in the South for the reason that at a time the Southerner had very little of his money to devote to the buying of books, and there was a kinship perhaps between the life of Scott's Highland and the life the Southerner led after Reconstruction. They too were in the aftermath of a land which had been conquered and devastated by people speaking its own language, which hasn't happened too many times. And so every Southern household when they bought books they bought Scott. That was because you got more words for your money, maybe, could have had something to do with it. But every household that [at] all pretended to be literate had Scott.

Q. While we are on that literary angle, which we dreamed up a little bit on the literary side, do you feel that the subject Mr. Boggs raised about the literary renaissance, or whatever you want to call it, the flourishing of literature in the South, has been in any notable way indebted to the fact that a number of young people, writers, were resident in Paris came under French influence perhaps in the 'Twenties?

135

A. I don't know. It seems to me that very few Southerners were a part of that group of expatriates of the 'Twenties in Paris. Most of the ones I knew were Northerners. I don't remember a single Southerner that had any part in it. I would say that the reason for the renaissance in Southern writing was in the cards, in the making, long before that. I think this may have had a little to do with it: since the Civil War there has been a great deal of—misunderstanding is not quite the right word. The Northerner, the outlander, had a queer and erroneous idea of what Southern people were. It may be that that was an instinctive desire in Southerners to tell the outlander just what we were, just what we might have had that we felt was great, excepting four years of war in which we knew we had no chance to win it. To say, This is what we had that we thought was worth that, or, This is what we actually are. I don't know, that's probably valid. I imagine there are so many things that went into it that probably nobody could say, This is where the resurgence of writing in the South came from. I myself am inclined to think it was because of the bareness of the Southerner's life, that he had to resort to his own imagination, to create his own Carcassonne.

Q. In that connection, would you mind commenting on this question? You said a minute ago, facetiously, that Southerners don't read books, they write them. It has long been known, of course, to literary historians that Southern writers both before and after the Civil War counted pretty largely on Northern readers. And—Hayne, for example, as a notable example, and Lanier is another example. Do you suppose that has been in the consciousness of the average Southern writer and could possibly have influenced his work in any way?

A. Yes, it has. It's in his consciousness that the man who will publish his book is a Northerner, and he is never unaware of that. That the publisher, and to an extent his readers, are Northerners. I think that most Southerners know that his home folks ain't going to like what he writes anyway. That he's not really writing to them, and that they simply do not read books. They are good people but they just do not read books.

136

Q. . . . If part of the renascence in Southern writing is due to an urge to explain the Southern—the South to explain itself, is it not also true that once we get out of the moonlight and magnolia school that various of the non-writing Southerners do not like what the writing Southerners do . . .?

A. Yes, that's quite true. The non-writing Southerner, the non-reading Southerner, he wants the sort of brochure that the Chamber of Commerce gets out. There are things in his country that he's not too proud of himself, but to him it's bad manners to show that in public.

Q. Does any locality like to read the books that are written about that locality, do you think? Isn't it characteristic that a locality is generally offended when it finds itself in a novel or a story?

A. The—an element of the locality, but didn't the people of his own country have a sort of a fierce pride in people like Thoreau and Emerson? Or was that just the educated, intellectual New Englander that felt that?

Q. I don't know—

A. Well, I always thought that everybody—they might not have approved so much of all that Emerson or Thoreau said, but they had a fierce, almost provincial pride in— . . . Can a man write about ideas excepting in the provincial terms of his background?

Q. I suppose they certainly must affect him.

A. Could Emerson have written Emerson—would it have been the same Emerson if he'd been a Mississippian, say, or a Texan or a Californian?

Q. Well, I think not. But still when you are writing about self-reliance in general, it could apply all over the world.

A. But would a Californian in a climate that don't change, where you don't need even a warm house to live in—what would he care about self-reliance?

Q. That reminds—that brings up this question, Mr. Faulkner, in my mind, that I often—Carlyle says Walt Whitman—he says Walt Whitman thinks because he lives in a big country,

137

he's a big man. Do you suppose—I gather that he thought—that Whitman thought that the climate and the general landscape, background of—the geographical features of a place had some influence on the person who grows up in that, whether he be a writer or not. Do you suppose there's anything in that? In the South, for example, what—how does that turn out in the South?

A. Well, I would say that Carlyle's and Whitman's definition of a big man were completely different. Carlyle's an islander, a small country. His idea of a big man is a big individual man. I should think that Whitman's idea of a big man is one that is lucky enough to belong to a race of giants, if he's one too. I wonder if Whitman believed that he was a bigger man than anybody else in America?

Q. What I was getting at was whether the peculiarities of Southern climate and topography might possibly have any influence on the nature of the writer?

A. It would have to, just like the language the man knows to write in would have some influence. But I don't think that the topography, one topography will produce a writer where another topography won't. But of course—

Q. You don't think there's any relationship then between the lack of roads in Yoknapatawpha County and the difficulties with your sentence structure?

A. No sir, because the lack of roads in Yoknapatawpha County isn't near as complex as Madison Avenue or 42nd Street. Though of course that depends upon who is looking at each one. Yoknapatawpha County ain't nearly as complex as the Empire State Building.

Q. Mr. Faulkner, I spoke to you about your long sentences and asked you if one reason for them were not that you were trying to give the past and the present and the future more or less all at the same time, to throw light on the present actions by referring to the past and to the future. And I understand why throwing light on the past would throw light on a present action. And I think I understand why reference to the future would do it. But I am not sure that I do understand,

and I would like to ask you why you feel it is necessary to bring in your future while you are telling the present. Why is that significant? It's not going to happen yet. So why bring in something which has not yet happened while you are recount-ing something that is happening?

A. Well, a man's future is inherent in that man—I—in the sense that life, A.D. 1957, is not the end of life, that there'll be a 2057. That we assume that. There may not be, but we assume that. And in man, in man's behavior today is nineteen fifty—two thousand and fifty-seven, if we just had a machine that could project ahead and could capture that, that machine could isolate and freeze a picture, an image, of what man will be doing in 2057, just as the machine might capture and fix the light rays showing what he was doing in B.C. 28. That is, that's the mystical belief that there is no such thing as *was*. That time *is,* and if there's no such thing as *was,* then there is no such thing as *will be.* That time is not a fixed condition, time is in a way the sum of the combined intelligences of all men who breathe at that moment.

. . .

Q. You have various children—you spoke of Benjy—there is—and also of *The Sound and the Fury* and Vardaman. I was thinking, been thinking recently about this boy who partici-pates in the telling of the story in *The Town.* I don't know, I'm not sure that I know how you would explain the function of Charles Mallison in this last novel, whether he has, whether he is—his part of the story is supposed to have particular value because he is a child or—and whether—and then Ratliff. There are three people, you see: there is yourself—and I haven't been able to see at the moment, and I've only read it one time, quite as well as I do in *The Sound and Fury* the dis-tinct values which come from the three points of view. I don't know whether I make myself clear or not. You can comment on that problem.

A. That was simply a—well, I don't like the word "trick," but it was used deliberately to look at the object from three points of view. Just as when you examine a monument you will walk around it, you are not satisfied to look at it from just one side. Also, it was to look at it from three different

139

mentalities. That was—one was the mirror which obliterated all except truth, because the mirror didn't know the other factors existed. Another was to look at it from the point of view of someone who had made of himself a more or less artificial man through his desire to practice what he had been told was a good virtue, apart from his belief in virtues, what he had been told, trained by his respect for education in the old classical sense. The other was from the point of view of a man who practiced virtue from simple instinct, from—well, more than that, because—for a practical reason, because it was better. There was less confusion if all people didn't tell lies to one another, and didn't pretend. That seemed to me to give a more complete picture of the specific incidents as they occurred if they could be [viewed] three times.

Q. And yet you didn't mean that Charles Mallison was quite as much of a child or an innocent as some of these other children?

A. Well, he changed. He grew up in that book. And of course, his point of view changed.

Q. One other question about that book. Someone has said recently—and I don't present this as my view, it is something that I would like you to comment on if you will—that Gavin Stevens in *The Town* is a less mature, a less responsible— somehow or other—a less likable person than he appears in some other places, as the stories of the *Knight's Gambit*.

A. Well, he had got out of his depth. He had got into the real world. While he was—could be—a county attorney, an amateur Sherlock Holmes, then he was at home, but he got out of that. He got into a real world in which people anguished and suffered, not simply did things which they shouldn't do. And he wasn't as prepared to cope with people who were following their own bent, not for a profit but simply because they had to. That is, he knew a good deal less about people than he knew about the law and about ways of evidence and drawing the right conclusions from what he saw with his legal mind. When he had to deal with people, he was an amateur, he was—at times he had a good deal less judgment than his nephew did. Which is not against education. Probably the passion he had for getting degrees, for trying this and trying that and going all the way to Europe to get more degrees, to study more, was in his own nature, it was the same character that made him shy away from marriage, he was probably afraid to be married. He might get too involved with the human race if he married one of them.

Q. Did you mean Gavin Stevens to be like that in *Intruder in the Dust?*

A. No, these people I invent and after that I just run along and put down what they say and do. I don't know always what they are going to develop into myself.

Q. I mean, is Gavin at the same stage of development in *Intruder in the Dust?* Is he younger in *The Town?*

A. *Intruder in the Dust* happened after *The Town. Intruder in the Dust* happened about 1935 or '40 and *The Town* began in 1909 and went to 1927. Probably Stevens learned something from *The Town* to carry into *Intruder in the Dust.*

Q. Mr. Faulkner, the fight that Gavin has with de Spain in *The Town* reminded me in some ways with the fight that Quentin had when he was in Cambridge. They both seemed a little bit like Don Quixote—

A. Yes.

Q. —fighting for the honor of a lady. Is there any such similarity there, in character, between the two men at that time?

A. No, that's a constant sad and funny picture too. It is the knight that goes out to defend somebody who don't want to be defended and don't need it. But it's a very fine quality in human nature. I hope it will always endure. It is comical and a little sad. And Quentin and Stevens were that much alike.

Q. Mr. Faulkner, what did you start with in *Intruder in the Dust?* Was it the idea of a single character . . .?

A. Well, it began with the notion—there was a tremendous flux of detective stories going about at that time and my children were always buying them and bringing them home.

141

I'd stumble over them everywhere I went. And I thought of an idea for one would be a man in jail just about to be hung would have to be his own detective, he couldn't get anybody to help him. Then the next thought was, the man for that would be a Negro. Then the character of Lucius—Lucas Beauchamp came along. And the book came out of that. It was the notion of a man in jail who couldn't hire a detective, couldn't hire one of these tough guys that slapped women around, took a drink every time he couldn't think of what to say next. But once I thought of Beauchamp, then he took charge of the story and the story was a good deal different from the idea that—of the detective story that I had started with.

. . .

Q. We discussed Joseph Conrad in the course that I teach. We frequently come up against you, and vice versa, and I was curious to know whether you saw any similarities.

A. I imagine if I went back over the work I could find similarities. I can find similarities between Conrad and Hardy. And I'm sure I can find Conrad in my stuff and find almost anybody else you could name.

Q. I was thinking of the particular thing of Conrad's effort to surround an event by throwing light on it from past and future as well as present. He seems to stop at a particular event and throw light from this character and that character, and from the front and the rear and the side in a way that I don't remember other novelists doing before his time.

A. I'm inclined to think that all writers do that, only most of them, except Conrad and me, may be a little more clever about it. Probably Conrad was because he deliberately taught himself a foreign language to write in. And mine may be because I never went to school enough to save myself the short-cuts of learning English. That we both are a little more obvious than the others for that reason.

. . .

Q. I know you admire Wolfe tremendously, but don't you feel that as Wolfe caught up to the present that he lost something that he'd had when he had a little more time between him and the event to digest?

142

A. Now that comes back to a more or less idle remark I made years ago. I have no particular great admiration for Wolfe. This is what happened in there, it was at a group years ago, somebody asked what I thought about my contemporaries, I said, We're not done writing yet, I couldn't say. And he said, Well, haven't you got any opinion at all about them? and I said, About who? He named Wolfe, Dos Passos, Erskine Caldwell, Hemingway, and me. I said, Well, I will— I would rate us this way, which I did [Wolfe, Faulkner, Dos Passos, Caldwell, Hemingway], and that's what that came from, and for about twenty years now I've been trying to explain that.

. . .

Q. Mr. Faulkner, in view of the fact that those people asked you for ratings when the horse race had gotten maybe to the first quarter mark, and we are now perhaps halfway around the course, would you feel inclined to make any revision in the order that you saw at this time?

A. No, because I made my estimate on the gallantry of the failure, not on the success or the validity of the work. It's on the gallantry of the effort which failed. In my opinion, my work has all failed, it ain't quite good enough, which is the only reason to write another one, because writing really ain't any fun, I mean the mechanics of putting the stuff down on paper is no fun, I can think of too many other things I'd rather do. And I don't see any reason to change that, no. After we have all written out, and if there's time to look back at it, then I could make a private estimate of the work. But right now, I think it's too soon. Of course, Wolfe is finished because he's dead, but the others are not. Caldwell seems to have written himself out years ago, which has nothing to do with the value of the first books and I think that the first books, *God's Little Acre* and the short stories, that's enough for any man, he should be content with that, but knowing writers, I know he's not, just as I'm not content with mine. I meant only that Hemingway had sense enough to find a method which he could control and didn't need or didn't have to, wasn't driven by his private demon to waste himself in trying to do more than that. So, he has done consistently probably the most solid work of all of us. But it wasn't the splendid magnificent bust that Wolfe made in trying to put the whole history of the human heart on the head of the pin, you might say.

. . .

Q. Mr. Faulkner, you said that Hemingway developed a method he could control. What do you think, what is your personal opinion of *Across the River and into the Trees*?

A. I would say it was—that he considered it a bad book. Just like he considers *To Have and Have Not* a bad book, probably. But then the man that wrote some of the stories in *Men without Women* and some of the early books, he can afford to write a bad book, whenever he wants to, I think. Miss [Nancy] Hale will agree with that, won't you?

Q. Oh, yes.

. . .

Q. Which one of Conrad do you read?

A. *The Nigger of the "Narcissus."*

Q. Do you read *Nostromo?*

A. Haven't read that in years.

Q. *Victory?*

A. Not in years. "Falk," "The End of the Tether." What's the one about the young man that was given command of the—

Q. *Lord Jim.*

A. —bark in—

Q. Deserted?

A. —Bangkok—"Youth."

Q. "Youth," yes.

. . .

Q. You were saying that you sometimes read something that you wouldn't ordinarily because somebody asked you to, or puts it in your hands. Are you besieged with aspiring writers who wish an opinion upon a manuscript or something of that sort?

A. Yes. Nobody can escape that, of course. But I think any writer that brings you a manuscript to read, you can save time by not reading that one because the ones that write the good ones haven't got time to bring it to you and say, Read this. They don't care whether you read it or not or whether you like it or not. They're the good ones.

. . .

Q. I will say this, sir. You speak of *Don Quixote* as one of your—one of the great books, one of the books that you most admire. It's a right long book, isn't it?

A. I hadn't noticed it. Just like *The Nigger of the "Narcissus"* is very short. I probably hadn't noticed that much either.

Q. Well, you have mentioned some of the novels that you like most. Is there any particular poetry that you think came closest to saying the truth in a few words?

A. Almost all of it. Burns, Keats, Wordsworth, now and then Whitman, Ben Jonson, Marlowe—almost all of it, Laforgue, Goethe—almost all of it. That's why people still read it, why the names are still known.

Q. Which do you suppose is the most difficult, the most unattainable, for an ambitious youngster who wants to write but doesn't know yet whether he is a poet or a novelist or what? I gather—I may be wrong—from what you say that in general you think that poetry is perhaps the most difficult thing to attain real attention.

A. Well, few are good ones. I don't think that difficulty is the word. It's a combination of a demon and a fire that you have. Difficulty or ease has nothing to do with it. I wish I did know exactly what it is that it takes to make a poet. I think that any writer is better off if he looks on himself as a poet—he's a failed poet, I agree with you—but to look on himself primarily as a poet. That he has found man's history in its mutations, in the instances in which it becomes apparent, his anguish, his triumph, his failures, the whole passion of breathing, is so strong and so urgent that it must be recorded. If he is very fortunate, he can do it as the poets did it. If he's a little less fortunate, he can do it as the short story writers do it—as Chekov did it. If he is least fortunate, he's got to go back to the clumsy method of Mark Twain and Dreiser.

145

Session Eighteen

May 15, 1957

UNIVERSITY AND COMMUNITY PUBLIC

. . . Q. Mr. Faulkner, I saw something not long ago that took *The Sound and Fury* in four sections and tried to draw a parallel between the id, the ego and super-ego and the author's person. Now don't you think that is indicative of what a lot of critics and scholars are doing today with the views of contemporary writers, making psychological inferences and finding symbols which the author never intended?

A. Well, I would say that the author didn't deliberately intend but I think that in the same culture the background of the critic and of the writer are so similar that a part of each one's history is the seed which can be translated into the symbols which are standardized within that culture. That is, the writer don't have to know Freud to have written things which anyone who does know Freud can divine and reduce into symbols. And so when the critic finds those symbols, they are of course there. But they were there as inevitably as the critic should stumble on his own knowledge of Freud to discern symbol [*sic*]. But I think the writer is primarily concerned in telling about people, in the only terms he knows, which is out of his experience, his observation, and his imagination. And the experience and the imagination and the observation of a culture are—all the people in that culture partake of the same three things more or less. The critic has a valid part in any culture. I think that it's—it might be a good thing if most writers were like me and didn't bother to read them. That is, the writer knows what is in his book and he knows whether it failed or didn't fail. It—and so it's possible that reading the criticisms

147

could do a young writer harm because it could confuse him, it could get him to think in terms of the symbolism which the critic,who is usually a good deal more erudite than the writer, can find in his work.

. . .

Q. Does it give the author as much pain as it does the reader to produce scenes such as when Caddy wanted to see her baby and Jason just drove by?

A. Yes, it does, but that's—the writer is not simply dragging that in to pull a few tears, he is—he puts that down as an instance of man's injustice to man. That man will always be unjust to man, yet there must always be people, men and women who are capable of the compassion toward that injustice and the hatred of that injustice, and the will to risk public opprobrium, to stand up and say, This is rotten, this stinks, I won't have it.

. . .

Q. Mr. Faulkner, do you believe that integration as defined by the Supreme Court will come in Mississippi at any time in the near future or future?

A. It won't come into Mississippi or anywhere else because of any decision of any court. That's something that's got to be settled by people. But the—yes, I think that whether —integration may possibly never come in the sense that people think of it. I think that equality for the Negro will come. I think if the Negro has political equality to vote, if he has economic equality, if he has educational equality, then he won't want to mix with white folks any more than white folks wants to mix with him, because I can't imagine any Negro after the—his experience with white folks wanting to be that close to them. But he has—will get equality. If it is given to him by a Supreme Court ukase and enforced with police, as soon as the police are gone then some smart white man, maybe some smart Negro, will take his equality away from him again. He has got to be taught the responsibility of equality. That the Constitution never said everybody is to have happiness. They only have the right to gain happiness if they could, and happiness or freedom is something that you have got to work for. If it were not to be worked for it wouldn't be worth having. It's

148

got to be worked for and defended. Who was the Irish Member of Parliament who said, "God hath vouchsafed man liberty only under condition of eternal vigilance, which condition if he break it, servitude is the consequence of his crime, the punishment of his guilt"?[1] Well, that's true of anyone. You can't have freedom unless you deserve it and work to keep it. That's —and equality, of course, is freedom.

. . .

Q. Mr. Faulkner, you've written for both TV and motion pictures. I wonder which you would prefer to work for?

A. I didn't work for either one seriously because that is not my bent, for the reason I stated that in either one it is a matter of compromise, a compromise with the actor, with the director, and mainly with the people that put up the money. It's so expensive, a TV show or a moving picture show. I've had a great deal of fun working for moving pictures because I liked the people I worked with, but I never took working for any of them seriously. It was just a pleasant way to get a check every Saturday night, to me.

Q. Mr. Faulkner, I would like to know what you think of Ernest Hemingway as a writer, what is your opinion of him?

A. He is a man who has never betrayed the—his integrity which one accepts to be a writer. He learned early in life a method by which he could do his work, he has never varied from that method, it suited him, he handled it well. If his work continues, then it's going to get better. His last book, I think, *The Old Man and the Sea,* was the best because he discovered something which he had never found before, which was God. Up to that time his people functioned in a vacuum, they had no past, but suddenly in *The Old Man and the Sea,* he found God. There was the big fish—God made the big fish that had to be caught, God made the old man that had to catch the big fish, God made the shark that had to eat the fish, and God loved all of them, and if his work goes on from then it will still be better, which is something that not all writers can say. Too many tragically write themselves out too

---

[1] John Philpot Curran (1750-1817).

149

young and then their lives are unhappy. That happened with Fitzgerald, happened with Sherwood Anderson, and so they go to pieces.

. . .

Q. Sir, what are some of your favorite books?

A. *Don Quixote,* some of Conrad, *Heart of Darkness, The Nigger of the "Narcissus,"* most of Dickens, *The Brothers Karamazov, Anna Karenina, Madame Bovary,* the Old Testament. I suppose I have about fifty that I read—I go in and out like you go into a room to meet old friends, to open the book in the middle and read for a little while, and I imagine over the course of every ten years I would have read all of them through.

. . .

Q. Mr. Faulkner, Sherwood Anderson and T. S. Eliot seem to feel that there has been no classic since Vergil's *Aeneid* and I wonder to what extent you have grown in that way in philosophy or ideas.

A. Well, I'm sure if I ever read Vergil—I can't remember whether I did or not—I'd have stolen from him too for the reason that the writer is influenced by everything he ever read, but I don't think that as long as the writer is busy writing he's got time to make any didactic statements about where culture stopped and where it didn't stop. That he's not really interested in culture or even interested in literature, until he writes himself out and he has been corrupted by books so much that he has nothing else to do with his time save to take up being a literary man. Most writers are not literary men. They're really—they're craftsmen.

Q. Then you believe that Mr. Eliot underestimates this culture, apparently?

A. No no. That he's perfectly—I'm perfectly willing for him to have his opinion, but to me I ain't interested in it.

Q. Mr. Faulkner, can a writer know when he succeeds or fails—and I gather you don't use the critics' opinion as a guide —what gives you the sense of having failed or succeeded in a book?

150

A. That would probably be the worst day the writer ever faces because then nothing remains but to cut his throat. I think that he would—the only way to express it is what Hemingway means by saying "to feel good." He finishes the job and there's nothing that is still dangling, nothing more he wants to do to it. It's finished, it's complete. As long as it's failed, there's always something you think, Now, if I could just go back and do this over I could do it better. But you know that's a waste of time. The best thing is to take a new story.

. . .

Q. Mr. Faulkner, do you believe that the American language is developing as compared to the English language . . .?

A. Yes'm, I think so. I don't know how many generations, aeons, before it will be too distinct, but any language if it is not changing will not last long. That is, the only alternative to change and progress is death. It may be with the world being condensed by rapid transportation there will be even less divergence to the two languages than ever, but I would say that there will be a change and in time there will be just as much difference between the English English and American English as there is between classic Greek and modern Greek, unless both have been abolished in the meantime and there is still another language that comprises both, which will also be in a state of flux and change and advancement. . . .

Session Nineteen

May 16, 1957

LAW SCHOOL WIVES

Q. . . . [What was the purpose of your] travel in the State Department . . .?

A. I think the purpose of the Americans that go abroad are the sort that without intending to they give foreign countries a poor impression of Americans and this country. They—Americans—we want to be liked, and we are a little uncouth, a little too quick to try to make ourselves to be liked and the European is not accustomed to that. He's accustomed to people that are a little more formal than we are and the purpose of sending other people apart from Chairman of the Board of General Motors and things like that is to let the Europeans see that there are other people in our country besides millionaires that have come up from nothing and in fifteen years and are now chairmen of very important boards. And so I was sent around not to deliver a particular message, but just to be myself, just to be a simple individual with no particular axe to grind, to talk to people, to try to communicate with people apart from the language, to communicate, you might say, human spirit to human spirit. It was interesting work. I would like to think that it has done some good, but I do think that what we should do is instead of trying to export America to foreign countries, we should bring the foreigners here and let them see what there is in this country that makes us like it. That when we try to export America it gets censored, it gets changed, it becomes a rehearsed, it becomes a—oh, what's the word I want?—well, anyway it's not America. That what we should do is to bring the foreigners here, especially the enemy. If I had charge of things I would establish a fund and issue a sort of scholarship. The first necessity would be that the young man or young woman would be a Communist, because we don't want to show our country to people that already agree with us. We want to show our country to the people that don't agree with us, that are our enemies. And I would bring them here. They must first be a Communist. Next they should have a wife and maybe one or two children. They would come to this country. The man should be given a job according to his capacity in his own country. To stay here for a year, let his children know America, which means the ability to go down to the corner drugstore and get an ice-cream cone, to go to the moving pictures, to play the games in the streets that American children do. Let them stay for a year. Let them pay the first installment on the deep freeze and the car. Then he must go back but his deep freeze will be kept in escrow for him. When he comes back again, he can finish paying for it and can get it. And every year, every two years, bring another ten thousand and just let them see it. Don't try to sell them anything.

. . .

Q. Mr. Faulkner, can you tell us why you in particular were chosen for this mission by the State Department?

A. I don't know. I had—to tell you the truth, I'd never thought about that myself. It's hard to think of a good reason. It may be because the writer in this country, the artist in America, really has no place in our economy, which is an economy based on success rather than on any quality of the human spirit, and they have tried to send a representative of this country to people who had acquired success in American terms, and that didn't work so well and I suppose that in something very like desperation they said, Well, let's try something we haven't tried.

Q. Other people have been sent . . . in the past? . . .

A. Yes, and also the Russians have been doing this for years. They have sent people who are simply members of ballet troupes, of theatrical groups, and writers. Of course, the Russian artist on the surface is a Communist first before he is anything else, and I imagine that it occurred to someone that it was a good policy, since the Russians were doing it, and also I would like to think it occurred to someone that we could show the world that the artist in America did not have to be an American first—he could be an artist first. He didn't have to be a Democrat nor a Republican. That he could be an artist, he could say in this country what he wanted to say. That what he believed was truth in his own terms. I would like to think that that was the reason that they chose—have chosen writers. They chose Mr. Frost—people like that.

Q. I read that you recently went to Greece. Have you been on other trips?

A. Yes'm. I was in South America, in Japan, in the Philippines, in Scandinavia, Iceland, and several times in western Europe.

Q. How did you meet the people? Did you just stand around and meet those at random or were they transported to universities and so forth for lectures . . .?

A. It took a certain amount of doing. The State Department had been in the habit of sending these people on very rigidly planned and conducted tours. I would have to explain to the people in charge that that might not be the only way to do that, that maybe if the individual could be let alone, he'd get along perfectly, and let alone to see what he could do. And the people in our State Department in Europe are intelligent people. They have learned by hard experience that the enemy, the opponent, is not the foreigner, it's in the State Department in Washington, the bureaucrats in Washington. And the very fact that someone said, Let's do something different from what the people back in Washington said to do, may have been something that helped them to change their notion, and so I would follow the routine set up by the people in Washington for half the time and then someone in the Embassy of the State Department in some foreign country would have the courage to say, Well, let him do it his way for a little while. And so they would give me an interpreter and let me go where I wanted to and let me talk to people, which would take a little while to draw the people out, to—for them to realize that I had nothing to sell, I just wanted to talk to them. But after that they would talk to me, they would ask me questions they really wanted to ask, not the questions that the State Department had told me they should be told, but the answers that they themselves might want. I would get an interpreter, I would go to the library, the schools in Japan where young people, I mean junior college age from seventeen up to twenty, twenty-one, that would never get into the gatherings in a country as rigidly formalized as Japan is. I'd never had a chance to see them, unless I would get out of the beaten track, and then they would ask me the questions that they wanted to know. The young women wanted to know if all the American women really did have washing machines, and if they really could vote and if their votes really did count in an election. And the young men would want to know how much longer American troops would stay in their country, why American troops were there, and I would explain to them that the American people didn't want to be there any more than they, the Japanese, wanted them to be there. That the American troops were there, the young men were there, only because their government believed that it was necessary that all free peoples should remain free, which seemed to be the first time anybody had told them. That was true in the other countries, in Iceland where there was a certain amount of bad feeling between the native people and the troops. In Iceland particularly, with a population of only a few hundred thousand, with five thousand foreigners in uniform it would be like having a million German or Russian or French soldiers suddenly move into New Jersey, say, fifty miles from New York City. You could imagine how the people would feel until someone took the trouble to explain to them that these young men didn't want to be there either.

Q. Mr. Faulkner, I don't know the feeling of the European about integration . . . What do you think . . . ?

A. Yes, yes, a lot of it. To the Latin, integration, the mixing of the black race with the white race, is not as important. That seems to be an emotional situation only to the Northern European, the white man of a Teutonic background. That the Latin seems to think that it was silly and foolish, a mountain made out of a mole hill. The Northern European could see that it was—well, he'd have some sense of the feeling which the American, the Southerner, might have toward the situation. That is, the Latin American thought it was just funny, in this sense, that You talk about liberty and yet you make a barrier, an impasse, out of a few, a handful of black people. The Northern European would say, Thank the Lord, it's your problem and not ours. Then there are so many other crises, problems, which are more important. I remember a gentleman, an Italian, said to me, he said—the Public Affairs Officer in Rome was a very brilliant Negro, a Harvard man, he was a linguist, spoke seven or eight European languages, he was a Ph.D. And this Italian said, You Americans know the Italian attitude toward women yet you send us a woman for an Ambassador. We know your attitude toward Negroes yet you send us a Negro for your Public Affairs Officer. Which is not too important—it's simply an indication of the sensitivity to conditions which the European has which the American doesn't have because the American is too fired always by the emotional situation.

. . .

Q. Mr. Faulkner, what are the most important sources of people's opinion about us there—the movies or books? Where do they get their information?

A. They get it from the moving pictures. In American moving pictures nobody ever works. The moving-picture idea which the European gets that people spend all their time in dress suits chasing one another over roofs with pistols. From the books—but mostly it's from the badly edited and the badly directed propaganda which is sent out from the agencies established for the purpose of showing a true picture of America. That apparently the American is incapable of showing a true picture of himself, because he himself don't know what he is. That he wants mostly to be liked and he is ashamed of things in his culture which he should not be ashamed of, but he thinks that other people might not like it so he tries to hide it, and the whole picture of America that goes abroad from our moving pictures, the books which are selected and sent abroad, are false pictures. They are not America at all. Which is the reason

157

I think the only scheme that would work is to bring the foreigner here and let him see what we can't tell him. Let him see what there is about this country to make us like it.

Q. Mr. Faulkner, do they ask you about the American public . . .?

A. Yes, they have an idea that Americans don't read good books, that Americans themselves, all they see are the sort of moving pictures being sent to Europe and the American reads only the sort of books, American books, which are sent to Europe. That I would have to explain that that is not so, that Americans read books and . . . that there apparently are enough Americans to be given the Nobel Prize every few years to indicate that there are a few Americans that know a little more about books than the sort of books that are sent to Europe. That nobody has taken the trouble to explain to them before because of that desire of our country to be thought well of, to be admired, and the only way we know to show people that we are to be admired is to show people how successful we are. That we don't realize that to the European, the people of an old tradition, success is not too important.

Q. Sir, do you find that the European is much . . .?

A. Yes, they have much more respect for the American writer and the American literature than we have. That they know much more about the background of American literature, the trends, the tendencies, the influences of the old country writers, than a lot of Americans know, because in Europe the cultured man has a definite position in the culture, in the economy. That sooner or later the member of the French Academy will have a place in politics or some foreign policy, which don't happen in this country. That's what the European can't understand, how anyone can be well-known in Europe as a writer and have no place in the American culture. That's almost impossible to explain to the European, and the fact that it is difficult to explain that he has none hurts the European's concept of this country, gives him a false idea of this country because he is using for his standard the rigid pattern of an old, old culture. That it is difficult for him to understand that this country is as new as it is. That it can have gone as far as it has gone and still be as new and as raw as it is.

Q. Mr. Faulkner, were you able to talk to other writers in other countries and have satisfactory conversations with them . . .?

A. Not too often. Writers—I doubt if one writer ever has a satisfactory conversation with another writer. I mean by that that the writer unless he is written out is too busy trying to say what his demon drives him to say before he dies to have time to talk shop with another writer, and so they will talk about conditions, man's condition, and it don't matter whether two writers talk about man's condition or two artisans or two lawyers or two doctors. That actually no writer has very much in common with another writer. Well, it—that he only is driven by the same demon. The writers I have known, the foreign writers, have not been as literary people because the American, to me, anyway, I find so much more ignorant than the European. I mean by that, less disciplined up here, with less knowledge of a long tradition of culture, which we don't have. Anyone with a knowledge of a long tradition of culture in this country has got to have crossed the ocean from one hundred and fifty to two hundred years ago. The Frenchman, the Italian, he has had that tradition that has gone back eighteen or nineteen hundred years. That he is more secure in the background of his culture than the American, because his culture has been in the land that produced him, the land that will feed him, that his children will spring from. The ones I've known, the ones I like, are not on any literary basis at all, because we have a certain—find a certain interest in man to talk about.

  . . .

Q. You believe—I think, from reading—that a demon must be your basis for being a writer. Can that demon be acquired or is it inborn?

A. I would say that that demon is inherent. You are born with it. It may be that you have to cultivate it, baby it and feed it and water it and nurture it a little, but I don't believe that you could acquire the demon in the sense that the actually

159

illiterate man like myself has been able to write. That one with a sensitivity toward literature, who has a true desire to add to the fine store of literature, can train himself to be a competent writer, and he may in the process acquire the demon, but if he don't acquire the demon he can still be a first-rate writer in that he will tell only the truth, that he will tell it in the most effective way he can. It's more—it's easier, it's—you're luckier if you have that demon from the first, then you don't have to bother about style or anything else. You're too busy writing.

Q. Well, don't you think then, in your opinion at any rate, the value of the writer depends a great deal on this quality?

A. I don't believe so. The value of one specific writer, one individual writer, might very possibly, but there are so many more things to write about other than the creation of fiction. That is, it's necessary to express ideas, it's necessary to some mentality which is capable of it to take the idea, to sift it, to reduce it to its absolute truth and show the rational process by which it arrived at that part of absolute truth, and to put that down, and if he is driven by a demon, very likely he is going to be too slovenly and too careless to do that properly, to do that well. So I think in some cases the writer needs only that demon and in other cases he needs the erudition, he needs the discipline of training, he needs the education. That's assuming that all writing is not to the same end, to the same purpose. That some is to show the several—the momentary anguish or passion or beauty or grief or comedy of man's condition, other [writing] is to show the background, the pattern by which man's condition reached that moment of passion or beauty or truth or comedy. That it takes one thing to make an Einstein today and it takes something other to make a Balzac. I think that Flaubert may have had a demon but that was an extremely French demon he had . . . but that Flaubert was that demon's master. It would take the Northerner with a capacity for delusion or mysticism, to believe in dreams, to be simply ridden by a demon. There's no check on it.

. . .

Q. Mr. Faulkner, could you comment on the level of the post-war European writers? Were there any—have been successful possibly without finding God?

160

A. I don't think so. I think that no writing will be too successful without some conception of God, you can call Him by whatever name you want. I think of Jean-Paul Sartre, which was good writing in the sense of good writing but there was something lacking. That to me is the difference between Camus and Sartre, the difference between Sartre and Proust, the difference between Sartre and Stendhal. That Sartre has denied God. Hemingway for years, he didn't deny God but he assumed, he functioned, on the premise that it was not necessary, that God might be all right but let God let me alone. His people functioned in a vacuum until his last book. In his last book there was—God made the great fish, God made the old man that had to catch the fish, God made the shark that had to eat the fish, and God loved all of them, and I think that Hemingway's work will get better, I think that Camus will get better, but I think that Sartre will never be better.

Q. Mr. Faulkner, do you believe there is a place in politics for the writer?

A. Yes, but he will never get elected to it. I think there is a place in politics, in our economy, for the qualities that Stevenson had, but how much longer we will have to go before we finally admit that America is a great country but we just can't afford to run it like we do and people like Stevenson can be elected, nobody can say. But there is a place, and I think that in time we will come to the point where we will have to take someone who has dedicated his life to—well, maybe not dealing with but accepting the fact that the human spirit itself is a verity that can't be avoided. But how much longer that will be—maybe that won't come until we have exhausted our last natural resources. We've got down now to where about the only one remaining is a lot of people. We have used up the gold and the copper and most of the timber and the beaver are gone. Now people will take the place of the beaver and I look to the day when the Fifth Avenue mansions and vast fortunes will be founded on people just as the Astors and Vanderbilts founded theirs on beaver, and so the next Astors and Vanderbilts will be people like Mr. Meany and Dave Beck and Reuther.

161

Q. Mr. Faulkner, it seems that the Europeans have criticized us so much about the things you have said. Did you find anything that they really admired us for, any one thing that they felt we were particularly strong in that they were not, or did you hear anything flattering or . . . any real strong points?

A. Yes. There is everywhere in Europe a very—a minority, I suppose—maybe they don't speak too loud, maybe they dare not, maybe they're not enough of them—but there are people in all the countries of Europe that I visited that can see what this country wants to do even in its clumsy way—that it really does want to preserve a culture or condition which man can be individually free, that we go about in clumsy ways, but that we really are after that. That we want to— we are too prone to hope, to let our beliefs—to establish beliefs on what we hope will be so. But that basically we do want to preserve what freedom there is in the world and to increase it. They are not too hopeful, I don't know whether it is because they don't dare be, that it's unpopular to be, but even the ones that are the loudest critics of America take a certain security in the fact that they can criticize America and still depend on America. That possibly the critics realize that they have that chance to criticize only because America is—does represent something steadfast that does believe that man must be free and is willing to share what it has that man shall be free. That out of our sentimentality and our very clumsiness there is something very strong and very valuable.

Q. Mr. Faulkner, when they pin you down about the racial problem in the South, what do you tell them? Do you tell them that possibly we will be able to work them out, solve them here in the South without violence, or—?

A. Yes. I tell them what I believe, which is that it's an outrageous, an anomalous condition that simply cannot continue. That no nation can endure with seventeen million second-class citizen in it nowadays. It might have done that a hundred years ago or fifty years ago but nowadays it can't, and that the problem will be solved because it has to be solved. That the violence is a matter of blowing off steam by a vociferous and noisy minority. That right now there are people

162

that are willing to accept compromise and to give the Negro equality in economics and education, but they themselves are intimidated by the loud and noisy minority who have nothing to lose, who are making a Roman holiday of burning crosses and things like that. That that will have to exhaust itself. I don't know enough of history but I imagine that if one could go back through history one could find similar cases, since man's behavior . . . has a way of repeating itself, his problems never are problems that he never faced before. It's mainly to explain to the European that all Americans don't feel like the ones that make the most noise. Just like you would explain to Europeans that all Americans don't feel like Senator McCarthy used to sound. That all Americans don't feel like Huey Long used to sound. But they ask us then, Why don't you Americans do something about it, and you try to explain to them that that is one of the valid qualities of democracy, that one can be a fool in public if he wants to. That one can be outrageous, but on everything he does shines the hard fierce light of publicity and nobody can do a great deal of harm as long as that fierce light of publicity shines on everything he does, and that I think as much as anything else destroyed people like McCarthy, people like Huey Long. It wasn't that their ideas were bad that destroyed them, it was the fact that that hard fierce light of publicity which everybody hates shone on everything he did, everything he said. Which is a sad condition, too, that in order to endure we must accept the fact that individual privacy can no longer exist. Sometimes we think that's such a high price to pay for it, but again you've got to admit that it's not, that no price is too high to pay for it, security, freedom.

Q. Reverting to the subject of writers in political affairs, why is it that in Europe, in the French papers, for instance, one frequently sees articles by Maurois or Mauriac, or in England you see letters from the writer, but in this country we almost never see anything in the newspapers from the well-known American writers?

A. That comes back to what we just spoke of, that in our culture the artist actually has no place. That nobody expects

163

him to write a letter to the newspaper nor articles on sociology or economics. In Europe it is taken as a matter of course that anyone who is first in his own craft or his media in the arts will also be socially conscious enough to have a voice in the economy and the culture and also anyone who is wise enough to be first in his own art will also be wise in the condition of the state. In this country we haven't quite come to that yet because so far we don't need it. We have our own culture of success, a quick turnover of boom times, and so we haven't found yet that we need the artist, the philosopher. That's another curse of democracy. That the first impulse of democracy is to evict from any public office everyone with a clean shirt and a clean collar. That democracy is the refuge for your cousin or your uncle that failed in the peanut business. But we will outgrow that some day. I think that we are going pretty fast to outgrow that right now. To find that that no longer works. That that worked in the days when we could be isolate and secure by the simple breadth of water, but that don't work any more and I think that we are going to learn that. That the people that we choose to run our State Department have got to be trained for it. The people that are to be our ambassadors have got to be trained for it.

Q. Did you find the Europeans with their cultural background satisfied with their life, their way things were, or was there an envy or desire for the so-called American life, the American way?

A. No. The European with the background you speak of is not at all satisfied with the human condition. That's why in France the good writer is also noisy in politics. He hasn't time to bother nor to envy any other country. He is dissatisfied with the whole human condition, which must be changed, must be altered. Then he will think about whether he envies America or envies any other place. That the writer does think of the world in terms of one world. The American still thinks of the world in terms of hemisphere.

Q. Mr. Faulkner, I'm getting sort of tired of hearing about how the Europeans disapprove of the Americans that go over and spend their money and talk too loud and try to be friendly and buy all the things they have to sell and everything and help their economy. Don't they care if we're trying to be friends?

A. Well, not always. I'm sure that all Americans agree with you, but the problem is to show the European we've had a pretty rough time of it for the last half-century. He's been in two wars, he has seen between 1914 and '18 and between 1939 and '45 two wars, which is from his point of view [that] this country tried first to buy its way through it. He [the American] fought only when he found that he couldn't do anything else. That Europe saw that the only country that was steadfast was England. That we came in only when we saw we couldn't buy our way out any other way, and—I grant you that their point of view is bad, it's unjust, it's unfair, but you have got to consider what they have gone through with and wonder what you yourself would think if twice in the last fifty years this country had been overrun by the same enemy, and we held off for three or four years before anybody came to help us.

Q. Mr. Faulkner, do you think that they feel that with our foreign aid that we are still trying to buy them or do you think that they feel that we are actually trying to help them?

A. No, no. The French feel that we are actually trying to help them. The loud noisy ones are the same—they are the opposite number of the same loud noisy people who say that the white race has to be supreme in America by law. It's a minority, but they make the most noise because it's popular.

Q. All I wanted to ask was, don't you think that with America being in the driver's seat in world politics today as opposed to Russia that the natural feeling for the European or anybody else who is not in the driver's seat is to take pot-shots—

A. Exactly.

Q. —at the driver? So no matter what we do, we're going to still be the target of a lot of hostility.

A. That's quite true. For so many years the driver was the—a European country. Then suddenly we who in a way don't think as they do, don't have the same background and by

165

their light don't even have the same problems, are suddenly the ones who say, This is what we will do next. Yes, that's quite right. There should—that's just natural, normal human nature that there should be some jealousy, a little bitterness. But I'm convinced that that—the expression of that bitterness comes from the same ignorant mass which will burn the crosses and will make the outrageous and fantastic impossible statements about segregation. That they are the noisy minority that somehow justify their own condition by taking a—trying to take an emotional condition and make a rational stand out of it.

. . .

Q. Is there any general fear or distrust of our policies and strength—say especially, military—such as we hold of Russia? I mean do they have the feeling that we may come in at any time with our strength . . .?

A. Yes. Europeans are not as afraid of a Russian war as they think we are. That they don't believe that Russia is going to start a war. Their belief is that the economy of Russia, of the Soviet State, requires an expenditure of the things that the machine produces. That is, they can't let the people have too much of the goods which the machine produces because the people will become too smart and might revolt. So this has got to be exhausted by manufacturing things which themselves will become obsolete—tanks and guns and aircraft. And the European thinks that America is so afraid that Russia may start a war that the Americans might get frightened themselves and start one.

. . .

Q. Sir, earlier you spoke of your meetings, encountering the Communists at large meetings. Did you have an opportunity to speak to a Communist sort of man to man, human spirit to human spirit, perhaps an intelligent Communist, and could you give us a—if you did—perhaps a feeling for him as you have for the American abroad?

A. My experience is that it is impossible to speak to a Communist man to man. He is a Communist first and you don't know whether to believe him or not and the safe thing is to—not to spend too much time believing him. To let him say what he says and then watch what he does and see whether what he

166

says is so or not. I doubt if there is any way that one can touch him with human spirit to human spirit. I know I can't.

. . .

Q. Do you think that the Fulbright program, Exchange Program, has had an effect in bettering the European impression of America?

A. Yes, it has. Even if—I think that we are not always wise in the export of America to foreign countries but if one time we are right then that does a great deal of good because there are people in Europe that do want to see this country as it is, that believe that even when this country looks bad that basically there's something sound and good in what we want to do. And so every time that one good—one Fulbright scholarship out of a hundred does some good it's worth the other ninety-nine that failed. I still think, my own notion is that we should stop trying to export America but bring foreigners here to see our country as it is, and I would like to see the foundations instead of sending American missionaries abroad to bring the European here, let him alone, let him see this country. But any effort like that we make—U.S.I.S., or Fulbright Scholarship, anything—because of out of every hundred there will be at least one that will give a true picture or will disabuse the foreigner of some preconception about this country he has got through some unfortunate means, and that much will be accomplished.

. . .

Q. Well, I don't mean this to be a carefully rehearsed literary question, but I did notice in the paper where you mentioned that the Old Testament was among your old literary friends, or one of the ones that you like to browse in and re-read, and I realize it is a classic, but I was wondering why the New Testament didn't have as much to offer. Is it because it is so narrative or—some of it is—?

A. To me the New Testament is full of ideas and I don't know much about ideas. The Old Testament is full of people, perfectly ordinary normal heroes and blackguards just like everybody else nowadays, and I like to read the Old Testament because it's full of people, not ideas. It's people all trying to get something for nothing or . . . to be braver than they are

167

—just ordinary everyday folks, people, that's why I like to read that. That's apart from the fine poetry of the prose.

. . .

Q. Mr. Faulkner, although you primarily write about the South and Southern people, are you striving for universality? . . .

A. That's it, it's to use a locale which the writer is most familiar with, it saves him doing research. That is, if he don't know anything about California or Canada or Australia, if he don't do a little research first, he'll write something and somebody will say, Hold up here, that ain't so, this is the way it is in Australia. Where if he writes about what he knows nobody is going to bother him that way because he knows what he is putting down. People are the same, but the differences in their background, the milieu they function in, which is different, not their behavior. But of course the milieu, the background, the environment will change the terms of their behavior not the act itself, and so the writer simply uses the background he knows just as the carpenter uses the tools that he has at his hand. Rather than to go somewhere to borrow a hammer or a saw, he will use the one he's got, so he won't have to fetch one.

Q. Mr. Faulkner, I believe Somerset Maugham said at one time that he felt it was rather a sad thing in his own life and assumed it to be in the life of any writer in that he felt that he had to divorce himself from life itself to a certain extent in that he was continually observing and thinking in terms of writing down what he saw. And I think that possibly he felt a little deprived in that he had this demon that caused him to want to do this and that he could not live to himself more as ordinary people do and—well, in that he was more concerned with recording life as he saw it and living was more like a vicarious thing. Do you feel that that is true of most writers or do you—

A. Well, it's not true of me and I imagine it's not true of many other writers. It would be true of many other writers. I think that Maugham of an older culture had more time to be that objective about his own subjectivity, if you can accept that paradoxical statement. I think that maybe Henry James, for instance, had the same approach toward his work that Maugham

168

did but Henry James had not got far enough to realize that that was depriving him of something that he didn't want to be deprived of, that is, Henry James probably was quite happy to live detached from life, to write Henry James.

Q. I hesitate to ask such a broad question, sir, but what effect do you think McCarthyism has had on freedom of thought and expression in American universities?

A. I would say that McCarthyism, that whole thing, has had a good effect on American universities in that it has shown not the educated man but has shown a lot of uneducated people what that sort of thing can cause. That uneducated people have a greater belief in the—that thought—that the freedom of thought must be inviolable, that never thought about it before and so in that sense McCarthy served a purpose. It's too bad that that should be one of the curses of democracy too, that that purpose can, must be paid for with the three or four years of McCarthy. In a way democracy has the capacity to use somehow almost everything.

. . .

Q. Do you think that the artist in this country would benefit from some form of government subsidization? . . .

A. I don't think that an artist should be subsidized too much by anyone. I think that he has got to be free, and even a little hardship may be good for him. That—I'm assuming that most artists are like me and they are lazy and if they had too much money there would be that much less work. That if they ain't got much money—just enough to buy a little tobacco and occasionally a drink and something to eat that they might work a little more. If it was too easy for them they would put off the work. That—now that's different from the opera because opera, theater, requires so much more money than the cost of a ream of paper and three or four pencils, so theater has got to be subsidized and if private capital is ever obliterated then there will have to be subsidy to print the books, but the artist himself shouldn't be subsidized too much. He would be a little better off if he had to hold another job and wrote in his spare time because that would keep his work on the plane of the amateur, which it should be. That when he begins to think of

169

himself as a professional writer he is sunk. He's got to do it because it's fun. It's got to be hard.

Q. Sir, . . . you say that a writer must write truth and therefore he must search for truth. If Arthur Miller is found guilty of contempt on the grounds that as he claims it was his own moral character which kept him from revealing the names of other writers in the cell . . . , would you publicly come out favor of his position?

A. Sure. Yes, if there is something you believe is wrong to do then don't do it, no matter who else disagrees with you. That would have nothing to do with whether he writes from now on, whether he is in contempt of court or not. Whether he is sent to jail or not would have nothing to do with what he writes. Yes, if you believe that something is wrong to do, don't do it.

Session Twenty

May 20, 1957

Q. Was there something that influenced you to write this story [*Old Man*]?

A. Yes. The story I was trying to tell was the story of Charlotte and Harry Wilbourne [*The Wild Palms*]. I decided that it needed a contrapuntal quality like music. And so I wrote the other story simply to underline the story of Charlotte and Harry. I wrote the two stories by alternate chapters. I'd write the chapter of one and then I would write the chapter of the other just as the musician puts in—puts counterpoint behind the theme that he is working with.

Q. Well, why don't, in this story, none of the characters have names?

A. To me the story was simply for background effect and they didn't need names, they just needed to be people in motion doing the exact opposite thing to the tragedy of Harry and Charlotte in the other story. To me they didn't need names, that they were not too important.

Q. Well, I noticed that you do have some names, though, in your story. Some names are mentioned, such as Bledsoe the convict. Do you have them in for any reason?

A. Well, the girl that jilted him, she had to have a name to sign to the postcard. The other people—if—I don't remember the rest of the story because I haven't read it in about thirty years, but when they had names it was for that reason, as simple as that—that at the moment they had to have a name.

Q. Well, in the swamp, three of the men that lived in the swamp did have names—Tine and Toto and Theule, and I wonder if those names had any type of significance or were supposed to be any type of literary allusion. They're rather colorful names, I think.

A. No, I don't think so. They were names, you might say, indigenous to that almost unhuman class of people which live between the Mississippi River and the levee. They belong to no state, they belong to no nation. They—they're not citizens of anything, and sometimes they behave like they don't even belong to the human race.

Q. You have had experience with these people?

A. Yes. Yes, I remember once one of them was going to take me hunting. He invited me to come and stay with his kinfolks—whatever kin they were I never did know—a shanty boat in the river, and I remember the next morning for breakfast we had a bought chocolate cake and a cold possum and corn whiskey. They had given me the best they had. I was company. They had given me the best food they had.

Q. If I may ask a question. . . . I believe that early in your life that you did quite a bit of traveling, had a lot of experience as an apprentice seaman, I believe, and flying. Do you think that to any author or to be a little more general, to anyone who wants to formulate ideas about life and all, do you think that this is very valuable while younger to travel around and not be fixed down?

A. Well, it don't do you any harm but it's—you don't have to do it. Homer probably didn't do a great deal of traveling and he did pretty well as a writer. That is, the material you write from has got to be a good deal more than just what you can see and remember. It's got to be observation, experience which—and part of experience is what you read—plus imagination. So the observation don't hurt you—you may need it, but you can get along without it if you have to if [you have] the imagination and experience. I think the best source to learn to be a writer is to read—what the best, the giants of the past have done.

172

Q. Mr. Faulkner, did the tall convict in the *Old Man* believe in God?

A. He probably hadn't got around to that yet. His background would be the bucolic, provincial, Southern Baptist and it may be a debatable question whether that sort of Baptist believes in God or not. Probably when he got older and got out of the penitentiary, if he ever did, and he didn't need to spend too much energy trying to have fun any more, he might have taken up religion, might have been a professor of God whether he believed or not or even knew what God was. But at this time he would have said he did, and if anyone had told him he didn't he would have fought him, but he probably didn't know what God meant.

Q. It seems to me in reading the book that he was depending a lot on fate to lead his life. That he would be led by fate.

A. Well, he depended more on himself. That to him fate was just his bad luck, the sort of thing that shouldn't happen to a dog. But he depended on himself, that he knew what he wanted, which was to be secure, to be back in that penitentiary, that's where he was secure because he didn't mind hard work, he didn't know anything else. And suddenly he was flung out into the world with another woman and all he wanted was to get rid of that woman and get back there where he was safe. But he didn't depend—he was doing the best he could, he depended on his own efforts.

Q. Well, when he got back, sir, did he share this view with the others that it was ten years without women—I mean, do you think he minded this?

A. No, no, he had had enough of women. After that girl had jilted him, she was the one that put him there, it was to get a lot of money to buy her a lot more of the Woolworth bracelets and rings. If it hadn't been for her he wouldn't have been there, he would have been back at his Mississippi hill home working hard all day long and drinking a little corn whiskey on Saturday nights and gambling.

Q. Sir, I'm interested in your saying that. I had taken it

173

that he is more betraying more for the events than . . . the baby . . . rather than money.

A. No, he wanted to please that girl. He didn't need a lot of money. He was doing all right with his mule, his little piece of corn land, but suddenly he ran into a girl that wanted a lot of Woolworth rings and so he had to turn robber to get those rings.

Q. . . . The plump convict wound up in the penitentiary because he didn't want to face the raging woman with whom he had committed this crime. Do you mean this also to mean his desire not to face life and yet, as you say, to face reality, the return to the womb? You spoke of persons being chained by a "clanking umbilical." We talked about this in our class, this jacknife position and the whole idea of escaping from life— does the woman here, especially the pregnant woman, represent life in this sense?

A. Not to the convict—that is, not consciously. He—all he wanted to escape from was insecurity. He—anyone that could be taken over the jumps by the sort of girl that was—that got him into undertaking to be a bank robber couldn't have been very mature mentally. That convict was probably still about fifteen or sixteen years old. And like a boy of fifteen or sixteen, the first shock of disappointment in love, he thinks it's going to last forever. Of course it don't, but that's what he thinks, and the convict never had grown up yet.
. . .

Q. Do you think that if the convict had not been given the extra ten years, do you think he would have returned to the security of prison or to the security of his home?

A. Well, that extra ten years meant nothing to him because he was mentally about sixteen or seventeen years old and anything—any sum of time longer than one year is all the same when you're fifteen or sixteen years old. In another year you'll be an old man anyway, so what's ten years or a hundred years to you?

Q. Getting back to this security or insecurity, do you think that enough background was given of the tall convict before he was in the penitentiary, before he was sentenced? It seemed

174

—he didn't feel insecure when you think that the person became insecure when he was in the penitentiary for so long a time at being out of it . . . .

A. No, I would say that the insecurity came to him with a shock when that woman betrayed him, and he was frightened and he wanted to be where no other woman could catch him off balance and take him over the jumps again. And the place where he was safe from that was in that penitentiary, which wasn't so different from the life he would have led if he'd been home. He would have had to work very hard all day at home, he would have had very little for it, which was just what he got there, but at least behind that barbed wire fence he was safe from another woman that would get him into the highwayman business.

Q. Do you think he would have stayed on the island with the Cajuns—hadn't they had to leave?

A. No, no, he had to get rid of that woman, and the only way he knew to get rid of her was to bring her back to the folks that sent him to get her. Remember he's mentally only about fifteen or sixteen years old, and by his own lights he's quite honorable and dependable. They had sent him out with a boat to get two people and he did the best he could to get the two people and bring them and the boat back.

Q. Well, why—I know that you said that the woman was almost exactly like, I mean the same type of background and everything, and also the woman must have realized that he was trying to get her back, but don't you—with the woman also in this immature state that she didn't realize that she could get back more quickly when they were in this armory, which is where they had all these other people, she was glad to leave with him, and when she was just about ready to have a child, she made, as I recall, no cry to the people in this houseboat to let her come aboard. She was content almost, it seems like, to stick with him. What is this, I mean, why didn't she try to better herself?

A. She didn't know how, she was as ignorant as he was. She came from the same class of people that he came from, she was ignorant. She was afraid of strangers. Of course the convict was a stranger to her too, but they had been hurled together by a circumstance and it probably didn't take her very long to find out that all that convict wanted was to get her back where he got her from and get rid of her, and that's what she wanted too—to get back and find her husband, she probably had a husband, she may have had other children and she wanted to get back just as bad as he did, and since he was the man, her instinct was to let the man run things.

Q. . . . The miscarriage of justice by having the additional ten years . . . ?

A. That additional ten years was simply another quantity in fate just like the flood that he ran into. Once he was in it he had to accept the extra ten years just as he accepted the flood and worked through it and survived it. There was no more injustice than there was to the flood. It was just something that was in the culture, the economy of the land he lived in, just like that flood was inherent in the geography and the climate, and he was a man that said, Well, if this is what it is I'll do the best I can to cut through it. That would have been his philosophy.

Q. Sir, when you set out to start a novel such as this do you have a complete story in mind or is it just a thought that you build upon as you go along?

A. You remember this was counterpoint to the other story. This to me wasn't too important, that these were just the orchestration of sounds that the musician puts back of the theme of his symphony. That I didn't know where this story was going, I just wrote it. I was as surprised as anybody else to find where it was going. The story that I was trying to tell was the story of Charlotte and Harry.

Q. When you reached the point where he met the woman, what was your purpose in having a pregnant woman?

A. I thought that made it funnier. To me all this is funny. A little more comical to show this man who meant well to get involved in all sorts of things that would have made a weaker or a less centered man blench and falter, but not him. It was because he was just stupid and ignorant enough to bull right

176

on through this. To accept anything the gods threw at him without even knowing that he was being tried.

Q. . . . Why do you put the humor in where you do, for example, the woman—I don't recall the remark—but she's just about ready to have a child, and you say something about, Hold on a little longer. It's an impossible thing. And then he's been kicked, hit by the tail of the alligator and she asks him if he's been kicked, and he says, No, that he'd got hit in the rear end with a pea shooter. . . . There's humor all the way through, and then even in the end, do you still want the message of the seeming injustice of society against him to come through or is that secondary?

A. Well, it's—"secondary" is not really wrong because it was the injustice was necessary to make the story funny and so it's not secondary because it was quite important, to make the story funny. It's a fact, and if one begins to write about the injustice of society, then one has stopped being primarily a novelist and has become a polemicist or a propagandist. The fiction writer is not that, he will use the injustice of society, the inhumanity of people, as a—as any other tool in telling a story, which is about people, not about the injustice or inhumanity of people but of people, with their aspirations and their struggles and the bizarre, the comic, and the tragic conditions they get themselves into simply coping with themselves and one another and environment.

Q. Mr. Faulkner, I think you must have put a great deal of time behind choosing the title *The Old Man.* I know you took it from the river, but I wonder what else you had in mind. Possibly does the river symbolize any other things or maybe nature or something else?

A. No, it's not *The Old Man,* it's *Old Man.* That's what the Negroes along the river call the river, they never call it the Mississippi nor the river, it's just Old Man, and this had to have some title and so that struck me as being a good title for it. That refers simply to the river.

. . .

Q. In the book, you had elaborated on to some extent on the fact that the Old Man was fruitful and life-giving . . .

177

and what it was to the people who lived along the Mississippi through that area. It was fruitful and not a destructive force.

A. Well, the destructive quantity had to be accepted too. That country where this took place was—is alluvial, it's lower than the river itself. In the winter it stayed under water from the fall rains sometimes as late as June. That was why they had to build the levee, and so in the spring and the summer the river is higher than the land. There's a levee and then you look up in the sky and there goes a steamboat. If the levee ever gives way, the country will be flooded again. It's rich because the river for hundreds of years had deposited the rich silt on top of the ground, and so the river dominates not only the economy of that country but it dominates its spiritual life. That the river is Master, and any time the Old Man wants to he can break the levee and can ruin the cotton crop. That in a way you're—the planter is at armistice with him, and the superstitious planter believes that he has got to make libations, make sacrifices to him, that every so often he's got to let the Old Man come in and take that cotton crop to keep the Old Man in a contented frame of mind like the ancients with the dragon, the Minotaur, the symbols of destructiveness which they had to placate, sacrifice.

Q. In putting this woman in the boat with the convict, did you want to draw a point to the lovers in the novel that went along with it or did you just put her in the boat as sort of a hindrance to progress and—?

A. No, that was a definite parallel. The isolation, the solitude of the boat in that raging torrent was the solitude which Harry and Charlotte had tried so long to find, where they could be lovers—to escape from the world. They went to infinite labor and risk and sacrifice to escape from the world where this convict had been hurled out of the world against his will whether he wanted to or not. That he and the woman he saved had what Charlotte and Wilbourne had sacrificed everything to get. That's what I mean by counterpoint to the theme of the other book. That these two people had what Charlotte and Harry had given up everything—respectability, future, everything, for.

178

Q. Was the short fat convict placed in the book . . . just to emphasize the qualities of the tall convict?

A. That's right. Had to have somebody for the tall convict to—or to dig out of the tall convict what had happened. The tall convict would never have told this himself. He'd just said he was away for a while and had a pretty hard time but here he is. That's all he could have told about what happened to him.

Q. You said that the convict wasn't afraid of work so he returned, yet when he was in the swamp with Cajuns you say that he had forgotten what work was like or something like that. Do you make a distinction between work for the reward and then work simply for the sake of something to do?

A. He had been so busy trying to keep that boat from being swamped and to get them along from one day to another, which was terrific work, but to him that wasn't work, anymore than somebody falling off a roof that scrabbles at shingles and chimney pots would consider himself working. Work to him was the orderly work from sunup to sundown and then you rested and then tomorrow you worked again.

Q. But he did consider the work at the prison just as much as—?

A. Yes, but he had been gone from there a long time, to him. That must have seemed like years to him that he had been in that boat with that woman who was a nuisance.

Q. You sort of draw a line somewhere in there between the work at the prison and work with the alligators because he seemed to work hard just trapping the alligators because he was going to get part of the profits from the alligators.

A. That's right.

Q. Was there—did that make a difference in the work he was doing and the way he went about it . . .?

A. Well, work to him meant the orderly work of following a mule in a furrow. Catching alligators to him wasn't work in —by his lights anymore than struggling with that boat was work. That he simply—he didn't want the alligator, he simply

179

had to have some money and that was the only way he knew to get money. When he was in the prison, or even at home, he probably worked for his father, he got a new pair of overalls whenever the other ones wore out, he got something to eat every night or a pallet to sleep on, but the work was ordered, began at sunup and went on to sundown. This was different—there was something frantic and desperate about this, just like there was something frantic and desperate about having to keep that boat from capsizing, because all he knew was that if he turned up without that woman in that boat he'd be in trouble sure enough. I don't know what more trouble he could have got into than he did, but that was his business that he had to get that woman in that boat back or he would be in bad trouble.

. . .

Q. Mr. Faulkner, when the convict was working in the logging camp on his way back to the river he kept—you said he got in trouble with another man's wife. Was that to go along with the tone of *The Wild Palms* or was that just to show another of his conflicts with women . . .?

A. It was to underline the fact that he had for free what Charlotte and Harry had given everything for. That he had the woman and the solitude but she wasn't enough—he had to go and get into trouble over somebody else's wife.

Q. What did the tremendous wave signify? What caused it?

A. That simply is a physical fact in that country when a levee breaks. The water rushed through the crevasse and it came to the lowest place, which was a stream which up to that time had been flowing toward the river. This wave of water—at that time the river, the Mississippi, was forty feet higher than the country and when that levee gave way that mass of water that came through had to go somewhere and it broke on the east side of the river so that wave of water simply continued to go east until it spent itself and in this stream, which up until that time had been flowing placidly west, it turned around and went backward. That's just a physical fact of hydraulics and levee.

180

Q. Mr. Faulkner, it seems you draw a picture of yourself . . . . Do you do that in your writing itself when you are writing a book? . . .

A. Oh well, any writer that puts down what he sees and what he hears and that image and that sound come from the proper blending of observation, experience, and imagination. Yes, you've got to see what you—the scenes you describe. You've got to hear the voice speaking the speech that you put down. You have to hear the vernacular he speaks in, rather than to think of the speech and then translate it into the vernacular.

Q. Sir, . . . I noticed we are missing this Mississippi accent which is so prevalent in your people. You made no attempt to simulate that in the dialect. Is there any reason for that?

A. If the writer puts too much attention to transcribing literally the dialogue he hears, it's confusing to the people who have never heard that speech. That is, some of the words are difficult to spell. They would be—to a Mississippian, he would see the words spelled the way a Mississippian would spell it, he would know how it sounded, but to an outlander he wouldn't know, he would mispronounce that word wrong. You can go only so far with dialect and then there's a point where for the simple reason not to make too much demand on the [reader] to distract his attention from the story you're telling you've got to draw the line.

. . .

Q. When did you come into the close contact with the flood on the Mississippi that the text would indicate? I mean, when did you observe all these things, the way the flood happened and so forth? . . .

A. Why, I can't say. I've known it all my life. That is, this country is not very far from where I was born and have lived all my life, and I have known these people. I have known that country—every fall as long as I can remember we would go there to hunt bear and deer, which was close to the levee and so we would know these people [Cajuns]. They would cross the levee and come into our camp. They were lawless people. They would be beggars and on occasions they would be thieves, but if we were ever benighted—lost at night—we could go to their shanty boats or shacks and they would give us what they had to eat and let us sleep there at night.

Q. On several occasions the tall convict is plagued by this nose bleed that can't be controlled. This is usually following some period where he's had a great struggle and shown his bravery and strength, such as with the alligator. Is this help-lessness in the face of this nose bleed supposed to be a humorous contrast with his strength and his usual self-sufficiency? . . .

A. Well, to me that was just something else comical and bizarre that he should be afflicted with that also. With all his other troubles he had that—what's the name of it, the ailment when your blood won't clot?

Q. Hemophilia.

A. Yes, that on top of everything else he had to have that too.

Q. This is just one sentence that I wondered about. In the beginning of this final chapter you told—you sort of describe the Governor's emissary and you say that he just sat down on the desk—you say "almost between the warden and the caller, the emissary." This is the sentence: "Or the vizier with the command, the knotted cord, as began to appear immediately." Exactly what does that mean?

A. Oh, that's Eastern, from the Middle East, when the sultan decided he was tired of a courtier he would send his Prime Minister with a knotted cord to suggest that he choke himself to death. That's all.

. . .

Q. Sir, this is . . . toward another tangent. We were having a discussion in our class as to whether Ernest Hemingway's novel *For Whom the Bell Tolls* was didactic or not. Would you give your opinion of that?

A. I would say simply that Hemingway was writing—well, in a sense the same story—every writer in a way is writing one story. That he—there's one thing in man's condition that seems to him the most moving, the most tragic, and this time Hemingway was writing the story which still seemed to him

182

moving and tragic, which like all writers he never had told well enough to please him. This one was brought into urgency by the condition of Spain at that time. That he was not really writing primarily about the Spanish Civil War, but he was writing about the human condition which to him was moving and tragic in the terms of that war.

. . .

Q. Does the convict in *Old Man* gain any strength from the fact that he does have the mind of a sixteen- or seventeen-year-old . . . ?

A. No. I wouldn't say he gained his strength from that, I would say that he gained his strength because he had a very simple moral standard. That he made one aberration from it because he was tempted by Delilah, but he would never make that aberration again, and he—the reason for the security was, he would never be tempted, he would believe that he wouldn't, that his own strength would keep him from being taken over the hurdles by another woman like that but he wasn't too sure. He knew as long as he was in that penitentiary and he was expiating the crime—he did something wrong, he knew that—and he was expiating his crime, he was doing the best he could to lead a decent life while he was there, to expiate his crime against society. He had a standard of morals, and that was, I think, his strength. He had been sent out to rescue two people in a flood and he did the best he could to rescue both of them and bring them back. That took a certain sort of morality to do that. He could have escaped at any time but he didn't.

. . .

Q. Sir, you have painted his fellow convicts as being almost animals—they turn their backs to the rain and they crowd around the empty stove of the train and they seem to have absolutely no personality—they're just animals. Would the tall convict have been exactly the same?

A. He would, yes. That is the result of having been in prison. Being in prison makes a man an animal—what it deprives him of is the thing that differentiates him from the beast, which is the capacity for free will, for liberty, freedom. So of course they were animals to turn their backs to a rain

183

and hover over the symbol of heat and warmth. That's the bad thing about prison, about the deprivation of simple liberty and free will. It's the worst thing that can happen to you.

. . .

Q. Judging from that, sir, you might say your idea of a true author isn't one who sculpts his material toward the commercial side.

A. That's right. Yes, if what he wants is money, then there are probably easier ways to make money than being an author. I think that the young man or young woman that wants to write will have to make that choice. He has got to decide, Do I want to do this because I have a demon that won't let me alone or do I want to make some money at this? I think in the case of the men and women who have been the good writers, that choice never occurred to them. That they had never had to stop to decide, I have a choice to make—now, which shall I choose? because he has made that choice. The alternative has never occurred to him any more than he would choose, Now, shall I be a writer or shall I be a banker? That if he wants to be a banker he will be a banker but he will be a writer too. That if he wants to be a doctor he will be a doctor, but if he has a demon to write he will still be a writer too. He will find plenty of time to be a writer and be a painter and be anything else.

Q. Have you been approached, and I'm sure you have, to express yourself in a medium other than a book or a play? For instance, have you ever been asked to write a television play? . . .

A. Well, when I have needed money I have worked for moving pictures and televison but that was simply a pleasant way to get a check every Saturday night and it had nothing to do with writing. It was just a job.

Q. I was wondering, one of your short stories, "A Rose for Emily," what ever inspired you to write this story . . .?

A. That to me was another sad and tragic manifestation of man's condition in which he dreams and hopes, in which he is in conflict with himself or with his environment or with

184

others. In this case there was the young girl with a young girl's normal aspirations to find love and then a husband and a family, who was brow-beaten and kept down by her father, a selfish man who didn't want her to leave home because he wanted a housekeeper, and it was a natural instinct of—repressed which—you can't repress it—you can mash it down but it comes up somewhere else and very likely in a tragic form, and that was simply another manifestation of man's injustice to man, of the poor tragic human being struggling with its own heart, with others, with its environment, for the simple things which all human beings want. In that case it was a young girl that just wanted to be loved and to love and to have a husband and a family.

Q. And that purely came from your imagination?

A. Well, the story did but the condition is there. It exists. I didn't invent that condition, I didn't invent the fact that young girls dream of someone to love and children and a home, but the story of what her own particular tragedy was was invented, yes. . . .

185

Session Twenty-One

May 20, 1957

PRESS CONFERENCE

Q. ... What [do] you think of the generations of students that you've had contact with over the last four months here and possibly a year or so ago—well, let's limit it to the United States. Are they more conventional than they were when you were their age? Are they more seeking of conformity? What —are they less intellectually curious? Are they less daring?

A. No, I would say that they are more intellectually curious, they are more daring, but they have more pressure to conform, there's more and more constant pressure to belong to something, to be submerged into a mass, that they have got to struggle with. But I would say that they are more curious than they were. That they have more opportunities to be curious, to know, to keep up with what cooks, what does go on, but there is that tremendous pressure to conform, which I think they don't always realize is there.

Q. Well, do you think most of them are resisting it. . .?

A. I think that all young people resist it, but there's no ordered resistance for they themselves don't realize how much and how constant that pressure is or that they would confederate against it. They are given too many things that take the form of bribery to not resist it, to be unaware of it.

Q. What sort of bribery?

A. Well, the pleasant things of existence, of being a student, the motor cars, and the things that make the day-by-day life of a student simpler than it used to be when there was some question to keep warm in winter—you had to go to a little trouble of keeping a fire going if nothing else. There were— it was a little more difficult to find pleasure. You couldn't go out and go to the theatre by paying sixty or seventy cents at the moving-picture show every night. The books were not always available, and because things like that are available, the student is—the young man is tricked into not realizing the pressure on him to belong to a mass or group which wants to do his thinking for him, to give him the ideas that group—the overlords of the group and mass—want him to have. But I'm convinced he still resists it and it breaks out in all sorts of queer and unpredictable places.

Q. What are they, sir?

A. Well, I think of young Mr. Plowden-Wardlaw, whose avocation seems to be taking part in a Calypso band, yet suddenly he and his friends on the magazine here have thought of that [magazine] issue stating different notions about segregation. That's interesting. He should—they should do more with that. There should be more of that in the University, I think, than there is. But that's a good, a very hopeful symptom.

Q. You said something about wishing that the University of Virginia and the state of Virginia would take more leadership in the South. You were asked that question the other night in conversation.

A. Well, yes, that's because of the respectful, almost abject, reverence which the rest of the South has toward the State of Virginia and toward the University. That when the State of Virginia makes mistakes which should have been made not by Virginia but by Mississippi or Alabama, we are a little ashamed.

. . .

Q. Mr. Faulkner, last week you went to see a play written by one of the students here. I would be interested in any comments you would care to make on the play.

A. Hopeful. It was another instance of that pressure to conform. I think that a sad and tragic thing—condition which the young writer today has to face is that the middle class has

188

been broken down. It no longer exists as a homogeneous condition recognized by everyone everywhere. It exists but it exists as, you might say, individual cells. The best of the writing of the old days was not so much done by members of the middle class but it was about the tragedies, the problems which existed in the middle class, and now there is no middle class anymore as a definite condition recognizable everywhere to create those problems, and so the plays have a flavor a little too preciously proletarian. That they are concerned with conditions and not problems of the human heart. Mr. Coffey's play showed a—it was very hopeful, I think. It showed a sense of his craft and it was very well done to have been done by amateurs because that was pretty difficult for amateurs to do—that sort of thing—to make it believable.

. . .

Q. Mr. Faulkner, I'm interested in something that seems to have happened to you. It seemed to me, using the Nobel Prize as a mark in time rather than any special significance, that you seem to have moved to a certain extent from communicating only through your works to—well, for example, going to Japan or coming to the University of Virginia and going to other places for the State Department. I wondered if this marked any sort of change or departure in your own thinking, or sort of why you moved out?

A. Well, sir, you are constantly changing, your skin, your fingernails, are constantly changing. The only alternative, you know, is death, and let's hope that we won't have to keep on doing tomorrow what we are doing today. There wouldn't be much fun in it.

Q. Mr. Faulkner, in your talk to the students you said, as I remember, that it's a question whether Southern Baptists are religious, and I was wondering if you would elaborate on that and say if they are not religious then what are they?

A. Well, they're Southern Baptist. I think that is an emotional condition that has nothing to do with God or politics or anything else.

Q. What is involved in this emotional condition of the Southern Baptist?

189

A. It came from times of hardship in the South where there was little or no food for the human spirit—where there were no books, no theatre, no music, and life was pretty hard and a lot of it happened out in the sun, for very little reward and that was the only escape they had. I think that is the human spirit aspiring toward something. Of course, it got warped and twisted in the process.

Q. This condition—do you limit that to Southern Baptists or do you visualize something larger actually than the Baptist churches in the South?

A. Well, I imagine that it exists almost everywhere, though it may take other forms. It would exist wherever people have been starved, spiritually starved.

Q. Mr. Faulkner, one other question, can you—have you gotten anything particularly out of these four months in Charlottesville yourself? Can you at this point in any way distill sort of any feeling you might have about Charlottesville and about the University?

A. The writer writes from the three tanks I spoke of—observation, imagination, and experience. He's got to constantly replenish them and fill them, and so I couldn't say exactly what I've got from my stay here to replenish those tanks, though the tanks have been replenished because, as we agreed, life is in constant flux and in constant change and the time that you don't learn something new every day you are dead.

Q. Based on your four months here, I was wondering if your opinion of university education or college education has changed. As I understand, when you first came here you said that a university—a college education was good for some people and not necessary for others, and I was wondering whether your opinion has been modified at all.

A. No, because I've had that opinion for about fifty years. I think that all education in this country has got to be overhauled. I think that there's a—it's basically bad when its premise is that everybody must be educated willy nilly. That some people don't deserve to be educated, and if everyone is to be educated, unless enough money is spent on education to where the best student can have the best of the treatment, the best of the education, then he is going to have to be stultified and held back by a scheme which has got to take the one that is least fitted. Probably the ideal form of education would be one professor to one student, or one professor to no more than ten students.

. . .

Q. Mr. Faulkner, your statements that you think that education should be overhauled and you said that you thought it would be good if possible to have maybe one professor to one student or one to ten students, and that generally I believe is what colleges are trying to work for, and do you think they are on the right track generally or do you think they are making some mistake, and if so, what mistake?

A. I'm sure that they are working toward something like that or maybe even a better idea and I'm convinced too that with all the problems, the social problems which we face, which is the leisure that we don't know what to do with, with too many people, with the need for housing, that it's amazing that the colleges advance as they do. That is, if suddenly things could be stopped to give the colleges one year in which to make their plans, they might do something, but now they can't because here's another flux of young men and women that have got to go to school and they don't have any chance to stop and get their breath and take stock and make plans.

. . .

Q. Mr. Faulkner, you may have touched on this previously, but could you give some advice to young writers? What advice would you give to young writers?

A. At one time I thought the most important thing was talent. I think now that the young man or the young woman must possess or teach himself, train himself, in infinite patience, which is to try and to try and to try until it comes right. He must train himself in ruthless intolerance—that is, to throw away anything that is false no matter how much he might love that page or that paragraph. The most important thing is insight, that is, to be—curiosity—to wonder, to mull, and to muse why it is that man does what he does, and if you have that, then I don't think the talent makes much difference, whether you've got that or not.

Q. How would you suggest that he get this insight? Through experience?

A. Yes, and then the greatest part of experience is in the books, to read. To read and to read and to read and to read. To watch people, to have—to never judge people. To watch people, what they do, without intolerance. Simply to learn why it is they did what they did. . . .

Session Twenty-Two

May 30, 1957

UNIVERSITY AND COMMUNITY PUBLIC

... Q. Mr. Faulkner, your publishers have announced a sequel to *The Town*. ... I think this is the first time this has happened to you. Do you like being under that kind of pressure, or ...?

A. The pressure is not actually from the publisher. When I first thought of these people and the idea of a tribe of people which would come into an otherwise peaceful little Southern town like ants or like mold on cheese then—I discovered then that to tell the story properly would be too many words to compress into one volume. It had to be two or three. So the pressure has been on me before I ever told the publisher about it. That I would have to keep on writing about these people until I got it all told, and I assume that one more book will do it though I don't have any great hopes that it will.

Q. Mr. Faulkner, do you write in regular hours or do you write in irregular hours?

A. No sir, by nature I am completely disorderly. I never have learned to hang up anything or put anything back where I got it, and so I work when—well, as the athlete says, when I'm hot. And I don't like to work, I'm by nature lazy, I will put it off as long as I can and then when I get started it's fun, I think the reason anyone writes is because it's fun, you like it, that's just your cup of tea. And so I will write until I have got to make myself stop because I have found that the only rule for writing I have is to leave it while I'm still hot—while I'm still looking good, as *Gentlemen Prefer Blondes* put it—

193

so that I can pick up again tomorrow. But I have never had any order. Some people are orderly, they lay out a plot or synopsis first, they make notes, which is valid and satisfactory to them but not to me, I would be completely lost. Probably if I'd begun to make a few notes I could say, Oh well, that's all, you don't need to work any more, and I would quit. So I think I put off working as long as possible and do as much of the research and the note-filing up here and then begin to write.

Q. Mr. Faulkner, in your actual composition do you write everything out in longhand or do you type or have somebody—?

A. Yes sir, I write it out in longhand because I never have learned to think good on to the typewriter. That I've got to feel the pencil and see the words at the end of the pencil, then if it is the wrong word it's simple enough to scratch it out and try it again. I reckon I was—started writing too soon to have taken the typewriter as an extension of the hands, as the young man nowadays can do. I have to put it down on paper first. After that I do the rewriting on the typewriter but something has got to be on paper first for me to look at and get the feel of.

Q. How fast do you dash it off?

A. So fast that somebody said my handwriting looks like a caterpillar that crawled through a ink well and out on to a piece of paper. If I leave it until tomorrow I can't read it myself, so it's got to be put down quick and then typed quick.
. . .

Q. Mr. Faulkner, may I ask how much your daily variations of mood affect the actions of your characters? Suppose one day you get up feeling fine—do your characters seem to take on a cheerful aspect?

A. I don't believe so. I think that anyone, the painter, the musician, the writer works in a kind of an insane fury. He is demon-driven. He can get up feeling rotten, with a hangover, or with actual pain, and if he gets to work, the first thing he knows he don't remember that pain, that hangover—he's too busy. That his feeling—I doubt if that reflects too much in

194

his work. That he can wake up and go to work feeling good and the first thing he knows he doesn't remember whether he feels good or not—he's too busy. That he is in the clutch of a demon then.

. . .

Q. I want to ask you a question about *The Town*. The heroine of this story, Eula Varner Snopes, at the end commits suicide. What do you think was her reason for it?

A. It was for the sake of that child. She at that time had realized that every child, a young girl especially, needed the semblance of an intact home—that is, to have a mother and a father, to have the same things that the other children had. And she had reached an impasse where her lover would have demanded that she leave her husband and then that child would have found out that it had grown up in a broken home. Up to this time, whether the child loved Flem or not, at least he was the symbol of the father which all the other children had, and with—the mother felt that it would be better for this girl to have a mother who committed suicide than a mother who ran off with a lover. Which was—that may have been the wrong decision she made but that was the decision she did make. That at least this girl would have had the similitude of an intact though a tragedy-ridden home, just as other children did.

Q. Do you by chance have in mind writing the story of this daughter now?

A. Yes sir, that will be in the next book. She's one of the most interesting people I've written about yet, I think. Her story will be in the next book.

. . .

Q. Mr. Faulkner, in some of the statements published about you in news stories you have made the distinction between yourself and the demon who makes you write. Who or what is that demon?

A. Well sir, I don't know myself. Probably he harasses me too much for me to have a good chance to turn and look at him. It could be, as I say, a desire to leave some mark on the world so that people after you will know that for a little

195

while Smith was here, he made this scratch. It—well, I don't think it's for glory, it's certainly not for profit, because there are many more profitable things than being a writer. If—it's certainly not to change man's condition. If anything, I would say that's what it is, it's simply to leave a scratch on the earth that showed that you were here for a little while.

Q. When or how do you decide on the titles?

A. Titles, I think—well, in my case the good titles are like gentle lightning strokes, I don't know where they come from, suddenly there is just exactly the right title. The only time I ever hunt—I ever had to hunt for a title it was a bad one, it never did please me. The others I don't know where they came from. Suddenly the situation, the character, the book or something about it brings a title out of the mysterious unknown or out of the background or experience—I don't know where it comes from.

Q. Not always at the beginning or—?

A. Sometimes the title is the first thing, the title invents the story, sometimes the title appears in the middle of the story. I've never had but one that finished without a title, that I had to hunt around and invent one.

Q. In the title of *Requiem for a Nun,* does the *Nun* have to refer to Temple Drake Stevens or to Nancy?

A. The nun was Nancy.

Q. She was very separated from the world as a nun is?

A. Well, it was in the—that tragic life of a prostitute which she had had to follow simply because she was compelled by her environment, her circumstances, to be it. Not for profit and any pleasure, she was just doomed and damned by circumstances to that life. And despite that, she was capable within her poor dim lights and reasons of an act which whether it was right or wrong was of complete almost religious abnegation of the world for the sake of an innocent child. That was—it was paradoxical, the use of the word *Nun for* her, but I—but to me that added something to her tragedy.

196

Q. Mr. Faulkner, did your title *The Sound and the Fury* come from Shakespeare's *Macbeth?*

A. Yes, there must have been a dozen books titled from that speech. I think that I had the best one. But I can think of six or seven books all from that same speech.

. . .

Q. Do you feel that your characters are universal? . . . I know that you are a regional writer, and I just wondered—or do you care?

A. I feel that the verities which these people suffer are universal verities—that is, that man, whether he's black or white or red or yellow still suffers the same anguishes, he has the same aspirations, his follies are the same follies, his triumphs are the same triumphs. That is, his struggle is against his own heart, against—with the hearts of his fellows, and with his background. And in that sense there's no such thing as a regional writer, the writer simply uses the terms he is familiar with best because that saves him having to do research. That he might write the book about the Chinese but if he does that, he's got to do some research or somebody'll say "Ah! you're wrong there, that ain't the way Chinese behave." But if he uses his own region, which he is familiar with, it saves him that trouble.

. . .

Q. Mr. Faulkner, why are you so fond of the Compsons and the Snopeses?

A. Well, I feel sorry for the Compsons. That was blood which was good and brave once, but has thinned and faded all the way out. Of the Snopes, I'm terrified.

. . .

Q. Mr. Faulkner, these characters that you follow along, do they come to a natural conclusion, or do you have to kill them off, or do they tell the story and that's the end of it, or what?

A. No no, they exist. They are still in motion in my mind. I can laugh at things they're doing that I haven't got around to writing yet. No, that's where the rules of the craft come in, that someone, some editor, has got to give the whole thing

197

unity, coherence, and emphasis. To start at a decent starting-place and then stop it somewhere at a logical, reasonable place. But the characters themselves are walking out of that book still in motion, still talking, and still acting.

Q. Mr. Faulkner, because of your interrupted education, it makes me wonder if formal education. . . .

A. I think that nobody can know too much, can learn too much. I think that one can be a writer without the formal education. I think the formal education will not do the writer any more harm than anybody else, but I'm convinced that nobody can be taught anything, that you must learn it. And the value of formal education is that all the knowledge, the wisdom, the opinions on the wisdom, on the knowledge which makes wisdom, is there convenient for you to get. Otherwise, you've got to run from pillar to post to find what is right there offered to you. But nobody can teach anybody anything, I'm convinced of that. You've got to want to know it. You've got to want to know it.

Q. Sir, you mentioned love and money and death as the three subjects of fiction. Isn't there something else, above that, such as represented in your novel about Thomas Sutpen, who was motivated by something other than those three things, involved in something higher than they?

A. I mean that love and money and death are the skeletons on which the story is laid. They have nothing to do with the aspirations and the conflicts of the human hearts involved. But the story has got to have some skeleton, and the skeletons are love or money or death. In Sutpen's case, there was—he needed the money in order to satisfy his aspiration. And it was his foreknowledge of death which compelled—impelled in him the haste to be completely ruthless to do it while he still could. The love was a part of his conflict too. He wanted that son for vanity, of course. But you—vanity is not really enough. You've got to love the thing that you can be vain because of, or proud because of. It had to be *his* son, not just—he could have adopted a child, you see, and carved out a plantation. That wasn't enough, it had to be his, not only to be proud of, but to represent his own blood, his own passion.

198

Q. You spoke of titles before, Mr. Faulkner. I'd like to ask you about the origin of *Light in August*.

A. Oh that was—in August in Mississippi there's a few days somewhere about the middle of the month when suddenly there's a foretaste of fall, it's cool, there's a lambence, a luminous quality to the light, as though it came not from just today but from back in the old classic times. It might have fauns and satyrs and the gods and—from Greece, from Olympus in it somewhere. It lasts just for a day or two, then it's gone, but every year in August that occurs in my country, and that's all that title meant, it was just to me a pleasant evocative title because it reminded me of that time, of a luminosity older than our Christian civilization. Maybe the connection was with Lena Grove, who had something of that pagan quality of being able to assume everything, that's—the desire for that child, she was never ashamed of that child whether it had any father or not, she was simply going to follow the conventional laws of the time in which she was and find its father. But as far as she was concerned, she didn't especially need any father for it, any more than the women that—on whom Jupiter begot children were anxious for a home and a father. It was enough to have had the child. And that was all that meant, just that luminous lambent quality of an older light than ours.

Q. Is "A Rose for Emily" all fiction?

A. Yes sir. Yes sir, that's all fiction, for the reason I said, too. If any time a writer writes anything that seems at all familar to anybody anywhere, he gets a letter about it, and if they think he's got enough money, he's sued, too, so he's awful careful not to write anything he ever saw himself, or anybody ever told him.

Session Twenty-Three

June 5, 1957

UNIVERSITY AND COMMUNITY PUBLIC

Q. Mr. Faulkner, in this book, *The Town*, we come across so many of the characters we've met previously. Are those four snakey Snopeses new?

A. Are the what Snopes new?

Q. The four snakey Snopeses, in the last chapter.

A. Not to me. I thought of these people thirty years ago and the more I thought about them the more Snopes they invented. It's simply that I haven't got around yet to telling about them. There's one more volume which I hope will be the last but I haven't no assurance that it will be. It may be that when I finish that there will still be another. But they are not new to me. They have been in—alive and have been in motion, I have hated them and laughed at them and been afraid of them for thirty years now.

Q. Mr. Faulkner, who's that poetess quoted in the passage you just read?

A. That was Djuna Barnes.[1] She belonged to one of the first minute precious expatriate groups back in the—when was that?

Q. The twenties?

A. Twenties. Yes, the early twenties. Djuna Barnes it was. I don't know if she's still alive or not—do you know?

[1] *The Town* (N. Y., 1957), p. 317. In conversation, Mr. Faulkner also identified the poet whom Gavin Stevens quotes in *Intruder in the Dust* (N. Y., 1948), p. 195, as Djuna Barnes.

201

. . .

Q. Mr. Faulkner, you often have referred to male authors that you have enjoyed. Are there any women writers you esteem?

A. Yes. Any number—Brontë, Willa Cather, Ellen Glasgow—any number. I think that when I refer to authors as males I'm simply using "he" as sort of a simplified term to express an individual. Yes, any number of good ones.

Q. Was *Wuthering Heights* one of your favorite books? I remember you gave us a list and I don't remember them all.

A. I don't really have favorite books. I have books that I read many times over and over but it's not for the book it's for the people in it. There are certain people that I like to read about just as you like to go into a room and spend thirty minutes with an old friend, and *Wuthering Heights* is a book that I have admired for its craftsmanship but there's nothing in it that I would ever read again probably, though some day I might.[1]

. . .

Q. Mr. Faulkner, would you give us your definition of poetry?

A. It's some moving, passionate moment of the human condition distilled to its absolute essence.

Q. Considering the Sherwood Anderson connection, had he written *Winesburg, Ohio* when you met him?

A. Yes. Yes, he was working on *Dark Laughter* then. He —that was after *Winesburg* and *The Triumph of the Egg*— his two best, I think.

Q. Well, his best character seems to have been George Willard, and isn't it a bit tragic that he left him in *Winesburg* and never revived him?

A. I don't think so. That George Willard is alive enough. That there's no need to harass and worry the man to death, he is quite alive and as you say he's the best character—that's enough.

[1] Mr. Faulkner read or reread *Wuthering Heights* in February 1958.

Q. Mr. Faulkner, you have been called, among other things, Christian humanist. I was wondering if you could tell me what you consider your relationship to the Christian religion?

A. Why, the Christian religion has never harmed me. I hope I never have harmed it. I have the sort of provincial Christian background which one takes for granted without thinking too much about it, probably. That I'm probably—within my own rights I feel that I'm a good Christian—whether it would please anybody else's standard or not I don't know.

. . .

Q. Mr. Faulkner, do you find that you can write almost anywhere, on a train, or riding in the back seat of a car or in an office?

A. Oh yes, sure, just anywhere. I put it off as long as I can and when I can't put it off any longer I can write anywhere, on anything and with anything except a typewriter. I'm not much good with a typewriter.

. . .

Q. You must have a phenomenal memory?

A. Well, it's a phenomenal memory in the sense that the muscle remembers. That it's not anything that's really catalogued into the mind, it's catalogued into whatever muscles of the human spirit produce the book or the music or the picture, and we'll assume that there are muscles in the spirit that do that. That the artist is—well, it's a little more than kleptomania—it's a little of kleptomania, but rather more of whatever it is that makes the magpie pick up everything or the packrat pick up anything that's loose. I think that's the way the writer goes through life, through books and through the actual living world too. That he misses very little, not because he's made up his mind before breakfast not to miss anything today but because those muscles work for him, and when that need comes he digs out things that he didn't know where he saw—which to him don't matter, he may have stolen it— he probably did—but to him that's not important. The important thing is if he uses it worthily. If he makes some base use of it then of course it's a shame. But he wants to—when he steals he wants the owner that he stole from to approve of what he did with it or not to disapprove too much.

. . .

Q. Your demon sounds relentless. Is there any hope for anyone learning to write if they have a part-time demon?

A. Well, I think that there's a limitless supply of demons just like germs that hang around maybe just looking for lodgment in anyone that shows any aptitude for ink. That—that's —as I said, it's a vice and it's a virulent sort of vice too. If you ain't careful it'll get you.

. . .

Q. Mr. Faulkner, do you feel that a writer might be hampered by a college education? Keep him from creating the characters—?

A. No sir, I do not. I think that a college education is not going to hamper anyone. I think that a lot of people are subject to it that don't deserve it and can do nothing with it, but it's not going to hamper anyone. I think that the college education will save the writer a great deal of trouble which he would have to go to in simply learning about man, about the history, the recorded history of man, that is available to him in the university which otherwise he has got to get out and dig for himself, and I'm sorry that I didn't have a college education myself. I think that if you have the demon you're going to write anyway, nothing is going to stop you, and it may be you don't want things too easy. But I never heard of anyone that was hurt by a college education and any writer that says, I would have been a good writer except—I put no stock in that because I believe that the "mute, inglorious Milton" is a complete myth.

Q. Mr. Faulkner, in spite of what happens to General Compson and Colonel Sutpen and Colonel Sartoris, there seems to be a heroic quality about them. Do you think that it is still possible for that kind of heroism in the time in which the story in *The Town* is set?

A. Yes. I think that although man is not always matched with his finest hour, I'm convinced that the hour, the need finds the men it requires. That the men like Compson and Sutpen who had the desire to be heroic—they failed through lack of character or absence of things in their character which should not [*sic*] have been there but at least they tried. But I'm

204

convinced that the hour will find the men it needs. Though the tragedy is the man who didn't find his hour, didn't find his chance to be what he could have been and might have been—he's tragic.

. . .

Q. Have you ever received any rejection slips?

A. Yes'm, for the first few years when I'd try to write short stories I got plenty of rejection slips.

Q. How did it affect you? Or did it?

A. Well, I would be frustrated and enraged in the time when I hoped I could get a little money for it, but if I didn't need money at that time it didn't make much difference, I'd send it somewhere else or I was busy still writing another one. I'd probably—that's—

. . .

Q. Mr. Faulkner, what became of those stories that were rejected in the first few years you were writing? Did you just abandon them?

A. No, I kept them and after a while the folks that rejected them bought them.

Q. Mr. Faulkner, this demon that follows you, could it be described as one that insists on your writing a certain story, one story, or is it one that suggests lots of different stories and you have to use your rational mind to select?

A. No, it's the sort of demon that is like the mosquito that won't let you sleep. You want to say, Oh, go away, let's be quiet a while, what's the use in going to all this bother and trouble just to write books and stories? but it won't let you sleep. It's not that it says, You must tell this story, it's just that it won't let you alone. That it keeps on whispering to you, If you wake up, this is a lot of fun, come on, wake up and try it now.

. . .

Q. Do you see any faces as you describe characters? Do you see a physical person as you write?

A. Yes. Yes. I don't always hear a name but I always see a physical face, a body, mannerisms, and quite often they name themselves, but not always.

Q. Where do you get your names?

A. The characters usually name themselves or the situation names the characters. I've never had to hunt around and say, Now let's see, what shall I call Smith this time? That he has said, This is who I am and this what I'm going to be called.

Q. Have you usually known people with these names?

A. No, I try not to use a name I've ever heard because once you do it, two days later you get a letter saying, Dear Sir, I have just turned this matter over to my lawyer. How much money—? And so any writer is awful careful not to put down any name he ever heard or to describe any incident he ever actually saw.

Q. Mr. Faulkner, I read that you admired Mr. Wolfe's, Thomas Wolfe's work very much. Just what about it—what do you admire about his work?

A. Now that was an unfortunate remark I made. It was a group of students. They asked me what I thought about my contemporaries. I said, It's too soon to say, we're not done writing. This was twenty or thirty years ago. They said, Well, don't you have any opinion of them at all? I said, Opinion of who? He named Wolfe, Caldwell, Hemingway, Dos Passos. And I said, Well, I think we all failed, so I will have to rate us on what I consider the splendor of our failure and so this is the way I would rate us, and ever since that I've been trying to explain that or live it down. But that's all it was. To tell the truth, I haven't read much of Wolfe. I've read one or two of his stories. I've opened his books and read pages or paragraphs, but that was an opinion on the tremendous effort that he had gone into to try to put all of the history of the human heart on the head of the pin. That is, to tell all in each paragraph until he died as though he had a premonition of his own early death. That was what I meant by the failure. That he failed the best because he had tried the hardest, he had taken the longest gambles, taken the longest shots. I rated Hemingway last not on the value of the product at all but simply because of Hemingway having taught himself a pattern, a method which he could use and he stuck to that without splashing around to try to experiment. It had nothing to do

206

with the value of the work at all. It was simply on the degree of the attempt to reach the unattainable dream, to accomplish more than any flesh and blood man could accomplish, could touch.

. . .

Q. Sir, when you wrote either *The Sound and the Fury* or *As I Lay Dying*, did you—were you conscious of making the characters, the brothers and sisters and their relationships, somewhat similar? Would you think back—do you recall— it seems to me that there's a certain type of family relationship in each of the families which—I don't know which of the books you wrote first—

A. Well, yes, probably there is, due to the fact that in each one of them there was a sister surrounded by a gang of brothers. One, *As I Lay Dying,* was *tour de force.* I knew when I put down the first word what the last word of that would be. The other was anything but *tour de force.* I was completely submerged in the other one. I struggled and an- guished with it for a year. *As I Lay Dying* I wrote in about six weeks without changing any of it. If there is any relationship it's probably simply because both of them happened to have a sister in a roaring gang of menfolks.

Q. Mr. Faulkner, you spoke about *The Sound and the Fury* as starting out to write a short story and it kept growing. Well now, do you think that it's easier to write a novel than a short story?

A. Yes sir. You can be more careless, you can put more trash in it and be excused for it. In a short story that's next to the poem, almost every word has got to be almost exactly right. In the novel you can be careless but in the short story you can't. I mean by that the good short stories like Chekhov wrote. That's why I rate that second—it's because it demands a nearer absolute exactitude. You have less room to be sloven- ly and careless. There's less room in it for trash. In poetry, of course, there's no room at all for trash. It's got to be ab- solutely impeccable, absolutely perfect.

Q. More like playwriting? . . .

A. Yes'm, that's right. Of course playwriting has one more

demand that you're not going to keep your audience that long. With a book you can read that a while and put it down and then go back and read it, but a play you can't. If you don't use up your ticket tonight you've got to buy another ticket. . . .

Session Twenty-Four

February 20, 1958

RAVEN, JEFFERSON, AND ODK SOCIETIES

A WORD TO VIRGINIANS

. . . My tenure as Writer-in-Residence here might be a little better if we kept it informal, serious but not too concentrated and continuous. That is, when I'm on the fifth floor of Cabell Hall I'm Writer-in-Residence. When I'm not there, then I'm just a Mississippi citizen that likes and admires Virginia and Virginia people. I hope that now you will take me under those conditions, that I'm just a private citizen here that likes and admires Virginia, Virginia people, even when they may not like what I'm going to say. That is, as far as the University is concerned, I'm free home here. As far as you're concerned, I am free game, only do flush me first, don't shoot me sitting. . . .

A hundred years ago Abraham Lincoln said, "This nation cannot endure half slave and half free." If he were alive today he would amend it: "This nation cannot endure containing a minority as large as ten percent held second class in citizenship by the accident of physical appearance." As a lesser man might put it, this nor any country or community of people can no more get along in peace with ten percent of its population arbitrarily unassimilated than a town of five thousand people can get along in peace with five hundred unbridled horses loose in the streets, or say a community of five thousand cats with five hundred unassimilated dogs among them, or vice versa. For peaceful coexistence, all must be one thing: either

209

all first-class citizens or all second-class citizens; either all people or all horses; either all cats or all dogs.

Perhaps the Negro is not yet capable of more than second-class citizenship. His tragedy may be that so far he is competent for equality only in the ratio of his white blood. But even if that is so, the problem of the second-class citizens still remains. It would not solve the problem even if the Negro were himself content to remain only a second-class citizen even though relieved of first-class responsibilities by his classification. The fact would still remain that we are a nation established on the fact that we are only ninety percent unified in power. With only ninety percent of unanimity, we would face (and hope to survive in it) an inimical world unified against us even if only in inimicality. We cannot be even ninety percent unified against that inimical world which outnumbers us, because too much of even that ninety percent of power is spent and consumed by the physical problem of the ten percent of irresponsibles.

It is easy enough for the North to blame on us, the South, the fact that this problem is still unsolved. If I were a Northerner, that's what I would do: tell myself that one hundred years ago we, both of us, North and South, had put this to the test, and had solved it. That it is not us, the North, but you, the South, who have refused to accept that verdict. Nor will it help us any to remind the North that, by ratio of Negro to white in population, there is probably more of inequality and injustice there than with us.

Instead, we should accept that gambit. Let us say to the North: All right, it is our problem, and we will solve it. For the sake of the argument, let us agree that as yet the Negro is incapable of equality for the reason that he could not hold and keep it even if it were forced on him with bayonets; that once the bayonets were removed, the first smart and ruthless man, black or white, who came along would take it away from him, because he, the Negro, is not yet capable of, or refuses to accept, the responsibilities of equality.

So we, the white man, must take him in hand and teach him that responsibility; this will not be the first time nor the last time in the long record of man's history that moral principle has been identical with and even inextricable from practical

210

common sense. Let us teach him that, in order to be free and equal, he must first be worthy of it, and then forever afterward work to hold and keep and defend it. He must learn to cease forever more thinking like a Negro and acting like a Negro. This will not be easy for him. His burden will be that, because of his race and color, it will not suffice for him to think and act like just any white man: he must think and act like the best among white men. Because where the white man, because of his race and color, can practice morality and rectitude just on Sunday and let the rest of the week go hang, the Negro can never let up nor deviate.

That is our job here in the South. It is possible that the white race and the Negro race can never really like and trust the other; this for the reason that the white man can never really know the Negro, because the white man has forced the Negro to be always a Negro rather than another human being in their dealings, and therefore the Negro cannot afford, does not dare, to be open with the white man and let the white man know what he, the Negro, thinks. But I do know that we in the South, having grown up with and lived among Negroes for generations, are capable in individual cases of liking and trusting individual Negroes, which the North can never do because the Northerner only fears him.

So we alone can teach the Negro the responsibility of personal morality and rectitude—either by taking him into our white schools, or giving him white teachers in his own schools until we have taught the teachers of his own race to teach and train him in these hard and unpleasant habits. Whether or not he ever learns his a-b-c's or what to do with common fractions, won't matter. What he must learn are the hard things—self-restraint, honesty, dependability, purity; to act not even as well as just any white man, but to act as well as the best of white men. If we don't, we will spend the rest of our lives dodging among the five hundred unbridled horses; we will look forward each year to another Clinton or Little Rock not only further and further to wreck what we have so far created of peaceful relations between the two races, but to be international monuments and milestones to our ridicule and shame.

And the place for this to begin is Virginia, the mother of all the rest of us of the South. Compared to you, my country —Mississippi, Alabama, Arkansas—is still frontier, still wilderness. Yet even in our wilderness we look back to that motherstock as though it were not really so distant and so far removed. Even in our wilderness the old Virginia blood still runs and the old Virginia names—Byrd and Lee and Carter— still endure. There is no family in our wilderness but has that old aunt or grandmother to tell the children as soon as they can hear and understand: Your blood is Virginia blood too; your great-great-great grandfather was born in Rockbridge or Fairfax or Prince George, Valley or Piedmont or Tidewater, right down to the nearest milestone, so that Virginia is a living place to that child long before he ever heard (or cares) about New York or, for that matter, America.

So let it begin in Virginia, toward whom the rest of us are already looking as the child looks toward the parent for a sign, a signal where to go and how to go. A hundred years ago the hot-heads of Mississippi and Georgia and South Carolina would not listen when the mother of us all tried to check our reckless and headlong course; we ignored you then, to all our grief, yours more than any since you bore more of the battles. But this time we will hear you. Let this be the voice of that wilderness, speaking not just to Mother Virginia but to the best of her children—sons found and chosen worthy to be trained to the old pattern in the University established by Mr. Jefferson to be not just a dead monument to, but the enduring fountain of his principles of order within the human condition and the relationship of man with man—the messenger, the mouthpiece of all, saying to the mother of us all: Show us the way and lead us in it. I believe we will follow you.

Q. Sir, you spoke of the Negro as a child, more or less, who had to be taught how to live like the best white man. Don't you think before that that, well, the—awful lot of this trouble that's been caused for colored people are by irresponsible white people? Don't you think it would be a good idea to educate the white people to accept the Negro?

A. Yes, I do. Of course, this could go into—to great length. I was simply stating the proposition in its simplest terms as it seemed to me. I think that all that don't violently repudiate what I've said will agree that the white man is responsible for the Negro's condition, the fact that the Negro does act like a Negro and can live among us and be irresponsible. That the white man has got to be himself capable to teach the Negro to be more responsible than he is. Yes, I agree with you. But then, the Negro is not going to wait right now while the white man educates himself in order to educate the Negro. We've got to do both at the same time. The Negro is not going to wait any longer.

Q. Sir, in your talk you had an analogy comparing the Negro with unbridled horses. Well, if you tried to break these unbridled horses and you turned a lot of tame ones in, don't you think it's a possibility that you may wind up with just a big group of half-wild horses?

A. Well, of course I used the horse as a quick analogy to state a condition. What I meant by that was the horse that can be trained and maybe has been trained. We'll assume that while that horse was a slave that he was a docile, well-behaved horse. But then he was—the burden of slavery was lifted from him and he was suddenly free. That he is still capable of being a docile member of society, but the condition in which he was compelled to be a docile member is gone, and so we will have to establish a new condition in which he is docile not through pressure but because he himself wants to be. He has got to be taught that it's best for me to pull my share in the traces if that's what we've got to do, than to run wild.

Q. Mr. Faulkner, don't you feel that if Virginia did integrate that the people in Mississippi and Alabama and Arkansas and those places would sort of lose their respect for Virginians as Southerners and sort of classify them as sort of Northerners?

A. No sir, I do not. There's a noisy minority in Mississippi and Arkansas, and I rather think it's in Virginia too, that will go to any length before they will risk in any way improving the Negro's class condition, for economic reasons. That's what's so in Mississippi anyway. But there are people in Mississippi and in Alabama and in Georgia, in the middle of

213

where the Ku Klux Klan and Citizens Councils are active, that do agree that whether they like it or not that there's a situation now which simply will not go on any longer, and our choice is to either do nothing and be run over and trampled or take ourselves, try to take charge of these unbridled horses. And I think that if the people in Mississippi and Arkansas and Alabama could find that there were people in Virginia that would take the lead in this, they would follow for the reason that there is a respect, a feeling of veneration toward Virginia that exists, as I tried to explain, everywhere in the rest of the South, whether it's valid or not I don't know, and from some of the things that I have seen Virginia do since I have been here I may agree that it's not too valid, but I think that basically there is that feeling and I believe that there is in Virginia the capacity to take the first step in solving this problem, and if it is taken in Virginia, the people in Mississippi and Alabama will follow when they wouldn't follow Alabama nor Mississippi.

Q. Mr. Faulkner, the subject of race relations seems to me to have been in the United States in such polarities, that is, the only view tolerated is an extreme view. If you agree with this premise of mine, would you say that there will be a resurgence of a moderate view on this subject, and what is your conception of that view?

A. I would say that the Negro doesn't want to mix with white people any more than white people want to mix with the Negro. The Negro simply wants the right himself to decide not to mix. I think that he doesn't want to go to white schools just because they're white schools. I think he wants to go to them because he's under the delusion that white schools are good schools. I think from what I've seen of a lot of schools that no really industrious Negro would want to go to one. Now that's not true of all schools but it's true of too many white schools. I think that what he wants is mainly the chance himself to decide to be segregated, and that if he had that, with schools so good that the people in the schools would be too busy passing the work to care what color who's sitting next to them was, there wouldn't be any trouble about integration in school.

214

Q. Sir, would you consider one of the problems disregarding in—you mentioned that the Negro was fighting for the chance to be able to segregate himself, is it not true that that is what the white Southerner is fighting to maintain? In other words, if the Negro is fighting for the right of association, aren't the Southerners fighting for the equivalent right to disassociate? In other words, they don't feel like sacrificing their right completely in order for the Negro to achieve the same right. In other words, they don't feel that they are balanced. Do you think that is a valid cause for the Southern white to be fighting so strenuously to preserve his equivalent right of disassociation?

A. I would say it's valid assuming that the Southerner's fear is valid. I think that his violent attitude toward integration is based in fear. It's—in Mississippi it's mainly an economic fear, that he has trained the Negro to get along with inferior tools and bad stock and yet to make a living and to send his children to school. The white man is afraid that if the Negro has better tools and better stock, the Negro will take the white man's economy away from him. I think that he is afraid that if he gives the Negro a chance to choose to be segregated the Negro may not choose, that if he was just convinced that the Negro would want to keep his own churches and his own schools and not mix with the white people, then the white man would give him that chance, but I doubt if some of the white people in the South can ever be brought to take that chance.

Q. Mr. Faulkner, I believe you inferred in the earlier part of your speech that a good deal of the prejudice against the Negro was because of his color, and if that be so I wonder if you really think that integration is going to solve this prejudice?

A. I myself think that integration as they mean it now will never occur, that the Negro doesn't want it either. I would say though in five hundred years he would have vanished, and I imagine then anyone that wants to join the D.A.R. will have to prove that she's got somewhere a strain of Negro blood, that they'll be descendants of . . . , but as—I think as the N.A.A.C.P. preaches it, and as the White Citizens Councils preach against it, it won't occur because the Negro himself as a race doesn't want to mix with white people, he don't like white people that well. But I do think that all the laws in the world are not going to make the two races mix if they don't want to, just as all the laws in the world won't keep them apart if they do want to.

Q. Virginia, and I think several other Southern states, have laws which say that in case schools are mixed with colored and white, these schools will be closed. Do you think that when these schools are closed the communities will finally come about to deciding that it's better to integrate and educate or just do away with education?

A. I think they will come around to integrate for the reason that we have made our schools in this country to a sort of a national system of baby-sitters and by the time these children have been at home underfoot the parents are going to be willing for them to go to school no matter who else is there.

Q. Sir, what specific program would you advocate to implement this education of the Negro race?

A. I would say first to raise the standard of all the schools to the best. I would let everyone that can pass the board go to that school. He might have one chance to fail. If he fails, he goes to a trade school. If he fails there, he goes to the Army. I mean by that that education should be a privilege. It shouldn't be a duty that I'm made to do by law whether I want to or not. That is, the law can make me go to school but they can't make me do anything there I don't want to do. It should be a privilege, people should be willing to walk four or five miles to get to school.

Q. Do you agree with the administration's proposal for federal aid to the schools?

A. Yes, if the status of the schools were improved. I think that more money ain't going to improve the schools, that the schools themselves are going to have to begin to improve themselves. They're going to have to get rid of a lot of people that don't have any business in school. They've got to give

216

teachers better pay and give the teacher some pride in his job and some security that nobody will fire him. But yes, federal aid will have to go to the schools, because I think the communities can't or won't.

Q. At what age do you advocate this entrance examination for students, elementary school or high school?

A. That should—I should think the entrance examination would come only to give the failure a second chance, that he can go to school as he does now, the first time he fails he goes to a trade school, but he will have the right to swot up and take an entrance examination to get back into the grade that he lost. I think that at college it should be a board, yes. That no matter what credits he brings from his school he should pass a board examination to get into college, yes.

Q. Sir, do you think that the federal government will allow the Negro to make this choice that you're talking about?

A. The federal government, I imagine, will do whatever the most folks hollering the loudest at it insist on.

Q. Do you think that the various groups up North which are pushing integration so hard now will—should the South try to adopt this voluntary segregation—leave the, both the white and black alone then to make a choice, or do you think it's sort of wrapped up in power politics from large Northern cities, that we will continue to be a whipping boy, for better or worse?

A. I think that most of the noisy vociferous people in the North don't really know what they're talking about. If they would come down here and look at it, they would know a good deal more than they do now. And I think that they are going to learn, because there are more and more Negroes moving to the North. In my county there were 6,000 people moved out since the last census. There were something like 4,800 of them were Negroes. I was through the country last winter birdshooting, I would see houses empty, house after house. One family on my place gone to Chicago. How long they'll stay I don't know, I imagine they'll be back in a year, but they've—and I think when more and more of these people begin to

217

crowd in among the white folks in the North a lot of them that talk so loud now will begin to change their tune.

Q. Sir, if the Negroes are the wild horses which you imply they are, how are they to pass the entrance exams? It seems to me they'll all end up in the Army and we'll be right back where we started from.

A. Well sir, that was an unfortunate simile, but I used something that we were all familiar with to express quickly a condition in which ten per cent of the population were not allowed to be members of the population except under sufferance. That's all I meant, I didn't mean that they were horses at all. We could reverse it and say that a community of fifty thousand horses with five hundred loose men moving around in it if you like. I simply meant that we have got to find some mutual ground to meet on, not socially so much as economically, and of course that implies education, culture—that is, the Negro can be equal without having to come in and sleep with you.

Q. Mr. Faulkner, it seems that the need by the early first colonies, the need for an agrarian society to have labor, gave birth to this great problem, and it also seems that the continual effort and attempt to maintain the society even after 1865 has prolonged and added to the problem. Do you think, and this is my question, that the advent of industry in the South, the industrialization of the South, and the possible eventual destruction of the remaining—of agrarian society will have any effect upon this problem?

A. It will in that I think the agrarian culture was the only culture the white man went to much trouble to train the Negro in. As that vanishes the Negro becomes more and more of a problem, when that's completely gone he'll be still more of a problem, and for that reason the white man will have to do something to substitute that agrarian economy which took care of the Negro. I mean by "took care" which assimilated the Negro. The Negro had a definite place in that economy. Now the only contact the Negro has with the white man's culture is the time-payment ice-box and the automobile that he owns

218

some day if he don't tear it up before he finishes paying for it. There's no other contact with the white man's culture that the Negro has since he was—since he left the agrarian economy of slavery.

Q. I'd like to probe your question, your statement, that no nation can exist with second-class citizens. I'm not aware of any civilization either ancient or modern that has not in some form had second-class citizenry. For example, the Hellenic civilization probably reached its flower because the leisure of one class was made possible by the labors of one who were not only second-class citizens, but worse—I'm not defending second-class citizenship, but it seems that some civilizations exist not only in spite of it but in fact because of second-class citizenship. So I would like to know if there is historical precedent for your statement.

A. This: I don't know any of those civilizations that have not had a second-class citizenship, but I don't know of any of them in which that second-class citizenship was an arbitrary condition compelled on the second-class citizen by the others. He found his own second-class level. He was not compelled to it by the color of his skin. If that second-class citizen could rise from his second-class citizenship he was allowed to, there was nothing to stop him. In our economy it's pretty hard for the Negro to get very far. That's the only difference.

Q. In Egypt many thousands and tens of thousands and hundreds of thousands of workers were held in slavery, and they could not get out. . . .

A. True, but some of them broke out. You know Moses led a big gang of them out himself.

Q. . . . Don't you think that there should be a great attempt to encourage the Negro to vote as much as possible in the South when you think of what he's doing, rather than going to practically every means to discourage him as at present?

A. Well sir, in principle, yes, but I think that to give a man a vote when he has no conception of what he's voting for or against is not going to improve him nor his condition much. I still think that the education should come first, but then I agree that a lot of white folks that vote haven't got any business voting too, but just because they do vote it's not going to help things to give a lot of Negroes that haven't got any business voting the right to vote. I think that if we've got to start educating somebody somewhere, then let's start with what is amenable to it, and the Negro in his present condition, he wants to advance himself, he would be more amenable to education than the white man would because the white man has got spoiled by it, the white man says, My laws make me go to school and if it—I've got to have a good school that suits me, I have to have a good football team or I ain't going there. I've got to have cheer leaders or I may not like it. The Negro, I think, anxious to better his condition—and I hope that some of his leaders tell him it can be done only by education—might be more amenable to education, to realize the responsibility that he has when he has the right to vote.

Q. Sir, do you think that the integration policies in the North have been successful, and if not, why?

A. Well, probably no integration policies have been successful, but then most of the agrarian policies have not been too successful yet somehow agriculture advances, somehow the human condition in which Negroes and whites have to live has advanced slowly, it has gone backward since that Supreme Court decision, but since '65 it had advanced gradually and steadily and I think that it will continue to advance gradually and steadily.

Q. Sir, before you made the statement that the Northerners were afraid of the Negro. What are your reasons for that?

A. That conclusion drawn from experience I've had with the Northerners, they love the Negro in theory, but they don't want much to do with him. I've noticed that the Southerner, he don't love the Negro in quantities, but he will defend some particular Negro—it may be the Negro just owes him money —but anyway, whatever the reason is, he will defend him. And that's what I meant, I simply generalized from what I've heard Northerners say, they express so many to me bizarre reasons for the Negro's desire to advance himself, they seem to think that he's—wants to take revenge on long oppression

220

from the white race. That may be true in certain cases but I think in general the Negro don't especially want revenge on the white man, that his attitude toward the white man is something like the white man's toward him, he likes a few of them but he don't think much of all of them. But his low opinion of all of them is not worth going to a great deal of trouble to get revenge.

Q. Sir, I don't mean to suggest that I'm a Northerner, but . . . if we in the South have an opportunity to do something progressive, and I don't think that any of our leaders have ever come up with a good working plan yet, what do you think of that?

A. I agree with you. That's what I'm talking about tonight. I agree with you. But then, I don't know of any of the Northerners that have come up with a good practical working plan yet.

Q. Sir, as I understand it, you believe that much of the leadership problem that we've got today is caused by an active noisy minority in each state. If so, if I've understood you correctly, I wonder what your reasons are for believing, for thinking, for wondering why the hapless majority refrains or keeps from using their numerical superiority to overcome this leadership problem.

A. Well, one reason is they don't want to be mixed up in something unpleasant. Another reason is that people that compose that noisy majority—minority—in Mississippi anyway, if you say something or do something they don't like they may set your house on fire.

Q. Sir, if Virginia's plea for moderation was ignored once before with particularly disastrous consequences to her that you mentioned before, do you think there's much hope for Virginia particularly caring to take the lead in the South on this question?

A. It seems to me she should. It seems to me that Virginia should feel something of the same responsibility toward the other states of the South that the Virginia younger sons moved into with the surplus slaves two hundred years ago that the father might feel toward his sons. It's a—I would say maybe the strongest tie would be some tie, an attenuation but still intact, of blood, of culture, of thought, of having shared in the same disasters. I think it's—there's a definite tie. I think that Virginia, that what we'll, if you'll allow me, the soul of Virginia, feels the same tie toward Mississippi and Alabama and Georgia as the soul of Mississippi and Alabama feel of respect toward the mother stock in Virginia. I think that that's an actual condition.

Q. Sir, in the deep South, Mississippi and Alabama, the people seem to be controlling it, more or less, by the Ku Klux Klan—you mentioned houseburning and stuff like that, and do you think that any examples that we set, any reasons we give, are going to break through those members of the Ku Klux Klan that are backed, in a lot of cases, by the law enforcement agencies who are not—are pretty ignorant, a lot of them? Do you think that we can do anything to break through their attitude?

A. I think so, that's the point I make. If there was a definite quality of leadership in common sense, apart from emotion and any dragging out of old battle flags, that the South, the wilderness, the frontier part of the South could hear and know about, they would have some reason to feel that if we can throw off these noisy people too, that there are people in other parts of the South that feel as we do. The liberal in Mississippi, he's hemmed in more or less by the sort of people that burn crosses and whip Negroes and compose lynching parties and he's afraid to say anything—well, he knows that if he says too much something unpleasant may happen to him, then no matter what he says it may not do any good. But if he found out that there were people in other states that felt the same way as he does, just as the people that form Citizens Councils and the KKK, they find out that there are people in other states that feel the same way, so it builds them up. I think that's what we need. The people that will look on this as something that is going to change whether we like it or not—it may be that all of us curse the day when the first slave was sold into this country, but that's too late now—and to live in this country,

222

anywhere in the world today, and to be against giving a man what equality, cultural, educational, economic that he's capable and responsible for, is like living in Alaska and being against snow—you've got snow. It's foolish to be against it—you've got it.

Q. Sir, this is just a simple question. I wonder if you could tell us if there's any particular class or economic group in the South which the Klan draws its members from, or whether they come from all walks of life in the South.

A. By and large they come from the poor unsuccessful white man. He has worked hard by his lights, and of course he has worked hard, he never gets very far ahead, he knows that he never will, he sees the Negro with the same sort of land he's got, with poorer tools and not as much credit as he's got, make a better job of it, to raise his family, and they seem to be happier than he does. And he doesn't like that. He's envious, he hates the Negro because the Negro is beating him at his own poor game, which is to make a living on forty acres of poor land. His only superiority over that Negro is not economic any longer. It's because he's white and that Negro is not white and so he's going to do everything he can to keep that Negro black, because it makes him feel good. That's the only thing, the only edge he has.

Q. Mr. Faulkner, in the light of what you just said, you also said that the Negro won't wait any longer and that he will demand rights, and that there's not time to educate the white man, but don't you really think that it is a matter of time and a long time before the Mississippian or the south Alabamian will actually accept any sort of integration in fact?

A. Yes, I agree with you, I think it will be at least fifty years, I meant that the Negro is now in motion toward more equality and he's got a lot of white folks and government bureaus and courts behind him. I didn't mean he's going to either blow the country up or change it tomorrow. I meant that now he has got pressure, outside forces helping him move forward, and that is what I think we've got to cope with, either use it, direct it, or let it run over us. But it will be fifty years before,

223

at least, before the integration as N.A.A.C.P. talks about it if that ever does come, but he will—it will be less time than that before he gets more equality that he's got. I think it'll be less time than that before he can vote in Mississippi or before his— he has to pay the same interest on his borrowed money the white man does, that a white man can't cheat him, can't charge things on a farm commissary book and refuse to let the Negro add up the figures, as he can do now in Mississippi.

Q. Sir, a lot of Southerners argue that complete integration would greatly lower our standards of education, but don't you believe that within a few years after complete integration, if it worked moderately well, there would be an overall improvement in our standards of education?

A. I don't know. It seems to me to improve standards of education we've got to get some folks out of the schools, not get more in it that don't belong there.

Q. Sir, being a liberal in Mississippi, as it seems to me you are, you have probably had experiences with this vociferous group that seems to know only violence to accomplish its means. It seems to me that you might have had some experience with this group. My question is, have you, and if you have, could you relate what they were?

A. Well, quite often as individuals they are not too dangerous, they're just noisy. When enough of them get together, they can usually be handled as those North Carolina Indians got rid of theirs, that a little firmness will do a lot with them. Of course, that don't keep them from coming around at night and setting fire to the barn, that's just an occupational hazard you've got to live with.

Q. Since you say Virginia must take the first step, how would you propose this, especially since the administration has closed the door as far as education is concerned?

A. Well, that would be something which Virginians must decide. What I hope is that Virginia will say, Something has got to be done about this, and you people in Mississippi and Alabama and Georgia, let's decide what to do, either to control it or let it run over us.

Q. We did have a vote here though, sir, and whether it was overlooked—the Gray Plan—just a start in the right direction . . . .

A. Well, the only answer to that is to vote again, and vote again, and vote again. If you tell people something often enough and long enough, whether they believe you or not they may follow you just to get you to hush.

Q. Sir, it seems to me that the main contention here tonight is that the economic and educational status of the Negro has propagated in him mores which are detrimental to our society. If this is so, why not, while segregated, raise his economic standard and raise his educational standard?

A. Good, I agree with you, that's what I'd like to do. I would like to give him such good schools that he wouldn't want to go to the white schools. I would like to give him so much equality in his own race and responsibility for it and make him have to spend so much time being responsible for his own equality that he wouldn't have time to bother with the white man's. Yes, I agree with you, that's what I would do.

Q. Sir, would you advocate letting the Negro pay his own taxes too?

A. Well, don't he?

Q. . . . we know.

A. Well, he—some of him does, he gets drafted into the Army just like he was a white man. He risks the same death as a white man does, and probably if he had the vote he'd vote for the same scalawag and scoundrel the white folks elect, but he would at least have the right to have voted for him.

Q. Sir, assuming that we in Virginia take the lead in this integration movement for the South, what guarantee if any do we have that incidents similar to those that just happened in New York in the last couple of weeks won't happen again down here? If we don't have a guarantee, what steps would you suggest that we take to stall off any such incidents . . . knifing, robbery, and so forth?

A. I would say that we train the Negro first into the responsibility of having the privilege of going to the white schools before we dump him into it. That he should be selected by rigorous examination before he was permitted into the white school. In the meantime white teachers should be sent to the Negro schools to train the Negro teachers how to teach the Negro schools to be equal, responsible for the right to go to the white schools. I think if that's—I'm sure what we all want not to happen is a thing like Little Rock or Clinton, to have troops with bayonets compel Negroes into white Virginia or Mississippi schools. That's exactly as I see it what we're trying to prevent, which if we don't do something, we will have.

Q. Mr. Faulkner, the Negro professional men of the South, doctors, teachers, and lawyers, themselves act as a blockade against the younger, better-educated Negroes. In . . . and medical societies, they won't let them pass board examinations, so what are we going to do about that? These old guard Negroes won't let the new, better-educated, the more liberal Negroes in as the leaders.

A. They will have to be by-passed, just like the old-guard white people that want to stop progress will have to be by-passed. We don't have time any more to wait around for the old mossbacks to die off. That might solve it if we had more time, but we don't, something's got to be done pretty soon, and they would have to be by-passed. And I'm quite sure there's a lot of that, that they prefer the status quo, they don't want to change and upset things, that probably they don't want a lot of smart young Negro doctors and lawyers getting in their hair. It makes them behave a good deal like white folks.

Q. Mr. Faulkner, as a foreigner I have regarded the Southerners and the Northerners all Americans, as members of the American nation, but here and elsewhere I have observed that there is a difference between the Southerner and the Northerner, but I see a problem here which seems to me greater or more dangerous than the problem of segregation against the Negroes. Would you please comment on this?

A. I think I understand what you mean, but I don't believe any problem can face this country that we won't drop everything and confederate on, unless it may be the abolishment of automobiles, but we are not going to confederate on the problem of segregation, that's the only issue that we balk at, but anything else is ephemeral, and the American don't take that seriously any more than he takes most of the stuff he talks seriously, that a great deal of his talk that sounds serious and meaningful to the foreigner, it don't to the American because he's never—occurs to him that anybody's going to really believe that, but . . . .

Q. I think this last comment is of some interest, and I was wondering if you felt that the problem which we face in Virginia and in the South has any strong international consequences insofar as the future of the Western civilization—that is, what do our neighbors across the oceans think of us in Virginia, let's say, as this young man has pointed out, when they've heard of our action in regard to Negroes?

A. I imagine that they have a very—pretty—very poor opinion of us, but I think that their opinion of us is not near as important right now as what we, Virginians and Mississippians and Alabamians, have got to think about ourselves. Let's look after our own opinion about our behavior, and then let's worry about what somebody else thinks about it.

Q. As slow and inefficient as it may be, do you feel that the best problem—the best solution to race integration would be race assimilation?

A. No sir, I don't think that that would solve many problems. The same amount of bickering would go on and they would find another subject for it. I think that the only thing that will solve that problem is not integration but equality, for the Negro to know that he has just as much and just as valid rights in this country as anybody else has. That his money is just as secure, his children have a right to just as good an education as anybody else does, his vote counts as much as anybody else's. That he don't have to pay any more for the Cadillac that he dreams of owning some day than the white man has to pay for it.

Session Twenty-Five

February 21, 1958

GRADUATE COURSE IN AMERICAN FICTION

. . . Q. I just wanted to know if [Sherwood Anderson] wrote in the same fashion you did. You said that you just let the story write itself and I was wondering if he did the same thing.

A. Yes, generally, yes. I think that all people write from—in—by the same method. It's a matter of imagining any number of things. The writer at the moment of putting it down has got to be a censor, to say, Now, this is right, this is wrong, and to throw away the wrong. Anderson didn't quite have that confidence in his own capacity to pick and choose. There was an instinct that would save him in the end. A lot of the stuff that went into his stories a man with a harder mind, more sure of himself, would have stricken out and would have gotten rid of some of the sense of fumbling and clumsiness, the heavy-footedness which was in Anderson's stories which he himself didn't like but in my opinion it had a great deal to do with making his stories, the very fact that they did sound clumsy and not quite strained but a little puzzled. That the truth did come out of all the heavy-footedness and the fumbling, the —whatever it was that made him go to the length of reducing some of it to the sort of *First Reader* statements, gave something to the final result that no imitator could match probably. But it was much more of an unhappy strain to him, that he never got the pleasure of, out of writing that a more facile craftsman could have done. It had nothing to do with the result, of course, it just was—

. . .

Q. . . . One critic suggests that Sherwood Anderson felt a particular kinship with Gertrude Stein. Miss Stein is spoken of so frequently in connection with the writers of the Twenties. I would be interested to know whether you recall any discussions by Anderson of her, her work, and its influence upon himself.

A. Yes, he had the unlettered man's boundless and almost baseless respect for literacy, for education, and she was an extremely versatile creature that way, she spoke two or three different languages, she came from a background of people that took the best of education as a matter of course, which he didn't have. Also, she was one of the few people that he could trust. I mean that when she said that what he was doing was good, he never doubted it, because he knew that she would never do anything to hurt him. Other people that told him it was good he never did quite trust, he said, Well, maybe they'll do something to hurt me tomorrow, I'm afraid of them, but with her he never was, because he knew that she was a—well you might say a lady, and wasn't—was never going to hurt him.

Q. Do you happen to remember how you first met Mr. Anderson?

A. Yes, I had worked in a New York book store, the manager was Elizabeth Prall, Miss Prall then. Later I had heard that she had married Anderson, was living in New Orleans, I happened to be in New Orleans and I had gone to call on her, because I wasn't going to bust in on Mr. Anderson without an invitation from him, I didn't think that I would see him at all, that he would probably be in his study working, but it happened that he was in the room at the time, and we talked and we liked one another from the start, and it was just the chance that I had gone to call on Miss Prall that I had known who had been kind to me when I was a clerk in a book store that I came to meet him.

Q. I'd like to follow that up just once, if I may, sir. We were talking about the background of Anderson's writing and all of the writing out of the Twenties and how people often gathered in groups in Greenwich Village and Chicago and New Orleans. Was there something in New Orleans that pulled you down there, or were you just making a trip?

A. Well, yes, I had heard of *The Double Dealer* and the people there for years. At that time I went to New Orleans to get a job in a ship and go to Europe, that was why I happened to be in New Orleans at that time. That I hadn't— it was no pull to be a part of a literary group, no. That I had felt the pull—I think that any young writer does feel that pull to be with people that have the same problems and the same interests as him, that won't laugh at what he's trying to do, won't laugh at what he says no matter how foolish it might sound to the Philistine, but that was the reason I was in New Orleans, was to get a job with a ship.

. . .

Q. To follow up an earlier question about how a writer of fiction draws on people in his mind, I would wonder if there wouldn't be some—if this might not constitute a test of demands on a good writer of fiction, that is, of how many people he can draw on. We have spoken of Mr. Anderson as making characters who are more or less mirrors of himself, whereas writers of fiction like Balzac and Dickens always seem to have such variety of human beings to use. Don't you think that this is pretty central, having full countries of persons to use when you're writing fiction?

A. Yes, it's to be preferred, but then Dickens and Balzac didn't have the self-doubt that Anderson had. Now whether that's because they lived in a culture that was less inimical to being an artist I don't know. It may be it took somebody a little tougher than Anderson to cope with America. That there was less in the culture of England in the time of Dickens, of France in the time of Balzac, to need to fend off and protect oneself from. That you could have either—you could carry your tender edges around without getting them bruised, or maybe a product of that culture didn't have the tender edges, I don't know which it would be. Anderson might have been happier if he had been a monk maybe, when he retired from the world if he could have retired completely into a monastery

231

to have written, where nobody could hurt him. Whether he would have written—yes he would, he would have written *Winesburg*, that was why he gave up the advertising business, but I think that what happened to the other books was that he was still trying to change his complete nature, he was still trying to write not another *Winesburg*, but he was trying to find the same passion and newness which he found when he quit being a successful advertiser and became an artist, and that never did repeat itself. That he didn't have the ruthlessness to, well, to rob from any and every source he wanted. He probably didn't have a concept of a cosmos in miniature which Balzac and Dickens had, that all he knew was this single man who was humble and ignorant and dreamed better than he was afraid he might ever reach.

Q. Because that was exemplified in his own life, wasn't it . . .?

A. Yes, that's right. Actually he knew too little about people, he wasn't interested in people in the way a writer's got to be, a writer must be interested in people the same way the surgeon's interested in cadavers—he don't have to like people at all, he can loathe people, but he's got to be interested in them, and Anderson didn't know people, he was afraid of people.

. . .

Q. In your article on Sherwood Anderson you mention stories about half-men, half-animals who lived out in a swamp. I don't remember seeing these in any of your books. Do you recall any of these stories?

A. They were never printed. We invented those people and it was the sort of thing that you think of and you do so much talking and laughing about it that the desire, the will to put it down has evaporated. We never did get around to putting that down. We'd write letters to one another about it and just swap lies about it face to face, but we never did get things put down on paper.

Q. Do you remember any, by any chance?

A. Well, it was a son of General Andrew Jackson after the

232

battle of Chalmette that decided to stay in Louisiana and establish a sheep ranch. So he bought some land from a New Orleans realtor, but when he found it, it was all swamp, it had just a few islands and roots of trees that these sheep had to live on but he brought his sheep there anyway and the sheep gradually adapted themselves, they learned to swim and he could call them back up on his platform and feed them, but after a while there was a little trouble getting them to come in even to eat, and when you'd see them the wool had gone, they were developing scales, their legs atrophied, they had got fins, and actually they turned into fish. And one of them, which was the lineal descendant of the old gentleman, he turned into a shark and left that country, and girls in swimming along the coast would be annoyed by this shark, and everybody knew that was this Jackson boy because he was always after women. It went on like that—oh, we spent a whole summer laughing over it, talking about it. There's no limit to where that can go, you know.

Q. A little about your method of working. Do you go out, say like Ratliff, that character, and associate among the people?

A. Yes, not deliberately.

Q. In other words, . . . they don't know you're out doing it?

A. No, and I probably don't know I'm out doing it myself. I don't go out with a notebook, but I like these people, that is, I like to listen to them, the way they talk or the things they talk about. I spent a lot of time with my uncle, he was a politician, and he would have to run every four years to be elected judge again. And I would go around with him and sit on the front galleries of country stores and listen to the talk that would go on, with no notebook, no intention to put it down, I just—it was interesting and I remembered most of it, and I have known them in farming and in dealing with horses and hunting, things like that, but without carrying a notebook at all, just to remember.

. . .

Q. You called Wolfe's works magnificent failures. I wonder what you—what difference is there between Wolfe and Dreiser. Do you feel that Dreiser in such a book as *An American*

Tragedy is a magnificent success or would you put him in the same category as Wolfe?

A. I wouldn't say that *An American Tragedy* is such a good book. I would say that *Sister Carrie* is a much better book. I think that Dreiser knew exactly what he wanted to say, but he had a terrific difficulty in saying it, there was never any fun to him, any pleasure to him, he was convinced that he had a message, I don't mean an ideological message or political but he had to tell folks, This is what you are. That he wasn't writing for pleasure, he wasn't writing for fun, and he had a terrific time of it, which Anderson didn't have, he loved the writing. It was his own confusion that troubled him but he never hated it, but I'm—I can imagine that Dreiser hated the sight of a blank piece of paper. . . .

Session Twenty-Six

February 26, 1958

UNDERGRADUATE COURSE IN WRITING

Q. In writing such a story as that ["Race at Morning"], which must be about concrete things that you've experienced—I don't know whether you've had a collision with a grapevine or not when you were on a horse—do you see that kind of a story from beginning to end when you start writing? Do you have that story sort of in mind, the ending as part of the beginning?

A. No, I think a story like that invents itself as you go along. That one began with the picture of that little boy— been abandoned by his mother and his father, they were no good, and by rights he should have been no good too, but this man, Mr. Ernest, with all his ignorance could see that here is a human being, and a human being is capable of anything if he has a chance to do it, and the story came out of the fact that this crabbed old bachelor would see this waif and suddenly say, He's too valuable to leave in the woods there. And the story was simply a matter of showing incidents to show the relationship between these two people, that this old man suddenly had seen a duty and was going to do it, that he didn't know—he had probably never been to school himself, but he saw that something could be made out of this waif simply because that little waif was a human being.

Q. Sir, in other words, in the beginning we were shown the hunt, the way Mr. Ernest took the boy, this was showing how he sort of took him in and how he took him on things . . . and how he took him into his life?

235

A. Yes, and the interdependence. The man was deaf, he couldn't hear which way the dogs went. This little boy would ride behind him and say, They went that way.

Q. Well, then could you perhaps put the part at the end, where he took the boy after his parents had gone away, first say, and then have the hunt come afterwards, after we know that the man has taken the boy in?

A. Could, but I think that my way made a better story. That's a matter of opinion, but I think that mine, for the payoff to come last, was a little more effective. If anything, it makes the story seem a little more condensed, shorter maybe.
. . .

Q. When you were talking about the education being so that he could learn not only what was right, but, since he already knew what was right, were you being—was that supposed to be sort of comical?

A. No. This uneducated ignorant man was fumbling after something which he had realized late in his life was not only true but important. That no man can be an island to himself, that you have a responsibility toward mankind. That is, you may do right because—through instinct, or because it's been beat into you, but that may be all right for you, but you have a responsibility toward people that have not been trained to do right, they've got to know why they must do right, and only education can give you the rhetoric, the capacity to think on your feet, to explain to the ignorant, the intractable, why something is right, why he must do something because it's right. That was—in fact, the association with that child had done that much to the man. If they hadn't met, the man would have gone on and would have been content to be crabbed and ignorant and a hard farmer, to make a little money every year, but suddenly the responsibility of that child, that man too had entered the human race. In a way they were to be the salvation of one another, mutual salvation of one another.

Q. You think then that the boy will go to school?

A. I should think so, yes. He may—will probably never be a Phi Beta Kappa, but this man will see that he learns to read and write and with the hope, the idea that maybe once he learns to read he will of his own curiosity read enough to learn why man does right, himself.

Q. The boy then will be changed by going to school and the man will be changed also by having the responsibility of this orphan?

A. Well, the man would be changed by the responsibility of the orphan. The little boy at that age was pretty well started in the way he would go, all he needed was just an occasional prod and some directing, that already he was truthful and brave, and he was willing to give the devotion, fidelity. All he needed was education, to learn to read, to know more of the history of his race. The man was probably changed more than that little boy was. The little boy was not changed so much as saved.

Q. Then were they hunting not only the deer but in a way themselves too?

A. Well, of course, they didn't know that, but that's what they were finding. That is, the man had—in teaching the little boy that never to touch satiety was valid. Maybe he had never thought of that before, that his notion was to take the two weeks off and get out there and kill every deer that got up in front of him, until suddenly his responsibility for the little boy made him stop and think, Well, what is better, to just drag the dead meat in or to see the beautiful splendid creature run in its native element?

Q. I thought I heard a little bit of wistfulness for the time when a man didn't have to do anything but farm and hunt, that maybe this—you said, "Time was when all man had to do was farm and hunt."

A. Surely, nobody really likes responsibility, it may be this man hated the fact that he couldn't stay in his home at night and go to sleep and let that little boy, which he knew was lost and abandoned in a hut in the woods, shift for himself, but he couldn't, he had to go and get him. And, yes, he probably thought it, I wish we could go on like it used to be, where people didn't have to be responsible, where a man could be an island unto himself, but once he realized that he couldn't, he realized that neither could this little boy, neither could any other human being. That the responsibility—the acceptance of the responsibility increased all of us, just like the refusal of it diminished all of us.

. . .

Q. Mr. Faulkner, when you put that title down, "Race at Morning," did you think of the appropriateness of that title on really various levels, that is, the fact that the "morning" is the boy, the "race" means human race as well as the literal race in the hunt? You can interpret that title in various ways. I was just thinking about it as you were talking. . . .

A. No, the title is in the little boy's terms, the morning of his life, and it happened in the morning, and I used the word "race" to—the exuberation—the exuberance of speed. That to him was that life at that age never does go slow, when it begins to slow up you get bored, it's that—always at top speed. No, I hadn't thought of it in reference to humanity. It was just— that was his title, his terms.

Q. Sir, do you find it best that, once you get an idea, to sit right down and write it, or is it best to think it over and sort of let it jell?

A. After you have been properly snake-bit with writing, you don't have any spare time to sit down and think something over. You get one idea while you're in the middle of getting another one down, and the new idea has simply got to take its chance, unless it's, as they say, so hot at the moment that you will put down what you're doing to take it up. But probably some sort of a—you might call it protective coloration, that that idea don't come into the mind as new until subconsciously it has been hovered over for a while, that it has begun to take its final shape before it ever comes into the conscious mind as an idea to write. That you don't know where you got it, you don't know how long you've had it, that it was an egg, or a hen that's been sitting over that single egg for the—whatever length of time it takes to hatch the thing out before it comes into the conscious mind.

238

. . .

Q. I was just wondering, if you have this—have a story, then your purpose is more producing something that's enjoyable to be read, but if it has a theme in it, in order to focus on the theme, in order to make the theme as fully developed—I should think you'd have to keep that in mind, keep what the—

A. If I understand you right, in that case the message would be one of the craftsman's tools, that—well, that's perfectly valid. A message is one of his tools, just like the rhetoric, just like the punctuation. That's quite valid, but you don't write a story just to show your versatility with your tools. You write a story to tell about people, man in his constant struggle with his own heart, with the hearts of others, or with his environment. It's man in the ageless, eternal struggles which we inherit and we go through as though they'd never happened before, shown for a moment in a dramatic instant of the furious motion of being alive, that's all any story is. You catch this fluidity which is human life and you focus a light on it and you stop it long enough for people to be able to see it. . . .

Session Twenty-Seven

April 24, 1958

THE ENGLISH CLUB

A WORD TO YOUNG WRITERS

Two years ago President Eisenhower conceived a plan based on an idea which is basically a sound one. This was that world conditions, the universal dilemma of mankind at this moment, are what they are simply because individual men and women of different races and tongues and conditions cannot discuss with one another these problems and dilemmas which are primarily theirs, but must attempt to do so only through the formal organizations of their antagonistic and seemingly irreconcilable governments.

That is, that individual people in all walks of life should be given opportunity to speak to their individual opposite numbers all over the earth—laborer to laborer, scientist to scientist, doctors and lawyers and merchants and bankers and artists to their opposite numbers everywhere.

There was nothing wrong with this idea. Certainly no artist —painter, musician, sculptor, architect, writer—would dispute it because this—trying to communicate man to man regardless of race or color or condition—is exactly what every artist has already spent all his life trying to do, and as long as he breathes will continue to do.

What doomed it in my opinion was symptomized by the phraseology of the President's own concept: laborer to laborer, artist to artist, banker to banker, tycoon to tycoon. What doomed it in my opinion was an evil inherent in our culture itself; an evil quality inherent in (and perhaps necessary though

241

I for one do not believe this last) in the culture of any country capable of enduring and surviving through this period of history. This is the mystical belief, almost a religion, that individual man cannot speak to individual man because individual man can no longer exist. A belief that there is no place anymore where individual man can speak quietly to individual man of such simple things as honesty with oneself and responsibility toward others and protection for the weak and compassion and pity for all, because such individual things as honesty and pity and responsibility and compassion no longer exist and man himself can hope to continue only by relinquishing and denying his individuality into a regimented group of his arbitrary factional kind, arrayed against an opposite opposed arbitrary factional regimented group, both filling the same air at the same time with the same double-barreled abstractions of "peoples' democracy" and "minority rights" and "equal justice" and "social welfare"—all the synonyms which take all the shame out of irresponsibility by not merely inviting but even compelling everyone to participate in it.

So in this case—I mean the President's People-to-People Committee—the artist too, who has already spent his life trying to communicate simply people to people the problems and passions of the human heart and how to survive them or anyway endure them, has in effect been asked by the President of his country to affirm that mythology which he has already devoted his life to denying: the mythology that one single individual man is nothing, and can have weight and substance only when organized into the anonymity of a group where he will have surrendered his individual soul for a number.

It would be sad enough if only at such moments as this—I mean, formal recognition by his country of the validity of his life's dedication—did the artist have to run full-tilt into what might be called almost a universal will to regimentation, a universal will to obliterate the humanity from man even to the extent of relieving him not only of moral responsibility but even of physical pain and mortality by effacing him individually into any, it does not matter which as long as he has vanished into one of them, nationally-recognized economic group by profession or trade or occupation or income-tax bracket or, if nothing else offers, finance-company list. His tragedy is that today he must even combat this pressure, waste some part of his puny but (if he is an artist) precious individual strength against this universal will to efface his individual humanity, in order to be an artist. Which comes at last to the idea I want to suggest, which is what seems to me to be the one dilemma in which all young writers today participate.

I think that perhaps all writers, while they are "hot," working at top speed to try to get said all they feel the terrific urgency to say, don't read the writers younger, after, themselves, perhaps for the same reason which the sprinter or the distance-runner has: he does not have time to be interested in who is behind him or even up to him, but only in who is in front. That was true in my own case anyway, so there was a gap of about twenty-five years during which I had almost no acquaintance whatever with contemporary literature.

So, when a short time ago I did begin to read the writing being done now, I brought to it not only ignorance but a kind of innocence, freshness, what you might call a point of view and an interest virgin of preconceptions. Anyway, I got from the first story an impression which has repeated itself so consistently since, that I shall offer it as a generalization. This is, that the young writer of today is compelled by the present state of our culture which I tried to describe, to function in a kind of vacuum of the human race. His characters do not function, live, breathe, struggle, in that moil and seethe of simple humanity as did those of our predecessors who were the masters from whom we learned our craft: Dickens, Fielding, Thackeray, Conrad, Twain, Smollett, Hawthorne, Melville, James; their names are legion whose created characters were not just weaned but even spawned into a moil and seethe of simple human beings whose very existence was an affirmation of an incurable and indomitable optimism—men and women like themselves, understandable and comprehensible even when antipathetical, even in the very moment while they were murdering or robbing or betraying you, since theirs too were the same simple human lusts and hopes and fears uncomplicated by regimentation or group compulsion—a moil and seethe of humanity into which they could venture not only unappalled and welcome but with pleasure too and with no threat of harm since the worst that could happen to them would be a head bumped by what was only another human head, an elbow or a knee skinned but that too was only another human knee or elbow which did the skinning—a moil and seethe of mankind which accepted and believed in and functioned according, not to angles, but to moral principles; where truth was not where you were standing when you looked at it but was an unalterable quality or thing which could and would knock your brains out if you did not accept it or at least respect it.

While today the young writer's characters must function not in individuality but in isolation, not to pursue in myriad company the anguishes and hopes of all human hearts in a world of a few simple comprehensible truths and moral principles, but to exist alone inside a vacuum of facts which he did not choose and cannot cope with and cannot escape from like a fly inside an inverted tumbler.

Let me repeat: I have not read all the work of this present generation of writing; I have not had time yet. So I must speak only of the ones I do know. I am thinking now of what I rate the best one: Salinger's *Catcher in the Rye,* perhaps because this one expresses so completely what I have tried to say: a youth, father to what will, must someday be a man, more intelligent than some and more sensitive than most, who (he would not even have called it by instinct because he did not know he possessed it) because God perhaps had put it there, loved man and wished to be a part of mankind, humanity, who tried to join the human race and failed. To me, his tragedy was not that he was, as he perhaps thought, not tough enough or brave enough or deserving enough to be accepted into humanity. His tragedy was that when he attempted to enter the human race, there was no human race there. There was nothing for him to do save buzz, frantic and inviolate, inside the glass walls of his tumbler until he either gave up or was himself by himself, by his own frantic buzzing, destroyed. One thinks of course immediately of Huck Finn, another youth already father to what will some day soon now be a man. But in Huck's case all he had to combat was his small size, which time would cure for him; in time he would be as big as any man he had to cope with; and even as it was, all the adult world could do to harm him was to skin his nose a little; humanity, the human race, would and was accepting him already; all he needed to do was just to grow up in it.

That is the young writer's dilemma as I see it. Not just his, but all our problems, is to save mankind from being desouled as the stallion or boar or bull is gelded; to save the individual from anonymity before it is too late and humanity has vanished from the animal called man. And who better to save man's humanity than the writer, the poet, the artist, since who should fear the loss of it more since the humanity of man is the artist's life's blood.

. . .

Q. May I ask you what moved you to write that essay? I find it very profound.

A. I reckon that anything you have devoted a great deal of your time to, any sort of craft, whether it's an important one or not, becomes pretty serious to you, and maybe when you get along you think, Well, I have—if it's not valid—I have wasted a lot of pretty valuable time, and so I prefer to believe that it is valid and it should continue, and the people to carry it on are the people that come after me, and if my thoughts about it are worth anything, whether they are or not, it had better be expressed so the young people after me can take a look at it and say, It's nonsense or not. I suppose that's the reason. That no particular need to improve writing or to better man's condition maybe, any more than any artist has, I think maybe it's not so much to better man's condition but maybe to uplift his heart, to give him pleasure, fun. Anyway, it becomes important to the one who's spent all his life laying the brick and he wants the trade of bricklaying to continue.

. . .

Q. Mr. Faulkner, Isaac McCaslin in "The Bear" relinquishes his heredity. Do you think he may be in the same predicament as modern man, under the same conditions that he can't find a humanity that he can fit in with?

A. Well, there are some people in any time and age that cannot face and cope with the problems. There seem to be three stages: The first says, This is rotten, I'll have no part of it, I will take death first. The second says, This is rotten, I don't like it, I can't do anything about it, but at least I will not participate in it myself, I will go off into a cave or climb a pillar to sit on. The third says, This stinks and I'm going to do something about it. McCaslin is the second. He says, This is bad, and I will withdraw from it. What we need are people who will say, This is bad and I'm going to do something about it, I'm going to change it.

. . .

Q. [Could you] compare Wall Street Panic Snopes and Holden Caulfield, please? What advantages or qualities are there in Wall Street Panic that Holden Caulfield has not now and never did have?

A. Wall Street Panic knew where he wanted to go, he knew that he could get there provided he observed a few of the rules of the game, which he did, and he got there. I think that Wall Street Panic wasn't really a Snopes, that probably, actually, he was not a Snopes, that his father's mama may have done a little extra-curricular night work, and that he really wasn't a Snopes, he was a—more of a simple human being than the other Snopes were. But he wanted to be independent, wanted to make money, but he had rules about how he was going to do it, he wanted to make money by simple industry, the old rules of working hard and saving your pennies, not by taking advantage of anybody.

. . .

Q. I've sometimes thought that the tragedy of Holden Caulfield was that he did not fall, in a way. That if he fell off into humanity he might have found it.

A. Well, he would have to have been tougher than he was. If he had been tougher than that there wouldn't have been any story in the first place. But his story was an intelligent, very sensitive young man who was—in this day and time was an anachronism, was almost an obsolescence, trying to cope with a struggle with the present-day world which he was not fitted for, when he didn't want money, he didn't want position, anything, he just wanted to find man and wanted something to love,

246

and he couldn't. There was nothing there. The nearest he came to it was his sister who was a child and though she tried to love him she couldn't understand his problem. The only other human beings he ran into he had preconceptions to doubt —the teacher which could have helped him, and he suddenly began to suspect the teacher's motives.

Q. Sir, this sounds an awful lot like a novel called *The Sound and the Fury*—Quentin Compson wanting to love people, and the same sort of relationship with his sister.

A. I don't quite agree with you, I don't believe that Quentin and Holden were very much alike in—except in being a little too sensitive and coming from a somewhat similar background of people that were over-intelligent but incapable of strength of mutual affection and tenderness, which, as I got it, was Holden's home.

. . .

Q. Don't you think nowadays that possibly there are a great many individuals whom you don't recognize as individuals because they don't seem to be doing anything, and that's where they are individuals—they're not belonging? . . .

A. I hope so, I hope there are a lot of them. I don't know very many of them that are free of the pressure to belong to something. There may be some, I would like to know that there are a great many of them.

Q. Well, I should think that probably in the teaching world, and universities and colleges, there might be more than elsewhere. Would you disagree with that?

A. No, I would say that there would be—that is the best, the happiest place, for the man to be an individual is in college.

. . .

Q. You'd feel that Salinger, for example, just hasn't created enough characters who seem to be part of this big human race, there isn't just a—there just isn't enough for Holden Caulfield to come in contact with before he can get anywhere.

A. He couldn't get to them, he tried—there was the chance with the professor that understood him and could have helped him, but there he had—right in there he had run into a preconception which was foisted on him that every man if he's not happily married he must be homosexual. That's the pressure to belong to a group, to be typed, that you can't be yourself, you've got to belong to something. He ran into two people that should have been a part of the moil and seethe of simple people which I spoke about, that was the prostitute and the pimp, and the only point they met on was that shabby five-dollar bill, that there was no human contact otherwise, even when the man hit him it might have been a door swinging into him, nothing human in it. The only human contact he could reach was with his little sister, who was too young to see that—she knew it, that he was in trouble, but she had no conception of what the anguish and trouble was. . . .

Session Twenty-Eight

April 28, 1958

...Q. Mr. Faulkner, were there—I'm sure there must have been a number of Confederate veterans around when you were growing up as a boy. Did you talk to them, hear their reminiscences?

A. Yes. I remember a lot of them. I was five-six-seven years old around 1904-5-6 and 7, old enough to understand, to listen. They didn't talk so much about that war, I had got that from the maiden spinster aunts which had never surrendered. But I can remember the old men, and they would get out the old shabby grey uniforms and get out the old battle-flag on Decoration, Memorial Day. Yes, I remember any number of them. But it was the aunts, the women, that had never given up. My aunt, she liked to go to picture shows, they had *Gone with the Wind* in at the theatre at home and she went to see it, and as soon as Sherman came on the screen she got up and left. She had paid good money to go there, but she wasn't going to sit and look at Sherman.

Q. Mr. Faulkner, at—toward the end of *The Unvanquished* Aunt Jenny tells Bayard about a blockade-runner she knew who used to have the toast, "No bloody moon." Was that so that he could get through the—

A. Yes.

Q. —ships undetected? And she passes it on to Bayard as kind of a "Good luck" thing, no doubt.

A. Yes.

Q. Now, why does he say it to George Wyatt the next day? I wonder. He meets him downtown, and is supposed to avenge his father. Is he just being humorous?

A. No. By that time in his concept that had begun—had become a gesture of well-wishing, it's almost like, Here's hoping, or May you have an ace in the hole, that sort of thing. It had no connection any more with moonlight, just a way of saying, May you win this gambit, May there be nothing—May the gods be good to you.

Q. Mr. Faulkner, how deep was Ab Snopes into Grumby's business and what jobs do you think he did for Grumby?

A. Probably not very deep, he was a hanger-on, he was sort of a jackal. Grumby in a way was a lion—he was a shabby, sorry lion—but Ab Snopes was never anything but a jackal, and I imagine that Grumby would have had little patience with Ab Snopes. Ab Snopes hung around the outskirts of the kill to get what scraps might be left. But nobody would have depended on Ab Snopes because Ab probably wouldn't have stuck, wouldn't have held together when the pinch came.

. . .

Q. Sir, in *Sartoris* it appears when Bayard, young Bayard, in the wreck after his grandfather's killed—that he commits a kind of cowardly act by running away. Why didn't he go back, to be more or less brave as the—to show his courage as the Sartoris family always had instead of running away?

A. I expect that that one of the twins really wasn't brave and knew it. His dead brother was the braver, I mean capable of the sort of rash recklessness which passes for physical courage. That the one that survived not only had suffered the psychotic injury of having lost a twin, but also he would have to say to himself, The best one of us died, the brave one died, and he no longer wanted to live, actually. He came back home but he probably had no good reason to live, or maybe he was —would have to salve himself by saying, Well, whether I'm brave or not, it doesn't matter and I don't care.

. . .

Q. Mr. Faulkner, could I ask a question of interest to many historians also interested in literature? You spoke of the three-fold fund—experience, observation, and imagination. When you write about—as you did in *The Unvanquished*—the period of the Reconstruction, do you find that works of historians about Reconstruction in Mississippi are useful or do they just clutter the issue and deaden the imagination? But to build up your knowledge of that period do you—did you find that you went naturally to historical works on the period or was that at all useful, that sort of thing?

A. As far as I know I have never done one page of research. Also, I doubt if I've ever forgotten anything I ever read too. The research I did was coincidental to the fact I was doing something which was fun, that is reading. I've never gone to these things to—for information. It's because I was reading about people in motion, alive, in the conflict of the heart with itself or with its fellows or with its environment. That what research I read, I read exactly as I do fiction because it's people, man, in motion, and the writer, as I say, never forgets that, he stores it away—he has no morals—and when he needs it he reaches around and drags it out, and if it don't quite fit what he wants to say he'll probably change it just a little.

. . .

Q. Sir, in *Sartoris* you sort of skipped over one generation of the Sartoris family between the old Bayard and the young Bayard. Is there any reason for that?

A. Dramatically, yes. Dramatically there was no—well, the twins' father didn't have a story. He came at a period in history which, in this country, people thought of and think of now as a peaceful one. That it was an optimistic one, nothing was happening. There would be little brush-fire wars that nobody paid much attention to, the country was growing, the time of travail and struggle where the hero came into his own had passed. From '70 on to 1912-14, nothing happened to Americans to speak of. This John Sartoris, the father, lived in that time when there was nothing that brought the issue to him to be brave and strong or dramatic—well, call it dramatic, not brave, but dramatic, nothing happened to him. But he had to be there for the simple continuity of the family.

Q. And yet if you thought of a story some time about that

father, something that he could have done, you would have a right to give it to him, wouldn't you?

A. Sure, he's already on record and he's in my stable too, I can run him any time I find . . . .

Q. Sir, did any of the three manuscripts you burned relate to that period?

A. No. No, none of them did.

Q. Mr. Faulkner, *The Unvanquished* was published originally as a series of short stories, I believe, and then revised for a novel form. When you were writing those short stories did you have the idea in mind that these would make a novel eventually, or did they just appear after they appeared in short story form to fit together so naturally it was necessary to make a novel out of them?

A. I saw them as a long series. I had never thought of it in terms of a novel, exactly. I realized that they would be too episodic to be what I considered a novel, so I thought of them as a series of stories, that when I got into the first one I could see two more, but by the time I'd finished the first one I saw that it was going further than that, and then when I'd finished the fourth one, I had postulated too many questions that I had to answer for my own satisfaction. So the others had to be—the other three or two, whichever it was, had to be written then.

Q. Has Hollywood ever expressed any interest in these stories?

A. Yes, they bought the book. That was a funny story too. A producer named David Selznick bought *Gone with the Wind*. M-G-M wanted to make it and he wouldn't let M-G-M make it. He wanted to use Gable, who was under contract to M-G-M in it, and they wouldn't let him have Gable, and he wouldn't let them have *Gone with the Wind*. So they bought my book and told him that if he didn't let them make *Gone with the Wind* they were going to make a *Gone with the Wind* of their own, they had no intention of making a moving picture out of my book, and so Selznick let them make the picture.

Q. I'm interested in both *Sartoris* and in *The Unvanquished* that were—the lines that were always talking about smell, there was lines about the smell of mules, and about the smell of the verbena, and people playing tennis were smelly, and thinks like that. I wondered why you did that all the way through both books.

A. I can't say unless maybe smell is one of my sharper senses, maybe it's sharper than sight. There's no reason, there's certainly no deliberate intent. That's a part of the environment which the writer is trying to describe. That to me is as noticeable as the ear which hears the turns of speech which could be simply because that's a sharper sense with me than maybe sight or hearing.

• • •

Q. Sir, especially in *The Unvanquished* and also in your other novels there seems to be a general loosening of tradition or a sort of rapid progress coming forth. What characters in general, what sort of people in your novels, do you think respond best to the progress?

A. They respond in different ways. The Snopes have responded to it and have coped with it pretty well. I would say that the one that is least troubled by change was the sewing-machine agent Ratliff. That he had accepted a change in culture, a change in environment, and he has suffered no anguish, no grief from it. In—for that reason, he's in favor of change, because it's motion and it's the world as he knows it, and he's never one to say, I wish I had been born a hundred years ago, or I'm sorry I was born now and couldn't have put it off a hundred years. Ratliff will take what's now and do the best he can with it because he is—possesses what you might call a moral, spiritual eupepsia, that his digestion is good, all right, nothing alarms him.

• • •

Q. . . . How much did you draw on Colonel Falkner to get the picture of Colonel Sartoris?

A. That's difficult to say. That comes back to what we spoke of—the three sources the writer draws from—and I myself would have to stop and go page by page to see just

253

how much I drew from family annals that I had listened to from these old undefeated spinster aunts that children of my time grew up with. Probably, well, the similarity of raising of that infantry regiment, that was the same, the—his death was about—was pretty close, pretty close parallel, but the rest of it I would have to go through to—page by page and remember, Did I hear this or did I imagine this?

Q. Sir, I wonder what—if you intended that, to make us think what the future of the young baby, John Sartoris, would be. I know—or whether it's just I read between the lines—I remember that Aunt Jenny said that when old Simon died, he was the last of the real Sartorises, and then again, Narcissa said that . . . when she wanted to change the name, Aunt Jenny said, You'd better not, he'll turn out to be one anyway. So, is there any prediction that you would make that he would turn out to be just like—as violent as all the rest or whether he would turn out to be a new generation?

A. Probably he wouldn't be as violent as the others. I think that what the old aunt meant was that these people were her kin and she would have to be on their side and have to see that all this was fine and gallant, but that they were obsolete, that the men, the Southern men, were the ones that couldn't bear being—having lost the war. The women were the ones that could bear it because they never had surrendered. The men had given up and in a sense were dead and even generations later were seeking death. And in her opinion the sooner this quality in the Sartoris men died out, the better for Sartoris, for the Sartoris clan, race, and she probably—she believed that this boy would have all the best of the Sartorises and none of the vices.

Q. Mr. Faulkner, toward the end of "An Odor of Verbena" she says to Bayard, "Damn you Sartorises," even though she seems to approve of his not going out and getting revenge. Is it some quality of heartlessness that she feels even in an act that she approves of?

A. No no. She loves these people, and they have constantly, all of her life, they have given her anguish and trouble. That she can't help but love them and she believes in them, not in what they do, and they do these reckless, completely self-centered things that have caused nothing but anguish and grief to all their womenfolk. That's all that meant. That she's proud of this boy but he too has done something unexpected, that when she expects them to act like human beings they act like Sartorises, then when she expects the next one to behave like a Sartoris he behaves like a simple human being, and she has no—will never have any peace from them. That's all that meant.

Q. When the boy's aunt says, Go upstairs until this blows over, it'll be all right—is she saying that because she just doesn't want him to get hurt?

A. Yes, that's it, that's the woman—this is the last one. And she knows that she expects him to go out and get himself shot, because he's a child compared to this man and he wouldn't come out of a duel with this man, and she's willing for him to be a coward just so he stays alive. She knows that he's not going to do that, but that's the woman, she's been his mother. She's telling him to do something that [she herself] probably wouldn't really want him to do.

Q. In that final section of *The Unvanquished,* are you developing a notion of a changing and developing tradition, and that Bayard doesn't reject the whole tradition, he keeps the honor and courage but he rejects the heart of the old tradition, and that is the vendetta. And I wondered if you—that if the sprig of verbena represented the old mechanical, unchanging tradition that he was building from and rejecting partly but not altogether. I notice that you present that sprig of verbena as having the petals stamped out as if by a machine. I wondered if you, in your mind, that meant that this was the mechanical, unchanging tradition that he was rejecting partly but he was growing away from, but still keeping the honor and courage.

A. No, the verbena—the fact that that sprig of verbena was alive, was an accolade, that the verbena, even though it looked like it had been stamped out by a machine and was traditional, was still alive, and there would be another one next year. And that was an accolade of optimism too, that she could have left a note scrawled on a piece of paper but that would have been dead paper and dead ink. This was alive, a promise of renewal for next year.

. . .

Q. Is there any romantic attraction between Drusilla and the boy?

A. I don't think so. They were nearer akin in age, but I don't think so. I think certainly Drusilla would have made no effort to bring that out in that boy because her husband— older than she though he was—was her knight, he represented the best of the masculine to her. To be ruthless and brave and to demand—to brook no insult, to demand blood for blood, that was exactly what she would have been if she had been a boy. And she probably never saw this boy other than someone who was close to her in age. And he had never felt of her romantically I am quite sure because his father had stamped the whole tone of that household with his, the father's, importance, that nobody would have dared tamper with his wife, for instance. And this boy, that would have—might have been the one thing he would have shot a man for, for an insult to his father's wife, not his mother necessarily, but his father's wife, because he would be preserving his father's honor.

Session Twenty-Nine

May 1, 1958

UNDERGRADUATE COURSE IN CONTEMPORARY AMERICAN
LITERATURE

. . . Q. Sir, Malcolm Cowley calls the novel *Mosquitoes* a
very bad early novel. Do you think that's a just criticism?

A. Yes, I think any criticism is just if the man is serious
about it, that a criticism is after all a personal opinion, and
any personal opinion on any work is valid because the work
itself is only the writer's personal opinion on a situation, on
a condition. Whether you agree with it or not, it's valid and
it's honest if the critic approaches it honestly. In that case
I'll agree with Mr. Cowley because I was still learning my
craft, but I think that some of the book, some parts of it,
are funny, but as a book it's—if I—I think that the writer
feels that if he could write it over again it would all be better.
That one, if I could write that over, I probably wouldn't write
it at all. I'm not ashamed of it, because that was the chips, the
badly sawn planks that the carpenter produces while he's
learning to be a first-rate carpenter, but it's not a—not an
important book in my list.

. . .

Q. I have heard you use the word "fun" several times, and
I'd like to know your idea of fun.

A. Well—fun—let's see if I can define that. In my own
case it is to accomplish something which makes me feel good,
which may make somebody else feel good, which won't hurt
anybody. Fun is to accomplish something which I thought that
perhaps I couldn't. That I might not be brave enough or

strong enough, and then I do it and I'm successful. I suppose that everyone has a different notion of what "fun" means, so I can tell you only what it means to me, and when I say that, to write for fun, it's to take man's dilemma, the old familiar things in which there's nothing new and can't be anything new, and by the light of my own experience and imagination and a great deal of hard work, to make something which was a little different, which wasn't here yesterday. People write about the same stories because there're so few to write about, but to take one—human beings in the old familiar dilemma and predicament—and by the imagination and the hard work to show them in some new, interesting, tragic, or comical instance of the struggle within the dilemma, that to me is fun. But then so is getting a horse over a fence that I wasn't too sure he could get over or that I would still be on him is fun.

Q. Is this fun for you right now?

A. Yes, because I am still making something which wasn't here yesterday, dealing with human beings, which are all of you and me and Mr. McAleer and classrooms like this, and then out of this I learn a little more about people, and I like to think that if some of you here want to write, and you may have learned a little more about how the writing gets done by someone who's been at it for thirty years. It doesn't have to be a very great new thing, but something new might come out of it, which is what I mean by the fun of being a writer, and then anybody likes to have a captive audience to talk to, probably.

Q. You have a great knack for creating atmosphere. Do you have to go about it consciously as Poe did or does it just sort of come natural?

A. Well there's—no writing comes natural, it's a great deal of concentration and hard work, because one's standards are pretty high, and I don't know, there are probably times when the writer's got to scrabble around and invent, create some atmosphere, then other times when the situation he writes about, the characters in it create the atmosphere. I think that every writer has sort of a storehouse of what he has read, what he has seen and smelled and heard and remembered.

After practice, after a few years of writing he don't have to go through his files to get what he wants, he sort of reaches one hand behind him and pulls out just what he needs for that moment, it'll be something that he remembered, the way a bird in a tree looked or sounded, the way an apple tree smelled, the way dirt looked that was just plowed, and suddenly he is putting that down before he has had time to say, Now, I need to write about how an apple tree smells. He's already done that.

. . .

Q. Sir, do you think Carson McCullers is supposed to be one of the leading writers in America today?

A. That's a question that is difficult for somebody like me to answer because I don't judge writers. To me the book is the important thing, it don't matter who wrote it. And some people—anyone is going to have bad days when what he writes is not good. The book is important, who wrote it means nothing. I will say that she's done some of the best work in our time, but I won't say that she is the best or the worst writer, or number three or number ten.

. . .

Q. Have you ever done any painting, Mr. Faulkner?

A. Not seriously. Occasionally when something comes to hand when they are painting barns and stables and things and I'll get a smooth piece of plank and knife or something to smear with and paint mules and people ploughing, things like that, but never serious. Dogs in the woods, that sort of thing, horses.

. . .

Q. Sir, I'd like to ask you a question about Sherwood Anderson's *Winesburg, Ohio.* In *Winesburg,* Anderson refers to— almost every character that he refers to is tall, like Alice Hindman and Elizabeth Willard and Wash Williams' wife. Is it some sort of symbolism or—?

A. It could be that that was his first book, the first writing he did, and probably more of his own subconscious wishes appeared in that than would have appeared if he had got in the habit of writing and discharging that younger. He was

259

getting along toward forty years old when he wrote that book. He was a short man that probably all his boyhood had wished he were bigger so he could fight better, defend himself. It could be that that is the reason, though it may be that he simply admired tall people whatever the reason that some people admire tall people. But it's just possible it was because he himself was short—when he was sitting behind a table like this he looked like a big man, but when he stood up he wasn't. And I think that he maybe would like to have been more imposing-looking, that at that time he didn't realize that probably it's not how high a man is, it's what's in his face that makes him imposing looking.

Session Thirty

May 2, 1958

UNDERGRADUATE COURSE IN CONTEMPORARY AMERICAN
LITERATURE

UNDERGRADUATE COURSE IN WRITING

GRADUATE COURSE IN AMERICAN FICTION

Q. Mr. Faulkner, is David Hogganbeck in "A Courtship"
the ancestor of Boon Hogganbeck in "The Bear"?

A. Yes, that would be Boon's grandfather, probably. 1812
to—yes, that would be Boon's grandfather.

Q. Mr. Faulkner, I have a few questions about your short
stories. The first one is, what is the relation of the chief,
Francis Weddell, to the Indians which we see in "A Courtship" or "Red Leaves"?

A. Simply another clan. They were the same Chickasaw
people. That was just another clan. They may have been
related by marriage, even by blood. But they had begun to
take white names by that time, when—as they became plantation owners and held U. S. commissions. That he was—belonged to the same lot of people as Issetibbeha and his descendants.

. . .

Q. Does the name T. P. stand for anything, sir?

A. No, that was just his name.

Q. Versh the same way?

A. Versh's name, back in slavery times, had probably been

Vergil. And then his people couldn't spell it and it passed from son to son and finally wound up as Versh. It may have gone from Vergil to Verge and then got to be Versh.

. . .

Q. Sir, we were talking about names—just as we learn that Eck Snopes was really named Eckrum, is there any longer name for I. O., Mink, and Flem?

A. No, that's like T. P.'s name, for I.O. and Mink. Mink was an orphan, he was raised by some kin-people and he himself had never heard himself called anything but Mink. Someone asked him in a book I'm at now, what his name is, he says, "Mink." He says, "Is that all the name you've got?" He says, "That's all I know." And he asks, "What did your mother call you?" And he says, "I don't know. She died." He doesn't know, that's all he's heard. Because he's raised, passed from hand to hand—anybody that would feed a child —like a stray dog.

. . .

Q. Speaking of symbolism, on the dust jacket of the first edition of *The Sound and the Fury,* two figures seem to be wrestling. A black one is pinning down a whiter one. Do you recall who the artist was, and whether anything in particular was intended?

A. No, I don't, I don't know who did that. Of course the symbolism was simply the powers of darkness and of light wrestling, struggling. I don't know whose idea that jacket was nor who did it.

. . .

Q. Did Quentin before actually have that conversation with his father about sleeping with his sister, or was that part of his—?

A. He never did. He said, If I were brave, I would—I might say this to my father, whether it was a lie or not, or if I were—if I would say this to my father, maybe he would answer me back the magic word which would relieve me of this anguish and agony which I live with. No, they were imaginary. He just said, Suppose I say this to my father,

262

would it help me, would it clarify, would I see clearer what it is that I anguish over?

Q. The feeling between him and his sister is pretty strong though, isn't it?

A. Yes, yes. But in Caddy's opinion he was such a weakling that even if they had been no kin, she would never have chosen him for her sweetheart. She would have chosen one like the ex-soldier she did. But never anybody like Quentin.

Q. Is Candace a common name in Mississippi, or—?

A. No. No, Caddy seemed a nice name for her and I had to think of something to justify it.

. . .

Q. Mr. Faulkner, I'm curious about Jason. . . . That Negro boy tells him to keep his hands out of his pockets, because he's falling on his face all the time, he stumbles. Why, was he fat and clumsy . . . ?

A. Probably. That was a mannerism, keeping his hands in his pockets, to me that presaged his future, something of greediness and grasping, selfishness. That he may have kept his hands in his pocket to guard whatever colored rock that he had found that was to him, represented the million dollars he would like to have some day.

. . .

Q. Sir, in *As I Lay Dying*, what was the significance of Darl's lying in front of his mother's coffin after it was saved from the fire?

A. Darl was mad. He did things which it seemed to me he had to do or he insisted on doing. His reasons I could try to rationalize to suit myself, even if I couldn't rationalize his reasons to please me I had to accept the act because Darl insisted on doing that. I mean that any character that you write takes charge of his own behavior. You can't make him do things once he comes alive and stands up and casts his own shadow. Darl did things which I am sure were for his own mad reasons quite logical. I couldn't always understand why he did things, but he did insist on doing things, and when we would quarrel about it, he always won, because at that time he was alive, he was under his own power.

Session Thirty-One

May 6, 1958

UNDERGRADUATE COURSE IN LANGUAGE

... Q. Mr. Faulkner, I'd like to ask you about your use of "ain't" in the dialogue of your characters, in particular in *As I Lay Dying*. When Anse Bundren is talking to Vernon Tull he says, "I ain't asking it of you," he says, "I can always do for me and mine. I ain't asking you to risk your mule. It ain't your dead; I am not blaming you." Now why do you have the switch from "ain't" to "am not"?

A. "Am not" is more positive.

Q. So you use the "am not" when you are definite—

A. Yes, to be very positive, yes. Otherwise they would have said "ain't."

Q. Mr. Faulkner, in *The Portable Faulkner* the editor says, "Incidentally the title of the novel has nothing to do with August sunlight; it refers to Lena Grove and her baby. In the Mississippi backwoods, it is sometimes said of a pregnant woman, but more often of a mare or cow, that she will be *light* in August or September." Is this how you meant it to be— the title?

A. No, I never heard of that. It refers to a texture of the light in August in my country, in a spell of two or three cool days we call "Blackberry Winter." It's the light. I had never heard that business of after the cow drops the calf she's light in August.

. . .

Q. Mr. Faulkner, this may sound like a typical question

from a proud Virginian, but how did you arrive at the name Jefferson for the town?

A. I told that in a book called *Requiem for a Nun.* It was —the mail carrier in 1811 or '12 it was, who brought the mail into what was then an Indian trading post, had been a tenant on Mr. Jefferson's place, one of Mr. Jefferson's places here in Albemarle County. It's an involved, long story, but it explains how they named the town Jefferson.

Session Thirty-Two

May 7, 1958

DEPARTMENT OF PSYCHIATRY

. . . Q. Mr. Faulkner, could you say a few words about what you might consider as irrational human behavior?

A. No, I couldn't. I've never tried to set up what might be a pattern to measure irrational human behavior. To me, all human behavior is unpredictable and, considering man's frailty, the—and—in the ramshackle universe he functions in, it's a—all irrational. It couldn't be very rational because his universe is not a very rational one, it seems to me. I think that probably no writer would set himself up to judge. If he'd begun to judge the people he writes about, his—oh, the— whatever the gods are that lets [*sic*] him do something which is his cup of tea—he likes—might withdraw the gift. If he began to preach or proselytize or pass judgment, that the fire might go out. Also, I think the writer is not really interested in bettering man's condition. He really doesn't care a damn about man's condition. He's interested in all man's behavior with no judgment whatever. That it's motion, it's life, the only alternative is nothingness, death. And so to the writer, anything man does is fine because it's motion. If he were not doing that he would do nothing instead. Maybe the writer has no concept of morality at all, only an integrity to hold always to what he believes to be the facts and truths of human behavior, not moral standards at all. But that man in his books does what man will do, not what man should do but what he will do, maybe what he can't help but do.

. . .

Q. Theoretically the psychiatrist also does not make judgments or—he simply takes man as he is, his life and the way it is, and tries to understand it. And yet . . . we think that we would be kidding ourselves—that we do nevertheless look at these things from our own perspectives. And certainly when the idea comes in of trying to do anything about it, which you said the writer doesn't do and which we theoretically do, attempt to do—we attempt to better the situation, we've got to think in terms of bettering it to what aim, to what goal, and those are essentially the goals that we have to hold at the present time, or at any given time. Can a writer really avoid personal judgments or value systems or—?

A. He can as long as he is a writer. I think that a writer is a perfect case of split personality. That he is one thing when he is a writer and he is something else while he is a denizen of the world. It may be that that's not—that he can't be really that split, that maybe he has a hope that what he does may improve man in the sense that it will give man some instance of man's fine record, being fragile and frail and not his own boss by any manner of means, yet out of that he has managed somehow to endure, to have accomplished a few things which have lasted. Maybe in that sense the writer has got to work for man's betterment, even if he's not deliberately trying to. I think that in a way the psychiatrist is doing that too. That I imagine a psychiatrist in—with one human being could learn about all he would need to know about what makes man do what he does. . . . And since he will devote his life to it, he must have some thought that somehow he will improve in the end man's condition.

. . .

Q. You don't have any idea of [where you learned psychology]?

A. No sir, I don't. Only what I have learned about it from listening to people that do know. What little of psychology I know the characters I have invented and playing poker have taught me. Freud I'm not familiar with.

Q. You apparently believe in extra-sensory perception.

A. Yes, I probably depend almost completely on it. I don't

268

have a trained mind, I've got to depend on extra-sensory perception.

. . .

Q. Most of your characters are certainly highly individualized human beings. Do you have any particular ideas on the so-called trend toward conformity, the loss of individualization in our current society?

A. Yes, I have very definite ideas about that, and if I ever become a preacher, it will be to preach against man, individual man, relinquishing into groups, any group. I'm against belonging to anything. Of course, when I was young I belonged to young people's fraternities and things like that, but now I don't want to belong to anything except the human race.

Q. Why is that?

A. I think that there's too much pressure to make people conform and I think that one man may be first-rate but if you get one man and two second-rate men together, then he's not going to be first-rate any longer, because the voice of that majority will be a second-rate voice, the behavior of that majority will be second-rate. And I think that a second-rate man to save himself at least won't be third-rate, but no second-rate man is going to become first-rate just by joining one or two more first-rate people.

Q. Can you go further and say how you rate people like that—first and second-rate?

A. Well sir, that would be a little difficult and maybe a little trite. I would say that a first-rate man is one—is a man that did the best he could with what talents he had to make something which wasn't here yesterday. And also to—that never hurt an inferior, never harmed the weak, practiced honesty and courtesy, and tried to be as brave as he wanted to be whether he always was that brave or not. I think that a man that held to those tenets wouldn't get very far if he were involved in a group of people that had relinquished their individualities to some one voice which would—could control their behavior.

Session Thirty-Three

May 8, 1958

SECOND-YEAR COURSE IN TYPES OF LITERATURE

GRADUATE COURSE IN AMERICAN FICTION

. . . Q. Mr. Faulkner, you seem to put so much meaning in the hunt. Could you tell us just why you hunted when you were a little boy, or what meaning the hunt has to you?

A. The hunt was simply a symbol of pursuit. Most of anyone's life is a pursuit of something. That is, the only alternative to life is immobility, which is death. This was a symbolization of the pursuit which is a normal part of anyone's life, while he stays alive, told in terms which were familiar to me and dramatic to me. The protagonist could have been anything else besides that bear. I simply told a story which was a natural, normal part of anyone's life in familar and to me interesting terms without any deliberate intent to put symbolism in it. I was simply telling something which was in this case the child—the need, the compulsion of the child to adjust to the adult world. It's how he does it, how he survives it, whether he is destroyed by trying to adjust to the adult world or whether despite his small size he does adjust within his capacity. And always to learn something, to learn something of—not only to pursue but to overtake and then to have the compassion not to destroy, to catch, to touch, and then let go because then tomorrow you can pursue again. If you destroy it, what you caught, then it's gone, it's finished. And that to me is sometimes the greater part of valor but always it's the greater part of pleasure, not to destroy what

271

you have pursued. The pursuit is the thing, not the reward, not the gain.

. . .

Q. Did [Sutpen] acknowledge Clytemnestra as his daughter?

A. No. Well, that would not have mattered because Clytemnestra was a female. The important thing to him was he should establish a line of dukes, you see. He was going to create a dukedom. He'd have to have a male descendant. He would have to establish a dukedom which would be his revenge on the white Virginian who told him to go to the back door. And so he—to have a Negro, half-Negro, for his son would have wrecked the whole dream. If he couldn't—if he had thought that that would ever be exposed that Bon was his son, he may have killed Bon himself. If it had ever come to that point, he would have destroyed Bon just as he would have destroyed any other individual who got in his way.

. . .

Q. I'd like to go back to Charles Bon in *Absalom, Absalom!* I have the impression that up until very near the end of the book that he does not realize he is part Negro. . . . At what point does he find this out and how does he find it out?

A. I think that Bon knew all the time that his mother was part Negress, but during Bon's childhood that was not important. He grew up in the Indies or in New Orleans where that wasn't too important. His mother was a wealthy woman. She could have called herself a Creole whether she had Negro blood along with the French or not. It became important only when Bon realized that it was important to his father. I think that Bon got into that business—well, of course, because he formed a friendship with Henry and felt that Henry, the ignorant country boy, had given him a sort of worship, an admiration and a worship which he enjoyed. Then when he saw the sort of stiff-necked man that Henry's father was and knew that that was his father too, he in a way had given his father a chance to say, I will acknowledge you, but if you—I do openly and you stay here, you will wreck what I have devoted my life to, and so take my love and go, I think Bon would have

272

done it. But this old man was afraid to do that. And Bon tempted him to hold him over the coals in—partly in revenge on his treatment of his—Bon's—mother, until Bon got involved too deeply. No, Bon knew that he was a Negro, but until he found it was important to Sutpen, that wasn't important to him. That he was a gentleman, had been well bred, cultured, much better bred and cultured than Henry himself was.

Q. Did Bon love Judith, or . . .?

A. I think he loved her, I think that he loved her, he knew that if she knew that he was part Negro, with her training and background it would have destroyed her too.

Q. Returning to *The Bear,* Mr. Faulkner, why did you put Part V after Part IV?

A. That story was part of a novel. It was—the pursuit of the bear was simply what you might call a dangling clause in the description of that man when he was a young boy. When it was taken from the book and printed as a short story, the publisher, who is very considerate, has a great respect for all work and for mine in particular, he would not have altered one word of that without asking me, and he didn't ask me. If he had told me he was going to print it separately, I would have said, Take this out, this doesn't belong in this as a short story, it's a part of the novel but not part of the story. But rather than to go ahead and do that without asking me—and I wasn't available at that time—he printed it as it was. It doesn't belong with the short story. The way to read that is to skip that when you come to it.

Q. Mr. Faulkner, in *Absalom, Absalom!* does any one of the people who talks about Sutpen have the right view, or is it more or less a case of thirteen ways of looking at a blackbird with none of them right?

A. That's it exactly. I think that no one individual can look at truth. It blinds you. You look at it and you see one phase of it. Someone else looks at it and sees a slightly awry phase of it. But taken all together, the truth is in what they saw though nobody saw the truth intact. So these are true as far as Miss Rosa and as Quentin saw it. Quentin's father saw what he believed was truth, that was all he saw. But the old man was himself a little too big for people no greater in stature than Quentin and Miss Rosa and Mr. Compson to see all at once. It would have taken perhaps a wiser or more tolerant or more sensitive or more thoughtful person to see him as he was. It was, as you say, thirteen ways of looking at a blackbird. But the truth, I would like to think, comes out, that when the reader has read all these thirteen different ways of looking at the blackbird, the reader has his own fourteenth image of that blackbird which I would like to think is the truth.

Q. Mr. Faulkner, Mr. Coldfield in *Absalom, Absalom!* retreats into the attic when the War between the States starts. Now, why did he do that? Was it because he was a sort of conscientious objector, or was he all or part coward?

A. No, he was probably by religious scruples a conscientious objector. Also, he was very likely a Unionist. That he hated that threat to the dissolution of the Union. That he hadn't enough courage to do anything about it except to hide his head in the sand. But I think that he was probably a Unionist. He probably came from eastern Tennessee, where the people were Unionists at that time. His background was a tradition of fidelity to the United States as it was. He had no agrarian tradition behind him in which slavery was an important part of it.

. . .

Q. Sir, speaking of those two books, as you read *Absalom, Absalom!*, how much can a reader feel that this is the Quentin, the same Quentin, who appeared in *The Sound and the Fury*— that is, a man thinking about his own Compson family, his own sister?

A. To me he's consistent. That he approached the Sutpen family with the same ophthalmia that he approached his own troubles, that he probably never saw anything very clearly, that his was just one of the thirteen ways to look at Sutpen, and his may have been the—one of the most erroneous. Probably his friend McCannon had a much truer picture of Sutpen from what Quentin told him than Quentin himself did.

274

Q. But it's still Sutpen's story. It's not Quentin's story.

A. No it's Sutpen's story. But then, every time any character gets into a book, no matter how minor, he's actually telling his biography—that's all anyone ever does, he tells his own biography, talking about himself, in a thousand different terms, but himself. Quentin was still trying to get God to tell him why, in *Absalom, Absalom!* as he was in *The Sound and the Fury*.

Q. Sir, I'd like some help on understanding what I call the bedroom scene in the fourth section of *The Bear*. You made one statement—"She is lost. She was born lost." Could you help me understand what was meant by that?

A. Who does that refer to?

Q. That refers to Ike McCaslin's wife, in that section. . . .

A. Yes, I think I remember now. She—from her background, her tradition, sex was something evil, that it had to be justified by acquiring property. She was ethically a prostitute. Sexually she was frigid. I think what he meant, he knew that there was no warmth that he would ever find from her, no understanding, no chance ever to accept love or return love because she was incapable of it. That's probably what he meant.

Q. And I wondered why she laughed and laughed. . . .

A. She realized then that he was going to give up the land. She married him because she wanted to be chatelaine of a plantation. And then she found he was going to give all that away, and the only revenge she knew was to deny him sexually. That was the only triumph she had. And she was going to make him suffer for that just as much as she could, to get even with him.

Q. So that she intended from the beginning of their marriage to deny him this one thing that he had requested until it was useful in blackmailing—

A. Well, she assumed when they got married that she was going to be chatelaine of a plantation and they would have children. And she was going to be as—according to the rules

275

of the book a good wife to him. She'd still be frigid and cold and a shrew probably but she'd still be a good wife. Then when he was going to throw the plantation away for idealistic folly, all she—the only revenge she had was that. At least he would have no children from her. He'd have no wife from her. And she—

Q. Well, Ike—excuse me.

A. And she hoped that it would make him grieve [?].

Q. Well, Ike says here. . . .

A. Did not mean what?

Q. That he would go back to the land.

A. She must have known that he was not going to retract and take his heritage. Yes, I'm sure she was convinced of that, no matter what he might have said.

Q. Mr. Faulkner, if she had been the kind of wife he needed, and had been able to give him love and companionship and had stuck by him and had children and had a home for him, do you think that his—that he would ever have compromised with his ideals? After all, he had no training, no way of providing for her.

A. I would say, since we are supposing, if she had been that sort of woman, she would have understood his hatred of of that condition, she might have been practical enough to say, This is the way we'll do it, we can't abandon these people, but let's do it this way, and he would have said, You're wiser than I, let's try it your way. That's possible, I would like to think that. But he would have stuck to his position, that I will not profit from this which is wrong and sinful.

. . .

Q. Sir, one of the most interesting aspects of *The Bear* to me is the conflict between man and the wilderness. I would like to ask you if you intend for the reader to sympathize more with Old Ben in his conflict with the hunters or towards the hunters in their conflict with Old Ben.

A. Well, not "sympathize." I doubt if the writer's asking anyone to sympathize, to choose sides. That is the reader's

276

right. What the writer's asking is compassion, understanding, that change must alter, must happen, and change is going to alter what was. That no matter how fine anything seems, it can't endure, because once it stops, abandons motion, it is dead. It's to have compassion for the anguish that the wilderness itself may have felt by being ruthlessly destroyed by axes, by men who simply wanted to make that earth grow something they could sell for a profit, which brought into it a condition based on an evil like human bondage. It's not to choose sides at all—just to compassionate the good splendid things which change must destroy, the splendid fine things which are a part of man's past too, part of man's heritage too, but they were obsolete and had to go. But that's no need to not feel compassion for them simply because they were obsolete.

. . .

Q. Sir, is that what you meant by the ending of this, then —that change must destroy all [goodness]?

A. Change if it is not controlled by wise people destroys sometimes more than it brings. That unless some wise person comes along in the middle of the change and takes charge of it, change can destroy what is irreplaceable. If the reason for the change is base in motive—that is, to clear the wilderness just to make cotton land, to raise cotton on an agrarian economy of peonage, slavery, is base because it's not as good as the wilderness which it replaces. But if in the end that makes more education for more people, and more food for more people, more of the good things of life—I mean by that to give man leisure to use what's up here instead of just leisure to ride around in automobiles, then the—it was worth destroying the wilderness. But if all the destruction of the wilderness does is to give more people more automobiles just to ride around in, then the wilderness was better.

. . .

Q. Mr. Faulkner, does the miscegenation and incest of Roth Edmonds in "Delta Autumn" complete a cycle of incest and miscegenation begun by old McCaslin and only interrupted by the goodness of Buck and Buddy and Ike in the middle?

A. Yes, it came home. If that's what you mean by complete a cycle, yes, it did.

Session Thirty-Four

May 12, 1958

REPRESENTATIVES OF VIRGINIA COLLEGES

Q. Mr. Faulkner, during our formal education we are taught to adhere to certain grammatical rules, punctuation rules, sentence structure, and so forth. Do you think that if a writer attempts to adhere to such rules, that his style is restricted or cramped in any sense?

A. No sir, I don't think so. It may be that his opportunities for experimentation are cramped. I think that any language must continue to be alive, that is, it must continue to change or be susceptible to change, and grammar, punctuation, are part of that fluidity. That by experimentation you find out if the old ways were the best or maybe the old ways might be subject to change. I wouldn't say that it restricts the style because style could be a part of the fluidity of the change. Style if it's—like anything else, to be alive it must be in motion too. If it becomes fixed then it's dead, it's just rhetoric. The style must change according to what the writer is trying to tell. What he is trying to tell in fact compels the style.

. . .

Q. Mr. Faulkner, in the novel—that novel *Pylon* does the title—could the title refer to the girl Laverne, the marker or beacon around which all the other—all the men gravitate?

A. Now there's some more of this erudite professorial symbolism gets into everything. I'm sure that you're quite right. I just hadn't thought of that. I'm glad to know it. I'll remember that and I'll use that sometime probably.

. . .

Q. You said you didn't deliberately write symbols but . . .

I'd like to ask you . . . if you saw a symbol in the bear in the short story *The Bear*.

A. Since I've been up here and discussed it I've seen lots of symbols that I was too busy at the time—

Q. [I wish you'd please] tell me one so that I could tell my class.

A. Well, one symbol was the bear represented the vanishing wilderness. The little dog that wasn't scared of the bear represented the indomitable spirit of man. I'll have to dig back and get up some more of those symbols, because I have learned around an even dozen that I put into that story without knowing it. But there are two pretty good ones that you can hold to.

Q. May I ask what you think of James Joyce?

A. James Joyce was one of the great men of my time. He was electrocuted by the divine fire. He, Thomas Mann, were the great writers of my time. He was probably—might have been the greatest, but he was electrocuted. He had more talent than he could control.

. . .

Q. Pertinent to that I'd like to ask why is it that Mississippi seems very active in a literary way and yet we don't find the same phenomenon in New Jersey.

A. Well, that's because Mississippi's in the South and New Jersey's in the North. I think that the wisest thing any nation can do when it gets itself into any sort of an economic muddle is to pick out some rich nation and declare war, and get licked and then be supported. The folks in the South write because the North has supported us ever since 1865. We had plenty of time to write.

Session Thirty-Five

May 15, 1958

WASHINGTON AND LEE UNIVERSITY

... Q. Did you find *Absalom, Absalom!* a very difficult novel to write . . .?

A. Yes'm, it was difficult. I worked on that next hardest to *The Sound and the Fury*, as I remember. Yes, I worked on that for a year and then put it away and wrote another book, and then the story still wouldn't let me alone and I came back to it. Yes, that was very difficult. There was a lot of re-writing in that.

. . .

Q. Sir, in the light of your friendship with Sherwood Anderson, are you as a writer indebted to him, and what is your opinion of his place in American literature?

A. His—he has never been given his rightful place in American literature. In my opinion he's the father of all of my generation—Hemingway, Erskine Caldwell, Thomas Wolfe, Dos Passos. Of course Mark Twain is all of our grandfather. But Sherwood Anderson has—in my opinion has still to receive his rightful place in American letters.

Q. I notice this year's Nobel Prize winner is a great admirer of yours, and I wonder if you could—what is your impression of Camus as a writer, if you're acquainted with him . . .?

A. Yes I know Camus best and I think highest of him. He is one man that has—is doing what I have tried always to do, which is to search, demand, ask always of one's own soul. That is my reason for saying that he is the best of the living Frenchmen, better than Sartre or the others. Malraux was a

281

—he became obsessed with politics, but Camus has stuck to his principles, which was always to search the soul, which I think is the writer's first job. To search his own soul, and to give a proper, moving picture of man in the human dilemma.

. . .

Q. How have you enjoyed your stay here in Virginia . . .?

A. Well, I have been in Albemarle County off and on for two or three years now, and I have seen a few Snopeses there. But I like Virginia and Virginians. The longer I stay in Albemarle County the more like Mississippians they behave, but they don't have some of the Mississippi vices. I said last year that I liked Virginians because they were snobs, and since they seem to think I'm all right then maybe I am all right.

Q. Are the Snopeses really taking over Jefferson, and is there any group that might hold them out?

A. The Snopeses will destroy themselves—I really can't afford to answer that question, sir, because you might not buy the next book if I do. They were—that's the artist's prerogative, I think, is to emphasize, to underline, to blow up facts, distort facts in order to state a truth. The—there's probably no tribe of Snopeses in Mississippi or anywhere else outside of my own apocrypha. They were simply an invention of mine to tell a story of man in his struggle. That I was not trying to say, This is the sort of folks we raise in my part of Mississippi at all. That they were simply over-emphasized, burlesqued if you like, which is what Mr. Dickens spent a lot of his time doing, for a valid to him and to me reason, which was to tell a story in an amusing, dramatic, tragic, or comical way.

Q. What is your opinion of Henry Miller?

A. Sorry, I don't know him. Should I? You must believe me, I do live in the country and I don't keep up with literary things, I ain't a literary man. So if I should know Henry Miller I'll find out about him.

. . .

Q. Do you think that the Snopeses are capable or incapable of participating in [civilized society] . . . ?

A. The ones which are incapable of it will be obliterated. Snopes will evolve into you might say an accepted type of Snopes. Either that or he'll have to vanish. That he will have to cope with his environment or his environment will destroy him.

Session Thirty-Six

May 23, 1958

UNIVERSITY AND COMMUNITY PUBLIC

Q. Do you think that there's a particular order in which your works should be read? Many people have offered a sequence. Do you think there's a particular sequence . . .?

A. Probably to begin with a book called *Sartoris* that has the germ of my apocrypha in it. A lot of the characters are postulated in that book. I'd say that's a good one to begin with.

. . .

Q. Sir, are there particular reasons why you do not go to the movies?

A. Yes sir, they come at the wrong time of day. That's the time of day I like to have two or three drinks and eat supper and then sit down and smoke and read. If the—if they had moving pictures—well, I don't know, I'd have something else better to do any time of day. I think maybe I'd rather read it than listen to it. I'd rather read Shakespeare than see it played.

Q. Would that apply to drama too?

A. Yes sir. I can count on my thumbs the plays I've seen in my life, and that's—one is *Ben Hur*, the other is—was *East Lynne*, I reckon I was eight or nine years old. I remember *Ben Hur* because it had live horses in it and a camel and I'd never seen a camel before.

. . .

Q. Who do you like best in the Old Testament?

A. Oh the story of Abraham. I like all of it. They were

285

scoundrels and blackguards and doing the best they could, just like people do now. I like most of it.

. . .

Q. Mr. Faulkner, in *The Hamlet* . . . I don't remember any one particular character that I had a great deal of sympathy for. Everyone seemed to be mad at somebody else for something. Is that typical of those people?

A. Only typical of the people in *The Hamlet.* They were a pretty poor set of people. But the writer doesn't judge people, he has compassion for all people or he wouldn't be much of a writer. And these people are unpleasant and I don't know that there are many of them that I could trust, but I would still be interested in what they did to wonder why they did it. They would still be people involved in the human dilemma.

. . .

Q. Sir, it means that your basic conception of life is optimistic?

A. Yes.

Q. But not of the individual.

A. Well, the individual is not too much, he's only a pinch of dust, he won't be here very long anyway, but his species, his dreams, they go on. There's always somebody that will keep on creating the Bach and the Shakespeare as long as man keeps on producing.

Index

289